Data Modelling
for Information Systems

Data Modelling for Information Systems

Carrie de Carteret

Richard Vidgen

Lecturer in Information Systems
Department of Mathematics and Computer Science
University of Salford

PITMAN
PUBLISHING

PITMAN PUBLISHING
128 Long Acre, London WC2E 9AN

A Division of Pearson Professional Limited

First published in Great Britain 1995

© C de Carteret and R Vidgen 1995

British Library Cataloguing in Publication Data
A CIP catalogue record for this book can be obtained from the British Library.

ISBN 0 273 60262 4

10 9 8 7 6 5 4 3 2

Printed and bound in Great Britain by Clays Ltd, St Ives plc

The Publishers' policy is to use paper manufactured from sustainable forests.

Contents

Part 2:   Object modelling

Part 3:   Theory and practice

Preface

We believe that a practical competence in data modelling techniques is essential to the development of robust and flexible computer-based information systems. A practical competence is gained by doing and a book cannot take the place of experience. However, by including a large number of examples and an extensive case study we hope to illuminate some of the practical aspects, while providing a rigorous introduction to the principles of data modelling. Although this book is concerned primarily with data modelling techniques, we recognize that in most situations a technical proficiency will not by itself be sufficient. Consideration must be given also to the organizational context in which the data modelling activity takes place.

Structure and rationale of the book

The structure of the book is shown in figure 1. In part 1 the fundamentals of data modelling are covered and built upon to show more powerful data structures and to consider problematic modelling situations.

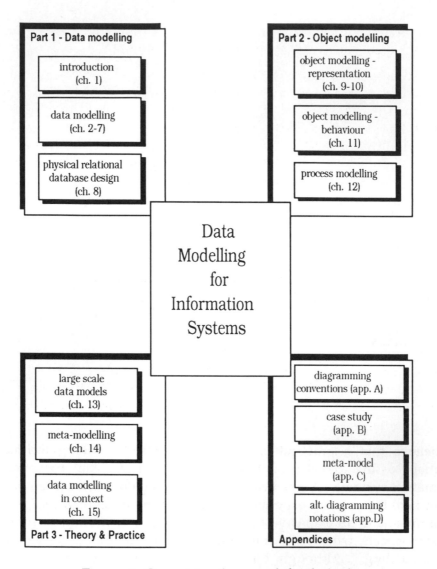

Figure 1: *Organizing framework for the book*

In part 2, Object Modelling, we relax some of the constraints that have origins in the relational model, the aim being to make the data model a more general and richer way of describing computer-based information system requirements. Object models and data models are compared and contrasted and a process for progressing from an object model to a logical data model is shown. Object-Oriented (O-O) principles are introduced in the object model, allowing behaviour to be added to data representation. The focus of the book is on data modelling, but because data models are used to support organizational activities a chapter on process modelling is included to provide a systems analysis context for data modelling.

It could be argued that a more natural point at which to begin this book would be object modelling, which is more general and less implementation specific than the data model. However, our experience of training data modellers has shown that the concepts entity and relationship can be difficult to grasp, and that it is easier for a student to understand the idea of entities and relationships at the conceptual level having first understood how they might be implemented. Making the entities and relationships visible and tangible helps achieve a level of understanding that can then be built upon.

In part 3 we consider firstly how the data modelling process can be managed and data models administered in the organization. We then tackle what can seem to be a rather abstract topic - meta-modelling. We believe that data modelling for business applications is an essential and practical exercise - we also believe that meta-modelling is essential (and practical) for anybody concerned with specifying requirements for a specific type of application - a repository that holds details of the data models developed in support of business applications. It will be seen by inspection of the meta-model that all of the foreign keys that are shown explicitly in chapters 2 to 6 are in fact derivable data that would not be held in a repository. All of the diagrams and attribute lists in this book should be thought of as reports that can be generated from a repository.

In the last chapter we attempt to locate data models, data modellers, and the process of data modelling within a wider context. We have no illusions concerning the technique of data modelling - it is a rigorous exercise and only once the basics have been mastered can those techniques be applied effectively and creatively. But technique alone is not enough and we argue that data modellers ignore the organizational aspects of modelling at their peril.

Appendix A contains a summary of the diagramming notation used in this book, providing a comparison of the class diagramming techniques and the entity diagramming techniques. Appendix B details a case study, The Gym, in which many of the techniques introduced in the book in fragments are brought together within a single data model. The case study is annotated to show how certain aspects could have been modelled differently and to give an idea of the strengths and weaknesses of the structures chosen to represent the case study requirements. In appendix C the meta-model introduced in chapter 14 is summarized and illustrated using sample meta-data. In appendix D the notation used in this book is compared with two known and widely-used notations: SSADM Version 4 and Oracle CASE*Method.

Using this book

Practitioners will probably find part 1 most useful and more experienced practitioners part 2. Students should work through the book serially; by the time the meta-modelling chapter is reached it should be possible for them to understand how part 1 of the book was constructed. Perhaps the quickest insight into the modelling notation can be gained by looking at the case study in appendix B (The Gym). Those familiar with SSADM or Oracle CASE*Method might like to begin by studying appendix D.

Acknowledgements

Carrie de Carteret would like to thank Geof Carrington, John Amos, Phil Black and Alison Neale, whose insights have helped develop her understanding of data analysis techniques, and Derek Meyer and Darren Furniss for their input to the chapter on physical relational modelling.

Richard Vidgen is grateful to Steve Hitchman of Cheltenham and Gloucester College of Higher Education, and Babis Theodoulidis and Peri Loucopoulos of UMIST for their comments on earlier drafts of this text and to colleagues at the University of Salford, especially Bob Wood and Trevor Wood-Harper, for their support and encouragement. Thanks are due also to Eddie Ellis who serves as an excellent model of professionalism in systems development.

1

Introduction

1.1   Modelling

Modelling is a process of representing a perceived reality in a simplified way. Any model, by definition, leaves out some of the complexity of the perceived world. A model railway doesn't have to have litter on the platforms or even leaves on the line if these are not the type of complexities that excite the model railway enthusiast. A data model is used in an attempt to reduce the universe to entities and relationships, which in the relational model become a number of two-dimensional tables that computers can use. To achieve simplicity, the data modeller is restricted to a small set of permitted constructs. These constructs may be combined in different ways to provide the complexity needed to achieve the model's purpose.

What is the purpose of producing a data model? In this text we have assumed that a data model is an input into the development of a computer system. It is a formal means of documenting a business's data structures so that they can be processed automatically. Logical data modelling is machine independent and independent too of the data management system which the application system will use. Because of this it can be done in a standard way from one project to another. When the computer system is to be implemented the logical data model will be succeeded by the physical model, which is based on its logical precursor but adapted to survive and perform in a given physical environment.

The quality of the logical data model has a critical effect on the value of the resulting system. A good data model will enable all the functionality that the users have asked for, provide enough flexibility for processes they haven't yet thought of, allow for maximum economy in code production and re-use and perhaps even lead an organization to think of its objectives in completely new ways. A bad one will hamper systems development to such an extent that most of the subsequent effort goes into overcoming its deficiencies.

1.2   Systems development lifecycles

A common way of representing the process of computer system development is as a lifecycle, as in figure 1.1. Because it represents systems development as a linear process it is also known as the "waterfall" model. In the waterfall model high-level data models are often used in support of strategy and might be prepared as part of a feasibility study. The development of a logical data model is a key activity within the analysis phase. The logical data model is transformed into a physical data model in the physical design phase, taking into account the characteristics of the implementation medium. One alternative to the waterfall model is to build prototypes in support of a rapid application development approach to systems development.

Regardless of the development model chosen, it is our view that the development process will take longer and result in less robust and flexible software if insufficient attention is given to data modelling. This is the case for large-scale mission-critical systems, the evolutionary development of prototypes and for data-based personal computing. Even spreadsheet design is enhanced by a basic awareness of data modelling. In a rapid prototyping exercise we might spend only half an hour (or less!) sketching a data model but even this small investment of time will yield a high rate of return, particularly if the data model is refined iteratively through successive prototyping cycles.

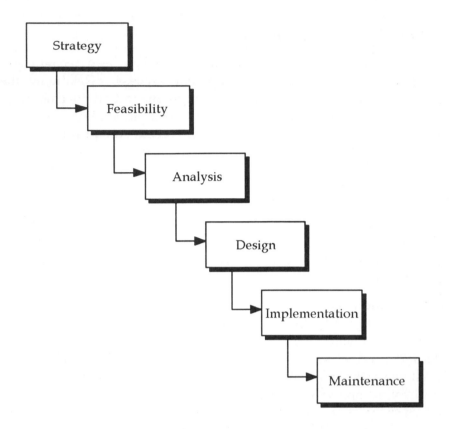

Figure 1.1: *Systems development lifecycle (waterfall)*

We are not suggesting that an ability to model data will necessarily allow a developer to produce a system in half an hour. Even the most optimistic of software development tools vendors would not be that rash. It can take a number of months for a data model to be completed and stabilized. This is the time it takes to gain an understanding of a problem domain and to arrive at an agreed computer-based solution; it does not indicate any inherent technical difficulty associated with data modelling techniques.

As with a lot of techniques, practice makes perfect (or at least competent). The ability to think in data structures becomes second nature after a time and it is much quicker and more rigorous than text-based descriptions. However, although the basic techniques of data modelling can be learnt on a one week course, it can take around eighteen months to gain a basic ability in data modelling and more probably three or four years to gain a deep and practical competency.

1.3   Development methods

Since the early seventies the logical data model has been recognized as a crucial input into the systems development process. Relational theory, although essentially a description of an implementation mechanism, also spawned the first techniques of logical data modelling. Structured development methods have traditionally seen data-centred systems development as fundamentally sounder than process-centred development because data structures were held to be more stable than process logic. Modelling data before process also allows organizations to plan computer systems which will all feed from the same pool of corporate data. The most recent developments in Object-Orientation may reject the assumption that data are necessarily more stable than processes but, by combining the behaviour of objects with their representation, they put the data model firmly back at centre stage. *methodology*

The most widely used structured development method in the UK, SSADM (Structured Systems Analysis and Design Method)[1], advocates a data-centred approach to the development of computer-based systems. SSADM provides lifecycle and product views of the development process. The lifecycle (or structural) view shows when and where different techniques should be used; the product view shows what deliverables should have been produced at the end of each stage. Logical data modelling is a technique used in the SSADM system development lifecycle, the resulting product being a logical data model.

Object-Oriented analysis methods, such as Coad & Yourdon and Object Modelling Technique (OMT)[2], are beginning to be adopted in mainstream development, although there is not currently the same level of infrastructural support for these as there is for more traditional structured methods such as SSADM and Information Engineering (IE).

1.4   CASE tools

A structured method, such as SSADM, is usually supported by a CASE (Computer Aided Software Engineering) tool[3]. CASE tools provide diagramming tools that support a variety of analysis techniques and should work from a shared and internally consistent repository of project data. Different CASE tools will cover different stages of the system development lifecycle: some CASE tools will cover the full cycle from strategy formulation through to code generation; other CASE tools might cover part of the lifecycle, for example analysis and design. Given the central nature of data modelling to structured systems development one would approach a CASE tool that did not support data modelling with suspicion.

CASE tools are not essential to data modelling - it is possible to develop data models using pencil and paper or, as is rather more likely given the availability of personal computers, a word-processor and graphics package. A CASE tool will not develop a data model for you. However, a CASE tool will make easier the task of amending and checking a data model as it develops over the life a project and should provide a path to physical database design.

1.5   Physical design and implementation

We are concerned primarily in this book with how logical models of data can be constructed and less with how those structures might be implemented in computer software. However, given the ubiquity of relational database management systems we have included a chapter on physical database design. By considering physical aspects we hope to show that a rigorous logical data model forms a very practical basis for the implementation of computer-based information systems.

1.6   Database management systems

At the time of writing, the great majority of IT developments can be expected to use a relational database, for example: IBM's DB2, Sybase, Gupta's SQLBase. Given the massive increase in the performance:price ratio of personal computers (PCs) and the increasing use of PC-based relational database management systems (such as Microsoft's Access and FoxPro, Borland's DBase and Paradox) we feel that a basic understanding and proficiency in data modelling will become an increasingly valuable skill. This skill can be exercised in teams performing traditional systems development, for groupware applications (such as Lotus Notes), or individually in the development of personal applications. Certainly we see no reason why a basic competence in data modelling should be the sole preserve of IT professionals.

Object-Oriented (O-O) databases, such as Gemstone and Ontos, are being used more widely in commercial applications and relational database providers are adding O-O extensions to their offerings. We have few doubts that the future for data-intensive applications will be Object-Oriented, but this does not mean that the principles of the relational model need be thrown away. In this book we describe modelling techniques that could be used as the basis for physical design and implementation on either relational or O-O database management systems.

NOTES

1. SSADM is owned by the CCTA (Central Computer Telecommunications Agency). At the time of writing SSADM version 4 is the latest release, for which numerous guides are available, including:

    Eva, M., (1994). *SSADM version 4: a user's guide.* Second edition. McGraw-Hill, England

    Skidmore, S., Farmer, R., & Mills, G., (1992). *SSADM Models and Methods Version 4.* NCC Blackwell, Manchester, England.

    Weaver, P., (1993). *Practical SSADM Version 4.* Pitman Publishing, London.

    The techniques described in this book are also applicable to other structured methods, for example IEM (Information Engineering Methodology) which is described in:

    Davids, A., (1992). *Practical Information Engineering: the management challenge.* Pitman, London.

2. See:

    Coad P., & Yourdon, E., (1991). *Object-Oriented Analysis* (2nd edition). Yourdon Press, Prentice-Hall.

    And for OMT:

    Rumbaugh, J., Blaha, M., Premerlani, W., Eddy, F., Lorensen, W., (1991). *Object-Oriented Modeling and Design.* Prentice-Hall, Englewood Cliffs, New Jersey.

3. Most structured methods are supported by CASE tools. For example, Texas Instruments provide IEF (Information Engineering Facility) in support of Information Engineering. IEF is described in:

    Texas Instruments, (1990). *A Guide to Information Engineering using the IEF (second edition).* Texas Instruments, USA.

Part 1

Data modelling

2

Entities and attributes

Introduction

The vocabulary of the relational data model is limited to two basic components: entities and attributes. This chapter defines entities and attributes and introduces several different ways of representing them. An attribute's optionality will be discussed, as will attribute roles. Finally the chapter investigates how to identify individual occurrences of entities.

2.1   Entities

Definition: An entity is a focal point for one or more pieces of information. Most entities are recognizable business concepts, either concrete or abstract, about which various data are stored.

An entity has a description which defines its scope. For example, the entity Vehicle could be described as, "A piece of equipment, powered by fuel, used to transport passengers and/or cargoes on public roads." Such a definition would include cars, lorries, motorcycles and tractors but exclude bicycles, tanks, trains, boats and aeroplanes.

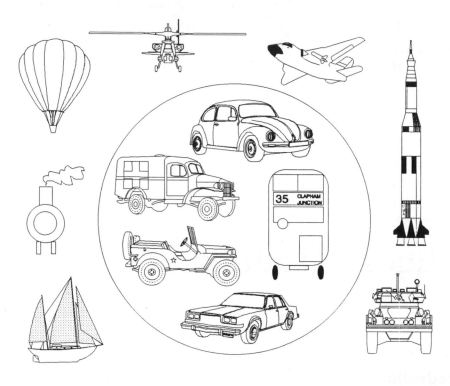

Figure 2.1: *Occurrences of the entity Vehicle are within the circle*

An entity also comprises a list of pieces of information it contains. For example, the Vehicle entity might hold details of make, model, colour and registration number. Each piece of information is held for every occurrence of the entity. An occurrence of Vehicle might be a midnight blue Volkswagen Polo with a registration number of J 166 CHM.

Throughout this book, entity names are formed from one or more words, run together, with a capital letter at the beginning of each word. For example, Vehicle, Product and LorryWithTailLift are the formal names of three different entities. When we talk about an occurrence of an entity we will usually use lower case and separate out the components. Thus we can talk about the vehicle with a registration number of J 166 CHM, or a lorry with tail lift with a registration number of M 918 WGH.

2.2   Attributes

Definition: An attribute is a piece of information at the atomic level - that is, in a form such that it cannot be subdivided into meaningful component pieces.

As with entities, attributes also have a description. For example, the attribute of Vehicle called registrationNumber might be described as, "The unique identifier assigned by the UK government's Driver and Vehicle Licensing Agency to a vehicle which is to be driven on the public roads of the UK during a period in excess of three months." In an occurrence of an entity each attribute takes on a particular value.

Attribute names are formed from one or more words, run together, with a capital letter at the beginning of each word except the first. For example, address, telephoneNumber, and dateRoadFundLicenceRenewable are the formal names of three distinct attributes.

2.3   Representing entities and attributes

This book will use three ways of representing entities and their attributes. Each is useful at different times.

2.3.1   The attribute list

An entity can be represented by a list of its attributes. This example shows the information needed to run a room booking system and to ensure that no room gets double-booked.

> RoomBooking
>   <u>roomNumber</u>
>   <u>dateRoomRequired</u>
>   <u>timeRoomRequired</u>
>   quantityDuration
>   nameBooks
> (o)   telexNumberBooks

The underlined attributes show an entity's primary key and (o) indicates an optional attribute: both concepts will be explained later in this chapter. The sequence of attributes in the list is unimportant.

This representation of an entity is particularly useful when all of its attributes need to be shown.

2.3.2   The relational table

Another way of representing an entity is as a relational table. In the relational table each attribute is shown as a column.

RoomBooking

roomNumber	dateRoom Required	timeRoom Required	quantity Duration	nameBooks	telexNumber Books (o)
2	12.11.93	12.00	2	Marsh	776109
14	12.11.93	12.00	1	Moon	
14	12.11.93	13.00	3	Girling	
2	13.11.93	09.00	1.5	Lowe	777443

The shaded column headings are used to show the entity's primary key attributes. Where column headings include the (o) symbol the attribute can be assumed to be optional. The sequence of columns in the table is not significant and nor is the sequence of the rows - this is a fundamental requirement of the relational model and is discussed in more detail in chapter 7. When a relational table has more columns than can be shown on the page this is indicated by three dots to the right of the table.

The relational table format has the advantage that it can be used to show a few sample occurrences of the entity.

2.3.3   The entity diagram

An entity can also be represented by a symbol on an entity diagram.

```
┌─────────────┐
│ RoomBooking │
│             │
└─────────────┘
```

Figure 2.2

The advantage of representing entities as symbols is that they can be linked together to form complete diagrams. Diagrams are a good way of communicating data structures in a concise way, both within a project team and to the outside world.

In this book the entity symbol is a rectangle. You may have encountered diagrams which use different shapes such as ellipses or rounded rectangles. Whether an entity is shown as a square, a bubble or a box is immaterial. What is important is that everyone in a project team agrees to adopt the same notation so that no time is wasted translating from one to another.

Data model diagrams do not get interesting until there are several related entities on them. Chapter 3 deals with the relationships between entities and details the authors' recommended diagramming conventions. A full list of the conventions is shown in appendix A. A data model diagram drawn up according to these conventions will convey each entity's primary key and foreign key structure (concepts which will be explained later in this chapter and in chapter 3) but no details of non-key attributes.

We tend to use both the entity diagram (for the power of its pictorial representation) and the attribute list (to show the details of the entities on the entity diagram). The relational table format is particularly useful when we want to give a tangible illustration of a particular data structure using sample occurrences.

2.4   Terminology

The terms used so far in this text are those most commonly used in describing the components of a logical data model. The table below shows terms used to describe closely allied concepts.

Logical:	Entity	Occurrence	Attribute	Relationship
Relational theory:	Relation	Tuple	Attribute	Relationship
Object oriented:	Class	Instance	Attribute	Association
Early physical:	File	Record	Field	Pointer
Database:	Table	Row	Column	Relationship
Spreadsheet:	Spreadsheet	Row	Column	Lookup

In part 1 of this text we shall use the terminology of logical data modelling. We shall introduce database terminology at the end of part 1 to show how each part of the logical data model is converted into its corresponding database component. In part 2 we shall map logical data modelling concepts onto those used in object modelling to see how far the parallels can be taken.

There is a good reason to include spreadsheet terminology in the cross-reference table. Spreadsheets are two-dimensional tables used for storing information in a standardized way - which is exactly what database tables are. Some spreadsheet packages already feature relational capabilities which are achieved by treating each spreadsheet as a table. However, although spreadsheets can be used to mimic relational databases, this is not how they are typically used and so the parallel should not be taken too far.

2.5   Attribute roles

The entity Vehicle has many occurrences and they are to be seen on the roads every day. You could go up to one of them and touch it. A particular occurrence of Vehicle may be a Vauxhall Astra with the number plate A 184 TGW. If you tracked down this car you might find that it was turquoise and that its tax disc had just expired. This information, being specific to the car, belongs in the entity Vehicle.

Opening up the bonnet, you might also find that it had an overhead camshaft. But you could have worked that out without locating it physically if you knew that all Vauxhall Astras have overhead camshafts. This piece of information belongs in another entity which could be called VehicleModel. The specifications for a Vauxhall Astra apply to all the cars of that type but to none of them exclusively. Analysing the characteristics of Vehicle and VehicleModel we might construct attribute lists something like these[*].

> VehicleModel
>   manufacturerName
>   modelName
>   quantityEngineCapacity
>   ifTransverseEngine
>   ifOverheadCamshaft
>   fuelType
>   countDoors
>   dateLaunched
>   quantityMaximumLoad

---

[*] The concept of a VehicleModel presented here has been simplified deliberately to illustrate basic modelling techniques. In reality, a number of model variants may exist to account for five-door models, diesel models etc. A fully detailed data model should probably also recognize optional extras such as power steering, sunroofs and compact disc players. An application which looks straightforward at first glance often yields a great deal of complexity upon further examination.

Vehicle
     <u>registrationNumber</u>
     manufacturerName
     modelName
     colourOfPaintwork
     yearOfManufacture
     dateRoadFundLicenceRenewable

Both entities have attributes which are dates: in the case of the VehicleModel, it is the date when the model was launched and in the case of the individual Vehicle the date its tax disc expires. Because both attributes are dates it is possible to see them as roles played by an attribute simply called date.

Attributes like date which typically play many roles are sometimes called **global** or **root attributes**. A root attribute's characteristics, such as its length and the format in which it is stored, are adopted by all attributes which are its roles.

2.5.1   Distinguishing attribute roles

One of the attributes of Vehicle was colourOfPaintwork: in the case of the Vauxhall Astra we record here that its paintwork is turquoise. But suppose we decide to store the colour of the upholstery inside the car as well.

Vehicle
     <u>registrationNumber</u>
     manufacturerName
     modelName
     colourOfPaintwork
     colourOfUpholstery
     yearOfManufacture
     dateRoadFundLicenceRenewable

The entity now has two attributes which are roles of the same root attribute, colour.

2.5.2   Roles of roles

Imagine that someone has now pointed out that there are cars with two colours of exterior paint. Two-tone cars have roofs which are painted in a shade which contrasts with the rest of the bodywork. We can store this information by introducing a further attribute.

Vehicle
>   registrationNumber
>   manufacturerName
>   modelName
>   colourOfPaintworkBody
>   colourOfPaintworkRoof
>   colourOfUpholstery
>   yearOfManufacture
>   dateRoadFundLicenceRenewable

The new attribute, colourOfPaintworkRoof, is a role of the attribute colourOfPaintwork which in its turn was a role of the attribute colour. The old attribute colourOfPaintwork now has a different name which specifies that it is the car's bodywork colour.

2.5.3   Occurrences without distinct roles

Consider a university which keeps records of its students. The university must know where it can send mail to a student both during termtime and during the holidays. Since most students at this establishment live in halls of residence during termtime and go back to their parents' homes in the holidays, the two addresses are likely to be different and therefore two separate attributes are required.

Student
>   studentNumber
>   nameFamily
>   nameGiven
>   addressTermtime
>   addressVacation
> (o)   grantGivingAuthority

Both addressTermtime and addressVacation are roles of the global attribute address.

Two of the students at the university are Michael Roberts and Ruth Carver. Michael was brought up in the town where he goes to university so he lives with his parents during termtime. Ruth is a mature student whose husband works in the town. They own their house and Ruth continues to live there during university holidays. For different reasons, both students have the same address during termtime as they do in the holidays. This does not mean they only have one attribute each for address. Every occurrence of the Student entity must have the same shape and the whole attribute list above applies to each student's record. Both students have two address attributes but in each case the two attributes take on the same value.

Returning briefly to the Vehicle example, note that most cars have roofs painted the same colour as the rest of their bodywork. Therefore most occurrences of the Vehicle entity will have the same value entered in the two attributes colourOfPaintworkBody and colourOfPaintworkRoof.

2.6   Optional attributes

The university needs to know the identity of the body which gives a grant to each of its students. This is because the university usually receives the student's fees directly from the grant-giving authority. However, not every student receives a grant. In this university there are overseas students and students from higher income families who don't qualify for grants and must pay their own fees. The attribute showing the student's grant-giving authority is therefore sometimes blank, as the last column in the table shows:

Student

student Number	name Family	name Given	addressTermtime	addressVacation	grntGvg Auth(o)
12573	Gupta	Ravi	7 Campus Hall	35 Market Road Leicester	LEIC
12728	du Pont	Linda	8 Campus Hall	51 Bishops Avenue London	
07543	Carver	Ruth	16 Hill Street Bath	16 Hill Street Bath	SERC
14171	Roberts	Michael	5 Vale Street Bath	5 Vale Street Bath	AVON
10944	Razak	Ali	3 Campus Hall	1093 Seri Begawan Brunei	

Attributes for which a value need not be supplied are allowed to remain empty, that is they may contain a **null** value, and are known as **optional attributes**. The rest are **mandatory** and must always contain a non-null value. Space characters (blanks) and zeros are not the same as null values.

Recall the RoomBooking entity.

RoomBooking
    roomNumber
    dateRoomRequired
    timeRoomRequired
    quantityDuration
    nameBooks
(o)   telexNumberBooks

Here the optional attribute telexNumberBooks shows that some bookings are received by telex and where this is so the booking clerk makes a note of the telex reference number. He has probably found from bitter experience that when a dispute arises because two people think they have booked the same room at the same time, it is useful for him to be able to produce a hard copy of their original requests. However, since most requests still come in by phone the attribute telexNumberBooks must be allowed to remain empty.

The attribute list notation indicates optional attributes with an (o) sign. The relational table uses the same notation to indicate optionality:

RoomBooking

roomNumber	dateRoom Required	timeRoom Required	quantity Duration	nameBooks	telexNumber Books (o)
2	12.11.93	12.00	2	Marsh	776109
14	12.11.93	12.00	1	Moon	
14	12.11.93	13.00	3	Girling	
2	13.11.93	09.00	1.5	Lowe	777443

Some occurrences of RoomBooking have null values for the attribute telexNumberBooks, confirming its optionality. Unless the attribute was optional such occurrences could not have come into existence. The attributes quantityDuration and nameBooks are both mandatory and we can imagine some of the difficulties the clerk would encounter were he to accept bookings that have no duration (when could he next book the room out again?) or booker name (whom should he contact to cancel a booking when a room's ceiling fell in?).

Problems will also arise if an attribute which should be optional is incorrectly specified as mandatory. This is a mistake sometimes made by data modellers who fail to think through the full life history of an entity. For example, a company stores details of its customers in an entity like this.

    Customer
        customerNumber
        name
        address
        telephoneNumber
    (o) creditRating

The firm receives most of its orders over the phone and these include orders from new customers. The telephone order clerk takes down the new customer's name, address and telephone number and enters this information to create a new occurrence of the Customer entity.

The firm has a policy that it will never ship goods to a customer until it has checked that the customer has a satisfactory credit rating - in other words, whether it has always paid its bills on time in the past. There is not much point asking the customer for this information. It can be bought from specialist agencies and once a new customer record has been set up the credit controller contacts one of the agencies to get a credit rating which she enters onto the Customer record. Often this check has to be done urgently so as not to delay the shipment of orders to the new customer. Nonetheless, there is a short period in the life of every Customer occurrence when the attribute creditRating is null and for this reason it must be designated as optional.

2.7   Avoiding derived attributes

If an attribute's value can be determined by looking at the values of one or more other attributes in the model then it is said to be **derived**. There is no place in the logical model for derived attributes. It is not until the physical data model is drawn up that derived data may need to be introduced for performance reasons: this is discussed in more detail in chapter 8.

The methods of deriving information are many and various. They range from straightforward copying of one attribute's value into another attribute to sophisticated calculation. In each case the danger is the same: that the stored value will get out of line with the value as recalculated from the raw data. To prevent such anomalies arising, attributes should be used to store raw data only.

Occasionally it is not easy to decide which of several attributes is the derived one. For example, a fashion buyer agrees to buy 100 pieces at £4.99 each, or a total of £499.00. Any two attributes out of the price, the quantity and the total consideration could be used to derive the third. Which two are actually held is a matter for the modeller's judgement. One factor which may tilt the scales is the required accuracy of the data. Rounding errors in the values of some attributes may matter less than in those of others: these are the ones that should be left out of the logical model to be derived by the application program.

Despite what has been said, there are a few categories of derived data that are almost certain to be introduced at the physicalization stage so they are usually foreshadowed in the logical model. One of these is shown below.

BankAccount
    <u>bankSortCode</u>
    <u>accountNumber</u>
    dateOpened
    customerNumberHolder
    currencyCode
(d)   quantityBalance

BankAccountTransaction
    <u>bankSortCode</u>
    <u>accountNumber</u>
    <u>dateOfTransaction</u>
    <u>timeOfTransaction</u>
    quantityOfTransaction

A bank account's balance could be derived by adding up all the amounts, positive and negative, of all the account's transactions since it was opened. Due to transaction volumes the details are unlikely to be held online for long. Even if they are available online, the time taken to sum them all might be unacceptable to a customer asking for an up to date balance. Although strictly speaking neither archiving policy nor performance has anything to do with the logical model, balance attributes are sometimes shown. Note that anything which can be construed as an account is likely to have a balance. For example, warehouses are physical accounts where quantities of product accumulate: the stock level of a given product in a warehouse is therefore a balance and hence it is logically derivable.

Any derived attribute which is included in a data model must be marked with a (d) sign.

2.8   Primary key attributes

So far we have looked at a variety of attributes which describe the entity of which they form a part. Each attribute contributes towards building up a picture of the entity as a whole. Primary key attributes have to do more than this: they must identify each occurrence of the entity.

Definition: An entity's primary key is one or more of its attributes which together uniquely identify an occurrence of the entity.

The primary key attributes can never take on a particular set of values in more than one occurrence of the entity. No primary key attribute can have a null value and thus every attribute in the primary key is mandatory.

Primary key attributes are indicated by underlining the attribute's name in the attribute list and shading the column name in the relational table.

2.8.1   Uses of the primary key

Whenever there is a need to identify a particular occurrence of the entity it can be referred to by its key attributes. For example, the primary key of the entity Vehicle is the single attribute registrationNumber. If we want to find out the value of any of the non-key attributes in an occurrence of Vehicle we can use the value of the primary key attribute to specify which occurrence we mean. It makes sense to ask, "What colour is the upholstery in vehicle registration number A 184 TGW?" Because only one car has that registration number we will get only one answer to our question.

The primary key's guarantee to represent no more than one occurrence of an entity is a powerful promise. All relational databases are predicated on this guarantee. Through its primary key - and by no other means - one entity can be related to others, as we shall see in chapter 3.

In order to maintain its guarantee of uniqueness, the database should reject any attempt to insert a new occurrence of the entity which has the same primary key as an existing one. For example, a new car with a registrationNumber of A 184 TGW could not be entered as an occurrence of Vehicle while that particular Vauxhall Astra's record exists. If necessary, the record can exist until long after the Astra is a heap of scrap.

In part 1 of this book we require that every occurrence of an entity be identified uniquely; in chapter 9 we will relax this requirement and consider object identity in a post-relational world.

2.8.2   Choosing a primary key

Let us consider an application which needs to hold information about adults from all over the UK. An attribute list for the Person entity has been prepared by the data modeller and is shown overleaf. No primary key has been selected and we must consider the possible candidates for the job.

First let us consider a combination of nameGiven and nameFamily. This combination takes on values such as "Ted Codd" and "Margaret Thatcher". It seems to us a very natural way of referring to another human being and presumably it was devised in the first place to fulfil a psychological requirement to be able to identify other individuals and refer to them in their absence. However, each culture has restricted itself to a limited set of names and partly as a result of this the name does not satisfy the requirement to be unique. In a school or workplace of any size there is almost guaranteed to be a duplicate. Within one family, where the inherited part of the name is going to be replicated anyway, even given names are passed on from one generation to another so that the only way of distinguishing between two members of the family may be to call one "William Pitt the Elder" and the other "William Pitt the Younger". This might make us think of adding dateOfBirth into the candidate key. It would solve many problems of duplication but it would still not be possible to guarantee that sooner or later somewhere in the country there wouldn't be two babies born on the same day and registered under the same name.

```
Person
        nameFamily
        nameGiven
        dateOfBirth
        gender
(o)     passportNumber
(o)     drivingLicenceNumber
(o)     constituencyName
(o)     wardCode
(o)     registerNumber
        nationalInsuranceNumber
```

What about drivingLicenceNumber? No two people in the UK have the same number and the coding system is controlled by an unimpeachable body of civil servants in Swansea. Surely this will provide a unique primary key? It would be fine were we certain that everyone we needed to record had got a driving licence. This might be true if the application system was intended to store members of an advanced drivers club, or people applying for motor insurance, but it is far too restrictive for most applications.

The same consideration disqualifies passportNumber. It is not compulsory to apply for a passport and there are plenty of people in the UK who can't afford overseas holidays.

A combination of constituencyName, wardCode and registerNumber will also uniquely identify an individual. There is always an electoral register in force and again it is maintained by a reputable government body. Every ward in a constituency has a two-letter code and within the ward registered voters are given unique numbers allocated sequentially along the length of each street. However, in the UK it is not compulsory to register to vote. Many people disappeared from the register during the Poll Tax era to reduce their chances of being tracked down and made to pay. It is impossible to register if you are homeless, insane or in the House of Lords. But the candidate key must be disqualified anyway because a person's number changes every time a new register is compiled. The changes would require every row of the Person table to be recreated and this change would also have to be effected in every other table to which the Person table was linked. A primary key must be stable.

This leaves nationalInsuranceNumber as the only serious contender. It is properly maintained by the UK government's welfare department and it is given to an individual for life. Unless they are employed as children, people do not receive a number until the age of sixteen, but this is not a problem because the Person entity is only required to store adults. In fact, national insurance number is used by some employers to identify their employees because it is one of the things an employer must find out from a new recruit. However it is not the sort of thing people expect to be asked when they first apply for a job or when they claim compensation for injury. Whether it is a suitable key or not therefore depends in the end on the nature of the proposed application.

If we have any doubts at all we should reject our last candidate. Since no suitable primary key has emerged from among the existing attributes, it is necessary to invent an artificial new one. It must be added to the attribute list as shown below.

        Person
                personIdentifier
                nameFamily
                nameGiven
                dateOfBirth
                gender
        (o)   passportNumber
        (o)   drivingLicenceNumber
        (o)   constituencyName
        (o)   wardCode
        (o)   registerNumber
                nationalInsuranceNumber

Although the sequence of attributes is not significant we shall adopt the convention of showing primary keys at the top of the attribute list in the interests of uniformity.

2.8.3   Natural versus artificial keys

All coding systems are artificial, including naming systems for institutions, geographical areas, people and objects. Many codes are allocated outside the sphere of influence of the system under development: because these cannot be controlled by the systems development team they are regarded as natural attributes. When a system generates its own codes however it is adding to the stock of artificial identifiers in existence. By and large this is best avoided, which is why we gave due consideration to the other candidates for Person's primary key, but it is sometimes inevitable.

While the grand generalizations, the fundamental entities with which all systems are concerned, often need an artificial identifier, it is important to avoid allocating them to lower level entities. Recall the RoomBooking example.

RoomBooking

roomNumber	dateRoom Required	timeRoom Required	quantity Duration	nameBooks	telexNumber Books (o)
2	12.11.93	12.00	2	Marsh	776109
14	12.11.93	12.00	1	Moon	
14	12.11.93	13.00	3	Girling	
2	13.11.93	09.00	1.5	Lowe	777443

Each room booking has a primary key of roomNumber, dateRoomRequired and timeRoomRequired. These three attributes are enough to ensure that a booking is uniquely identified[*]. It may have been tempting to give each new booking an artificial serial number but since room number, date and time all have to be held anyway they may as well serve in the capacity of primary key too.

Natural keys can get quite long and may involve ten or more attributes. Don't bottle out!

---

[*] The primary key of roomNumber, date and time ensures that once a meeting has been booked no other meeting can begin in the same room on the same date at the same time. However, another meeting could be booked to begin there one minute later. The primary key's function is to ensure uniqueness, not to prevent double booking. In a relational database application the program code would need to check all previously booked meetings, taking into account their durations before allowing a new one to be inserted. Other types of database may be able to store insertion rules like this themselves.

2.8.4   The sphere of uniqueness

We said earlier on that there is only one Vehicle with the registration number A 184 TGW, but is this true? Yes, as long as we are content to confine ourselves to vehicles registered in the UK. A system designed for Interpol (the International Police force) might need to record the number plates of cars registered all over the world and its Vehicle entity would require a country attribute as an addition to its primary key. Within the country, the registrationNumber is unique.

> Vehicle
> > <u>countryOfRegistration</u>
> > <u>registrationNumber</u>
> > manufacturerName
> > modelName
> > colourOfPaintworkBody
> > colourOfPaintworkRoof
> > colourOfUpholstery
> > yearOfManufacture
> > dateRoadFundLicenceRenewable

In a sense the Interpol Vehicle entity is a generalization. It is a merger of many existing entities: the UK Vehicle, the Swedish Vehicle, the Australian Vehicle and so on. The Person entity might be a generalization too, an entity created to recognize that employees, contractors, job applicants and claimants are all human beings and have something in common. It is probable that in the past there were different coding systems to identify each specialization. These coding systems may conflict with one another. For example, SMIT002 in the contractor file and SMIT002 in the claimant file could be two separate individuals, but JONE017 in the claimant file and 13785 in the applicant file might be one and the same. One solution would be to give a two-part key to the Person entity: the first attribute specifying which of the old coding systems the second attribute derived from. The two-part key would certainly be unique. But it would prevent the merger of separate records from the employee and claimant files to show that they really represented the same individual (say, an employee who suffered an industrial accident) and would thus defeat one of the major objects of generalizing the Employee and Claimant entities in the first place. The benefits of generalization, which is a particularly powerful technique in data modelling, are explained in chapter 4.

In the case of the international vehicle database it was acceptable to pad out the existing primary key with an attribute specifying which coding system it came from. This is because we assumed a vehicle could not be registered in Sweden and Australia at the same time. The specializations were mutually exclusive. A Person on the other hand could be an employee and a claimant at the same time. For this reason a new artificial key, personIdentifier, was invented.

2.9   Avoiding structured attributes

It is in trying to devise new artificial keys that we run the greatest danger of creating structured codes. Recall the definition of an attribute: it must be an atomic piece of data, not divisible into meaningful components. Structured codes defy that definition. A structured code is one into which several different attributes have been crammed.

Take for example an invented key for order in a new order processing system. A typical occurrence of the order code will have a value such as BR/94/P/0005, which shows that the order was taken in the Brighton office from a personal caller and that it was that office's fifth such order in 1994. This is useful information but it would have been more useful had it been held in four separate attributes. The individual attributes which should have emerged from the structured code - office taking order, year of order, order method and serial number - can be extracted from the structured code for use in selecting and analysing orders, but only at a cost of extra programming effort.

By insisting that every type of order taken in each individual office has its own serial number series, the organization is also committing itself to making an accurate assessment of the annual volumes of orders expected in each office in each category. The number of digits in the serial number part of the code will have to be big enough for the maximum volumes expected anywhere, even though that might seem excessive to some of the smaller offices. The organization will also have to arrange to reset all office's serial numbers at the beginning of each year.

If an artificial serial number is to be created at all then it should be forced to take on as much work as possible. Serial number alone could identify orders throughout the organization if all the offices could dip into a common pool of serial numbers and go on incrementing them until they have run out, say in five years' time. After five years it should be possible to start again at 1 without risk of confusion. However even if each office needed its own set of serial numbers - perhaps because the computers in each office are not permanently connected - then a key consisting of the two separate attributes, office code and serial number, should be enough to identify the order.

A structured code can be regarded as a variety of derived attribute. However, instead of replicating data already held in attributes elsewhere, it replaces them. The code BR/94/P/0005 is something which ought to be derivable from other attributes and therefore should not need to be stored in its structured form.

A similar type of structured code tends to afflict key-only entities which are used as domains. A domain is a pool of possible values from which the actual values an attribute takes on are drawn. Where two or more selection criteria must be specified the domain of possible values is an n-dimensional array. Instead of specifying the selection criteria independently the modeller may be tempted to force the entire contents of the array into one attribute. For example, a company sells fishermen's smocks by mail order. Each smock is either blue-and-white striped or red-and-white striped and the smocks come in a range of sizes from 32" to 44" chest. Instead of giving each Product a size attribute and a separate one for colour, the company has rolled the information together into a single attribute called productCode, with values such as B42 for a blue-and-white smock size 42". Effectively the values of productCode are the values in the cells of a matrix which holds all combinations of colour and size. When a new green-and-white smock is produced a number of new values must be added to the style domain - one for each available size. When the managing director demands some analysis of sales by size, regardless of colour, the size part of the productCode attribute must be stripped out before the work can be done.

It is true that both size and colour are required as attributes of a product so that its stock levels can be tracked. These two may both feature in the Product's primary key, but they should be held as two separate attributes.

There is one structured code that recurs so frequently as an attribute that it would be impossible to abolish it: that is date. A date such as 12/07/1992 is a code made up of a year, a month of the year and a day within the month.

2.10   Alternate keys

Definition: An alternate key is one or more attributes other than the primary key which, when non-null, uniquely identify an occurrence of an entity.

This means that the attributes comprising an alternate key will never take on a particular set of values in more than one occurrence of the entity, except where the set of values includes a null value.

In the process of choosing a primary key for an entity we often recognize the claims of competing candidate keys and attribute sets which provide unique identifiers whenever they are present. Although only one set of attributes can be chosen as the primary key, we should also register the fact that the alternate identifiers exist.

Each alternate key can be shown in a separate clause below the list of an entity's attributes.

```
        Person
                personIdentifier
                nameFamily
                nameGiven
                dateOfBirth
                gender
        (o)     passportNumber
        (o)     drivingLicenceNumber
        (o)     constituencyName
        (o)     wardCode
        (o)     registerNumber
                nationalInsuranceNumber
        Unique:     passportNumber
        Unique:     drivingLicenceNumber
        Unique:     constituencyName, wardCode, registerNumber
        Unique:     nationalInsuranceNumber
```

An alternate key will never get the job of representing the entity to the outside world, as the primary key does, but it can help to prevent inappropriate occurrences of an entity from coming into existence. For example, if we tried to create a second record of Person with the same national insurance number as an existing person, the fact that nationalInsuranceNumber was a known alternate key would cause alarm bells to ring.

Alternate keys are also instrumental in supporting some of the most useful structures available to the data modeller. We shall meet them again in chapters 3 to 6.

Chapter summary

The basic components of the logical data model are the entity and the attribute.

Entities can be thought of as two-dimensional tables like spreadsheets. Each column represents a different attribute. Each row represents an occurrence of an entity. A cell contains an attribute value specific to the occurrence of the entity.

Entities contain attributes that describe them. Some attributes are roles of other attributes. Attributes may be mandatory or optional. One or more of an entity's attributes form its primary key. An entity's primary key uniquely identifies an occurrence of that entity. For this reason, a primary key attribute can never be optional.

Sometimes a primary key must be chosen from among competing candidates. An attribute, or group of attributes, which would uniquely identify the entity but hasn't been chosen as the primary key is called an alternate key. Alternate keys are allowed to be null.

Questions

1. What are the differences between a logical and a physical data model?

2. Create a description for the entity ItemOfFurniture. List five things that would be occurrences of the entity according to your definition and five things that would not.

3. Draw up a relational table with at least five sample rows for the entity Vehicle.

4. An exam paper is completed by one person, marked by another and cross-checked by another. Draw up an attribute list for the entity ExamPaper which differentiates these roles.

5. Is a mandatory attribute allowed to contain the value zero? Can it take on the value of a space character(s)?

6. Mark the derived attribute(s) in the attribute list below, giving reasons for your choice.

> RockSample
>   sampleNumber
>   dateCollected
>   quantityVolume
>   quantityWeight
>   quantityDensity

7. What would be the advantages and disadvantages of making telephoneNumber an optional attribute of Customer?

8. Suggest a primary key for the entity Appointment in a system being developed for a group practice where several doctors hold surgeries.

9. The following are occurrences of attributes of a variety of entities. Explaining your reasoning, decide which of them are atomic and which are structured.

    (a) green
    (b) 16/11/1996
    (c) Dame Alicia Markova
    (d) 591.83
    (e) The Name of the Rose
    (f) New York, New York

10. Suggest an alternate key for the entity Property whose attribute list is shown below.

    Property
          address
          countOfBedrooms
    (o) quantitySquareFootageGarden
    (o) landRegistryNumber
          partyOwns
          yearBuilt

3

Relationships

Introduction

Until now we have studied isolated entities. This chapter shows how entities are formally related to each other in the relational data model. Linked data entities provide paths through a data model and invest it with its power to answer enquiries.

3.1   Making enquiries

We have already noted that the entities Vehicle and VehicleModel represent closely allied concepts. Now we shall see how they can be used together to answer questions.

When we needed to know the colour of the upholstery in A 184 TGW, we found the answer in the Vehicle entity itself since it has an attribute called colourOfUpholstery. How can we find out whether or not it has an overhead camshaft? The attribute which holds this piece of information is not in the Vehicle entity but in VehicleModel.

A VehicleModel is identified by the name of the maker (such as Vauxhall) and the name of the model (such as Astra). It makes sense to ask whether the Vauxhall Astra has an overhead camshaft because there is only one occurrence of the VehicleModel entity for Vauxhall Astra and we will therefore receive only one answer to the question. So, to find out whether A 184 TGW has an overhead camshaft it is first necessary to determine its make and model. This information *is* held in the Vehicle entity.

Vehicle

A TGW 184 →   registrationNumber
                    manufacturerName   → VAUXHALL
                    modelName   → ASTRA
                    colourOfPaintworkBody
                    colourOfPaintworkRoof
                    colourOfUpholstery
                    yearOfManufacture
                    dateRoadFundLicenceRenewable

VehicleModel

VAUXHALL →   manufacturerName
ASTRA →   modelName
                    quantityEngineCapacity
                    ifTransverseEngine
                    ifOverheadCamshaft   → YES
                    fuelType
                    countDoors
                    dateLaunched
                    quantityMaximumLoad

The original question, "Does A 184 TGW have an overhead camshaft?" had to be broken down into two parts: firstly, "What are the make and model of A 184 TGW?" and secondly, using the answer to the first question, "Does the Vauxhall Astra have an overhead camshaft?" Thus an enquiry that concerned a specific occurrence of the Vehicle entity was answered with an attribute value from the VehicleModel entity.

Sometimes we need to ask questions to which the answer is a list of values. For example, suppose the police have been asked to investigate an incident in which a car has filled up its tank with diesel at a filling station and then driven away without paying. The investigating officer might ask, "What are the registration numbers of all vehicles which use diesel as a fuel?"

Again the attribute, registrationNumber, whose values are required as answers lies in a different entity from the attribute, fuelType, whose value provides the starting point for the enquiry.

In each case, the enquiry was made possible by the fact that the Vehicle entity has the attributes ManufacturerName and ModelName which match the primary key of the VehicleModel entity. This is how a relationship is implemented in the relational data model.

Definition: An entity is related to another when the attribute list of one contains all the other's primary key attributes, or roles of those attributes.

3.2   Owners and details

The relationship between VehicleModel and Vehicle is not symmetrical. Every occurrence of VehicleModel describes thousands of related occurrences of Vehicle. A 184 TGW is one of many Vauxhall Astras. But for every occurrence of Vehicle, there is only one related VehicleModel. A car cannot be both a Vauxhall Astra and a Fiat Uno.

The entity which occurs once for each occurrence of the relationship is known as the **owner** and that which occurs many times as the **detail**. Note that entities are classed as owners and details only with respect to particular relationships. An entity can be the owner in one relationship and the detail in another.

Enquiries such as, "Does A 184 TGW have an overhead camshaft?" start at the detail end of the relationship and finish at the owner end, ensuring that a single attribute value is returned. Those such as, "Which vehicles use diesel?" start at the owner end and finish at the detail end, ensuring that a list of values results.

Relationships must be named so that they can be read from owner to detail. Our naming convention concatenates the words in relationship labels, like those in entity and attribute names, beginning the first word with a lower case letter. Naming a relationship often allows us to read a relationship as an English sentence such as "Department registers students". It is also permissible to give a relationship a second label so that it can be read from detail to owner. "Students are registered by department" is the inverse of "Department registers students": it conveys exactly the same fact. In either direction, the name can be used to signify either the relationship itself or a particular occurrence of it. Thus, "VehicleModel describes Vehicle", or "Volkswagen Polo describes J 166 CHM".

Relationships between owners and details fall into two categories. A foreign key relationship is one whose owner's key attributes appear among the non-key attributes of the detail. A primary key relationship sees the key of the owner contribute towards the key of the detail. A primary key relationship is a special case of a foreign key relationship, so we shall deal with the most general case first.

3.3   Foreign key owners

3.3.1   Diagramming foreign key relationships

On data model diagrams the symbols representing owner and detail entities are connected by a line, as shown.

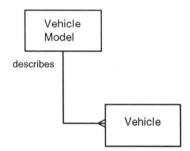

Figure 3.1

The crow's foot symbol at the detail end of the line indicates that there are many occurrences of the detail entity for each occurrence of the owner. It could be thought of as a visual mnemonic representing the multiplicity of the details[*].

Wherever possible entities are positioned on data model diagrams so that the owner is above the detail. Only when an entity is both owner and detail

---

[*] Sometimes an arrowhead is used instead of a crow's foot: this is perfectly acceptable although it lacks the mnemonic qualities of the many-toed foot and conveys instead misleading impressions of motion. Data do not move.

of another is this impossible. See chapter 5 for further exploration of such relationships.

3.3.2   Foreign key clauses

The attributes of the owner which appear in the detail entity and forge the link between them are called foreign keys of the detail. Foreign key clauses are shown by convention at the bottom of the attribute list. A foreign key clause is made up of a list of the attributes which form the primary key of the owner followed by the name of the owner entity.

> Vehicle
> > registrationNumber
> > manufacturerName
> > modelName
> > colourOfPaintworkBody
> > colourOfPaintworkRoof
> > colourOfUpholstery
> > yearOfManufacture
> > dateRoadFundLicenceRenewable
> Foreign: manufacturerName, modelName → VehicleModel

The foreign key notation should be somewhat reminiscent of the Unique clauses which were used to specify alternate keys in chapter 2. An alternate key identifies the listed entity itself, however, while a foreign key identifies a related entity.

3.3.3   Foreign keys on the relational table

Looking at an individual relational table such as Vehicle it is impossible to tell whether it has any foreign key relationships at all. The lines between objects on a data model diagram represent logical relationships. These are not necessarily implemented physically in a relational database, which is in essence no more than a collection of two-dimensional tables.

VehicleModel

manufacturerName	modelName	quantityEngine Capacity	ifTransverse Engine	ifOverhead Camshaft	...
Volkswagen	Polo	1300	Y	N	
Volkswagen	Golf	1600	Y	Y	
Vauxhall	Astra	1300	Y	Y	
Peugeot	205	1300	Y	N	

Vehicle

registration Number	manufacturerName	modelName	colourOfPaintwork Body	...
A 184 TGW	Vauxhall	Astra	turquoise	
E 358 OLL	Vauxhall	Astra	mustard	
NRK 156 P	Ford	Cortina	white	
J 166 CHM	Volkswagen	Polo	midnight blue	
OAL 50 W	Vauxhall	Astra	turquoise	
B 292 APN	Toyota	Carina	red	

Without a physical link between the tables then how does the relational database know which is the owner and which is detail? It is a property of the relationship that the detail entity has the owner entity's key amongst its attributes. The vehicle example shows why this has to be so: the attributes manufacturerName and modelName, as the key of the VehicleModel entity, can only take on the values Vauxhall and Astra together in one row of that table. But they are not the primary key attributes of Vehicle, nor an alternate key of the entity, so in the second table they can take on the values Vauxhall and Astra as often as they like.

By joining these tables on the common attributes we can answer enquiries such as those discussed in section 3.1.

3.4   Primary key owners

Sometimes the primary key attributes of an owner entity appear among the primary key attributes of the detail. For example, an invoice with several lines could be represented by the following data structure:

Invoice
        invoiceNumber
        dateRaised
        customerNumber
Foreign: customerNumber → Customer

InvoiceLine
        invoiceNumber
        invoiceLineNumber
        productCode
        quantity
        dateOfDespatch

Foreign: invoiceNumber → Invoice
Foreign: productCode → Product

The fact that the key of Invoice appears among the attributes of InvoiceLine means that the two entities are linked and that Invoice is the owner. Since the key of Invoice is wholly contained in the primary key of InvoiceLine, we say that this is a **primary key relationship**.

Diagramatically, primary key relationships are shown entering the top of the detail object. This distinguishes them from the foreign key links which enter the detail from the side. It does not matter where the link leaves the owner object.

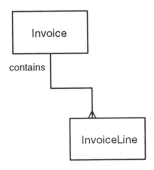

Figure 3.2

3.5   Key-only owners

The invoice data model diagram shows that InvoiceLine has inherited part of its primary key from that of Invoice, but it doesn't reveal anything about the rest of the key. The diagram can be improved if we say that the other element of InvoiceLine's key is also inherited from an owner entity.

The other component of the entity's primary key is the attribute invoiceLineNumber. The entity of which invoiceLineNumber is the primary key is of no interest in its own right. It has no attributes other than its key and is known as a key-only owner. The entity would not be implemented physically as a relational table. Key-only owners are useful at the analysis stage and result in highly informative diagrams which can be used for formal verification of the attribute lists. Note that a key-only entity will never have any owners of its own and will always appear at the top of a data model diagram.

>   InvoiceLineNumber
>   <u>invoiceLineNumber</u>
>
>   InvoiceLine
>   <u>invoiceNumber</u>
>   <u>invoiceLineNumber</u>
>   productCode
>   quantity
>   dateOfDespatch
>   Foreign: invoiceNumber → Invoice
>   Foreign: invoiceLineNumber → InvoiceLineNumber
>   Foreign: productCode → Product

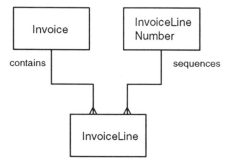

Figure 3.3

Definition: Every attribute which forms part of an entity's primary key should be the sole primary key of an entity of its own. Entities which come into existence purely to satisfy this rule are known as key-only owners.

In most data models of any size, Date becomes a key-only owner due to its presence in at least one other entity's key. So do its components, Year, Month and DayOfMonth. Time, SequenceNumber, Count and Quantity are common too. Once they become entities in their own right key-only entities should be shown on diagrams as foreign key owners. For example, Date becomes a key-only owner of both Vehicle Model and Vehicle, as shown in figure 3.4. This makes an entity diagram a very close guide to the entity's full attribute list while still retaining its visual force.

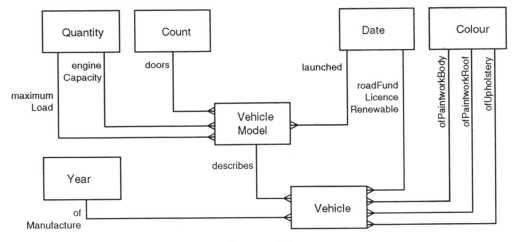

Figure 3.4

Foreign keys supporting relationships with key-only owners usually need to be rolenamed. Since the role of the attribute is determined by the nature of the relationship between owner and detail entities, we have used the convention that a foreign key attribute name is created by concatenating the owner's key attribute name (such as date) and the relationship name (such as roadFundLicenceRenewable). Under our convention, the modeller is not compelled to create rolenames for foreign key attributes whose role is already clear. Thus the attributes manufacturerName and modelName are inherited unadorned from VehicleModel by Vehicle.

        VehicleModel
                manufacturerName
                modelName
                quantityEngineCapacity
                ifTransverseEngine
                ifOverheadCamshaft
                fuelType
                countDoors
                dateLaunched
                quantityMaximumLoad
        Foreign: manufacturerName → Manufacturer
        Foreign: modelName → Model
        Foreign: quantityEngineCapacity → Quantity
        Foreign: countDoors → Count
        Foreign: dateLaunched → Date
        Foreign: quantityMaximumLoad → Quantity

Vehicle
    <u>registrationNumber</u>
    manufacturerName
    modelName
    colourOfPaintworkBody
    colourOfPaintworkRoof
    colourOfUpholstery
    yearOfManufacture
    dateRoadFundLicenceRenewable

Foreign: manufacturerName, modelName → VehicleModel
Foreign: colourOfPaintworkBody → Colour
Foreign: colourOfPaintworkRoof → Colour
Foreign: colourOfUpholstery → Colour
Foreign: yearOfManufacture → Year
Foreign: dateRoadFundLicenceRenewable → Date

3.6   Domains

Date, Time, SequenceNumber, Count and Quantity entities hold a potentially infinite number of values for the foreign key attributes of their details. Some key-only owners, however, exert more control over their details by holding a finite domain of permissible values. Any key-only entity with "Type", "Indicator" or "Flag" as part of its name is likely to be performing this function but this clue is not always there. Consider for example the diagram in figure 3.5.

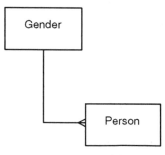

Figure 3.5

The attribute list for the Gender entity can be extended to incorporate a value clause that specifies legitimate values of the gender attribute.

Gender
gender
Values: 'male', 'female'

Since the entity Gender has only two occurrences the relational table below is complete. Its relationship with Person ensures that the Person's gender attribute is always filled with a value from the Gender table and never with anything else.

Gender

gender
male
female

Person

personId	nameFamily	nameGiven	dateOfBirth	gender	passportNumber (o)	...
0056964	Igbo	Benjamin	12/05/1971	male	006754114	
8975565	Harrison	Cora	08/06/1945	female		
7667786	Leung	Amy	16/08/1960	female	008767867	
5465001	Tew	Hermione	27/02/1896	female	000602155	

3.7   Cardinality

A relationship linking one owner occurrence to many occurrences of a detail is called a one-to-many (1:n)[*] relationship. The number of owners and details for each relationship is known as the **cardinality** of the relationship.

All the relationships in the examples in this chapter have been of the form 1:n: it is the workhorse of the data model. However, the term 1:n conceals subtle differences in cardinality.

3.7.1   Cardinality of the detail

We say that there are many occurrences of a detail entity for each occurrence of an owner - but how many is many? The usual assumption is that many includes zero, one and every positive whole number up to infinity. This assumption gives the data model maximum flexibility.

---

[*] Many texts use the abbreviation 1:M for a one-to-many relationship. We prefer 1:n as n is a standard mathematical abbreviation for a number which can take on any value.

For example, when a company sets up a record for a new customer it cannot be sure whether the customer is ever going to place an order, whether it will place only one order, whether it will order once a year or once a week. There is no minimum or maximum which a data modeller would wish to place on the number of potential orders for a customer. Therefore the minimum cardinality of the detail entity in this relationship is zero and the maximum infinity. The crow's foot symbol on the detail end of the diagrammed relationship shows the maximum cardinality of infinity; we have now added an o to show that the minimum is zero.

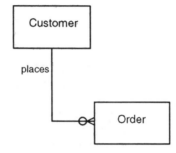

Figure 3.6: *Unrestricted cardinality of the detail*

Recall the company in chapter 1 which took telephone orders from its customers. It never set up a customer record until an order had been received from the new customer. A company like this may wish to restrict the minimum cardinality of the detail entity in the relationship between Customer and Order by stipulating that each customer must have at least one order. The bar beside the crow's foot on the diagram below shows that "many" no longer includes zero.

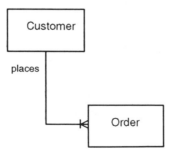

Figure 3.7: *Minimum cardinality of detail restricted*

This option is less flexible than the previous one and before it is implemented the entire life history of the owner entity, from creation to deletion, must be considered. If at any point in its lifecycle a Customer can exist without any orders then this structure is too rigid.

As well as increasing the minimum cardinality of the detail we can decrease the maximum from infinity to some finite positive number. Suppose a company which manufactures hi-fi equipment subjects each unit to a performance test as soon as its final assembly is complete. The test date and results are noted and any unit failing the first test is adjusted before being sent back for a second. If a unit fails three consecutive tests all attempts to fine tune it are abandoned and it is dismantled. The entity Test, a detail of Unit, can therefore occur a minimum of once and a maximum of three times for each unit. This is shown diagramatically by an annotation close to the crow's foot.

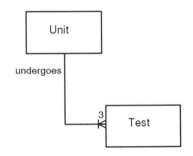

Figure 3.8: *Minimum and maximum cardinality of detail restricted*

It is possible to increase the minimum cardinality of the detail and decrease the maximum to the same value. Imagine an organization which engages in barter with other organizations[*]. Each barter trade involves the receipt of one kind of goods and the despatch of another. Receipt and despatch are both movements of goods (albeit in opposite directions) and the organization sees them as the same thing. A trade is effected by two and only two movements of goods. If Trade is the owner entity and Movement its detail, the maximum cardinality of the detail is not infinity but two, as is the

---

[*] This may sound like an obsolete example but the barter model is actually a useful way of looking at modern financial transactions.

minimum. On the diagram both minimum and maximum are shown beside the crow's foot.

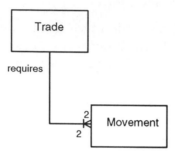

Figure 3.9: *Minimum and maximum cardinality restricted to same value*

Therefore the cardinality of the detail in a relationship can range from zero to infinity but in particular circumstances the minimum can be increased and the maximum decreased.

In some circumstances it is necessary to reduce the maximum cardinality of the detail to one. In effect this creates a one-to-one (1:1) relationship between the owner and the detail and it sometimes difficult to decide which is which.

Consider for example a financial institution which helps exporters to collect the proceeds of overseas sales. It records details of the exports in which it is involved.

    Export
        exportReference
        organizationCodeExporter
        categoryOfGoods
        quantityTotalValue
        currencyCodeTotalValue
    (o)   insuranceTerms
    Foreign: organizationCodeExporter → Organization
    Foreign: quantityTotalValue → Quantity
    Foreign: currencyCodeTotalValue → Currency

Some overseas sales involve considerable delay and uncertainty. Rather than wait until the goods have been shipped, unpacked and inspected and until the foreign currency payment has been received from the purchaser and converted at the prevailing exchange rate - which could be very different from that in force when the price was originally agreed - an exporting company may choose to receive its payment up front from the financial institution. Assuming the importer doesn't default the financier eventually receives the funds. In return for accepting the delay, the credit risk and the foreign exchange risk the financier is paid a commission by the exporter.

To the financial institution this kind of arrangement has a lot in common with other types of loan it offers so it records each one in its Loan entity.

Loan
       <u>loanNumber</u>
       quantityLent
       currencyCodeLent
       organizationCodeBorrower
       dateOfLoan
       quantityTerm
Foreign: organizationCodeBorrower → Organization
Foreign: quantityLent → Quantity
Foreign: currencyCodeLent → Currency
Foreign: dateOfLoan → Date
Foreign: quantityTerm → Quantity

Exports can exist without loans, therefore, and loans without exports, but when a loan is export-related the financial institution needs to record the link. To ensure that a relationship exists between the two entities the key of one must appear amongst the attributes of the other. In this case it is arbitrary which entity is chosen as owner and which as detail. It might be worth considering whether either is likely to become a true detail of the other in future - that is, whether the maximum cardinality at either end of the relationship is likely to be increased from one. Given a change in the rules, could a single loan be granted to cover more than one export? Could an export ever be financed by several distinct loans? Assuming the former is felt to be the more likely, Export becomes a detail of Loan, but with a maximum cardinality of one to reflect the existing rules.

Because the relationship is effectively a 1:1, a particular loan can finance at most one export. Therefore the attribute loanNumber can only take on a given value in one occurrence of Export. This can be stipulated in the Export's attribute list by the creation of a Unique clause.

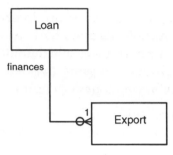

Figure 3.10: *Maximum cardinality of detail restricted to 1*

Export
      exportReference
      organizationCodeExporter
      categoryOfGoods
      quantityTotalValue
      currencyCodeTotalValue
(o)   insuranceTerms
(o)   loanNumber
Foreign: organizationCodeExporter → Organization
Foreign: quantityTotalValue → Quantity
Foreign: currencyCodeTotalValue → Currency
Foreign: loanNumber → Loan
Unique: loanNumber

While this pattern of cardinality is not common, it is used wherever two independent entities, each with its own key, need to be linked on a 1:1 basis. It also has particular value in some recursive constructs, as we shall see in chapter 6, and as chapter 4 shows, it provides a way for the relational database to simulate multiple inheritance from supertype entities.

3.7.2   Cardinality of the owner

In any 1:n relationship the owner has a maximum and minimum cardinality too. We say that there is one occurrence of the owner for each occurrence of the detail - but how many is one? Usually, one is one: that is, both the maximum and the minimum cardinality of the owner are set to one. This implies that an occurrence of the detail entity can't exist without a related occurrence of the owner. The owner is said to be mandatory. All primary key owners and many foreign key owners are mandatory[*]. For example, a Vehicle entity without a VehicleModel has been prohibited because it would stop anyone asking whether a particular Vehicle had an overhead camshaft. Mandatory owners are indicated on the diagram by a double bar at the owner end of the relationship.

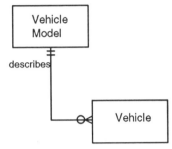

Figure 3.11: *Minimum cardinality of owner restricted to 1*

On the other hand, Telex as an owner of RoomBooking has a minimum cardinality of zero and a maximum cardinality of one. Any optional owner takes on this cardinality which is represented by an o (zero) and a bar (one) on the diagram.

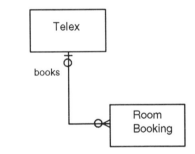

Figure 3.12: *Cardinality of owner unrestricted*

---

[*] This text maintains that primary key owners are always mandatory and that mandatory foreign key attributes on a detail imply mandatory foreign key owners. Other methods permit non-null attributes on a detail entity to refer to non-existent owners in the following circumstances. Imagine a workshop which takes orders for specialized engineering products, some of which are advertised in the company's catalogue and some of which are one-offs, built to the customers' specifications. Even one-off products are given product codes but the product record will not necessarily have been set up when the order is entered. Since an order has to have a product code it is given the next available number. Under these circumstances an optional owner is supported by a mandatory foreign key. The product code mentioned on the order must be non-null, but it need not identify a valid occurrence of Product.

From now on all relationships diagrammed in this text will have maximum and minimum cardinality shown at both owner and detail ends.

3.7.3   Cardinality combinations

In figure 3.13 the different combinations of cardinality have been illustrated using the entities Customer and Order.

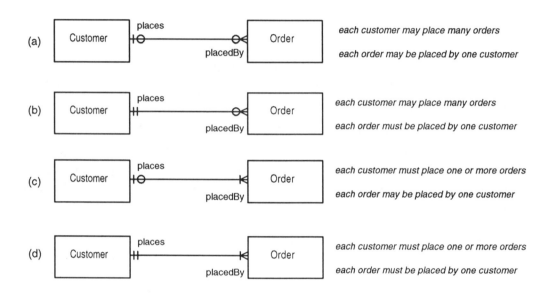

Figure 3.13: *Different cardinality combinations*

The combination shown in figure 3.13 (a) allows the most flexibility. When a company sets up a record for a new customer it cannot be sure how many orders the customer will place, if any. Therefore the minimum cardinality of the detail in this relationship is zero and the maximum infinity. Since the owner is not mandatory, it is permissible to establish an order that has no associated customer. The company might want to record over the counter sales without capturing the customer's particulars.

Figure 3.13 (b) restricts the model by requiring that all orders are associated with a customer. A computer system built on the basis of this data model would stop anybody entering an order unless a valid customer existed. Figure 3.13 (c) requires a customer to place at least one order before being entered into the system. Such a model might be appropriate if the organization only wanted to keep details of people who had actually bought something from them.   This structure does allow orders to be entered without a customer.

The model illustrated in figure 3.13 (d) is the most restrictive, as it increases the permitted minima for both owner and detail from zero to one. Each and every customer must have one or more orders and each and every order must have one customer. Such structures tend to be less common than those shown in 3.13 (a), (b), and (c) because of the severity of the restriction they impose.   Structure 3.13 (d) raises an interesting "chicken and egg" question: how can a customer be added unless it has an order and how can the order be added if the customer does not yet exist? To resolve this issue we need to think in terms of a logical unit of work in which a new customer is added and its first order entered. This logical unit of work must leave the database in a state that conforms to the rules expressed in the data model. In database terms a logical unit of work is referred to as a **transaction**.

3.8   Referential integrity

To enforce referential integrity in a database is to preserve the proper relationship between each owner and detail entity over time. Whenever an occurrence of one entity is to be added or deleted the proposed action is first checked to ensure that it will not violate any of the model's cardinality rules. If it will, the choice of reaction will be governed by referential integrity policy.

Note that the policy relates to the relationship between an owner and one of its details and therefore referential integrity rules are characteristics of the relationship rather than of either entity.

3.8.1   Deleting an owner

When an occurrence of an entity is to be deleted, its status as an owner is the main concern. For each relationship in turn we must ask whether it has any detail occurrences. If so, what will become of them?

If the owner's maximum and minimum cardinality are both set to one, then the owner is mandatory and details cannot be allowed to exist without a valid occurrence of the owner. There are two options.

- Prevent the deletion of the owner. This is known as a **restrict** policy. The owner could eventually be deleted but only after all the details had been individually deleted first.

- Delete all corresponding detail occurrences along with the owner. This is known as a **cascade** policy.

If the owner's minimum cardinality is zero one extra policy is available.

- Permit deletion of the owner occurrence, but change all the foreign key attributes' values on corresponding details to null. This policy is known as **nullify**.

Each policy has merits in different circumstances. Figure 3.14 models a situation in which all three are required. A restrict policy is used to prevent a customer organization being deleted while its orders remain in the system. A cascade policy ensures that, when a customer is finally deleted, the names of contacts on the staff of that customer are also scrubbed. A nullify policy ensures that, when a sales representative leaves the company, all his or her customers are left without a sales representative until they can be assigned to someone else.

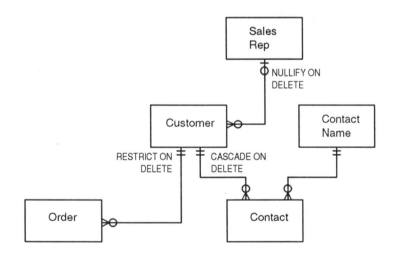

Figure 3.14: *Three policies for deleting an owner*

3.8.2   Deleting a detail

Normally a detail's cardinality will range from zero to infinity. When it does, no deletion of a detail will ever violate referential integrity rules.

However, if minimum cardinality has been raised to one or more, there should be a policy for handling deletions which threaten to reduce the number of details below the minimum level. Under these circumstances either the detail deletions must be prevented (a restrict policy) or the owner must be deleted along with the detail. This would be a cascade of sorts, albeit one which defied gravity.

3.8.3   Inserting an owner

Only when the owner has a detail whose minimum cardinality is greater than zero can the insertion of an owner occurrence threaten to violate integrity. Suppose that a barter Trade is to be recorded. Since the minimum and maximum cardinality of the Movement detail is two, then the owner occurrence cannot exist even momentarily without two details. The act of setting up the owner must cause the cascading creation of two details as part of the same database transaction.

3.8.4   Inserting a detail

If the detail has a mandatory owner - that is to say, one whose cardinality had a maximum and a minimum value of one - then any insertion of a detail for which a corresponding owner does not already exist threatens a violation of the rules.

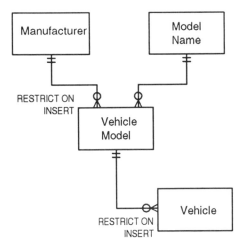

Figure 3.15

Say for example that someone is trying to insert an occurrence of the Vehicle entity which represents a custom car (figure 3.15). No occurrence of VehicleModel exists for this new design. According to the rules we have laid down, the insertion must be restricted. The database must ensure that a VehicleModel occurrence, holding details of the new vehicle's design, exists before the Vehicle does. Note that the VehicleModel insertion itself will be restricted until the inventor has been recorded as a manufacturer organization in the Manufacturer table, since Manufacturer is a mandatory owner of VehicleModel.

Where an owner is optional - that is to say, its cardinality extends from zero to one - then a new detail with a null value for the foreign key will always be permitted. A non-null foreign key must still match up with an existing owner occurrence, though.

If the owner is a key-only entity, the same rules apply. For example, someone trying to insert into the Person table an occurrence of a person who is neither male nor female should probably be restricted. The description of the key-only Gender entity should carry enough guidelines to decide a person's sex in all circumstances. These may not be straightforward. Chromosonal abnormalities and sex change operations have certainly confused bodies such as the All England Lawn Tennis Club and the International Olympic Federation who need to be able to make gender distinctions. But, however controversial, a particular definition must always exist.

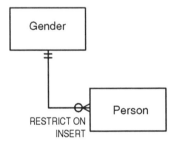

Figure 3.16

However, there are circumstances in which a key-only owner, even if mandatory, may be updated automatically to allow the insertion of a detail. Logically, if an invoice line were to be created on an invoice which contained as a result more lines than any previous invoice then an occurrence of

InvoiceLineNumber would also have to be created. This is another upward cascade.

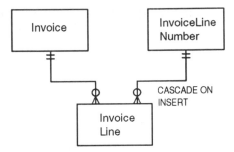

Figure 3.17

3.8.5   Transferability

The amendment of a detail occurrence sometimes involves the change of its foreign key attributes so that it refers to a different occurrence of its owner. Again a policy is required to determine whether the amendment should be allowed or restricted. If no alteration in the value of a foreign key is allowed then a relationship is said to be **permanent**. Otherwise it is **transient** or **transferable**.

A permanent relationship can be diagrammed as shown in figure 3.18.

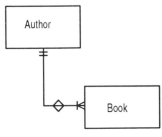

Figure 3.18 *A permanent relationship*

Chapter summary

Two entities are related when the primary key of one (the owner) appears among the attributes of the other (the detail). If the owner's key appears in the non-key attributes of the detail the relationship is a foreign key reationship and the boxes on the diagram are connected by a line joining the detail at the side. If the owner's key contributes to the primary key of the detail the relationship is called a primary key link and the line joining their boxes enters the detail from above.

Relationships are labelled so as to express the owner's contribution to the detail. A label which expresses the detail's use of the owner may also be held and should express the grammatical inverse of the owner-to-detail label.

An entity with only one attribute in its primary key has no owners. Other entities must inherit all of their primary key attributes. Entities which exist so as to endow their details with primary key attributes are called key-only owners. A detail entity which is not a subtype (see chapter 4) must have at least two owners by 1:n relationships.

A mandatory owner in a 1:n relationship occurs exactly once for each occurrence of the detail. All primary key owners are mandatory. A foreign key owner may be optional and need not occur for a particular occurrence of the detail. Details may exist none, one or many times for each occurrence of the owner. Upper and lower bounds can be placed on the number of detail occurrences. Where the number of details is constrained to a maximum of one, the relationship becomes in effect a 1:1 relationship and the owner's key becomes an alternate key of the detail.

The cardinality of each relationship is protected by referential integrity policy. This dictates the actions to be taken whenever cardinality rules are in danger of being violated.

Questions

1.   Do the following enquiries start at the owner or the detail end of a relationship?

   (a)   What fuel type does car J 166 CHM use?
   (b)   What are the registration numbers of all cars with transverse engines?
   (c)   What is the most popular upholstery colour among cars with

transverse engines?

(d)   What were the results of the tests on hi-fi unit 923674534/004?

(e)   What was the date of the second test on hi-fi unit 923674534/004?

(f)   Which grant giving authority (if any) funds Ravi Gupta's studies?

(g)   How many students get a grant from Kent County Council?

2.   How many attributes form the primary key of entity E?

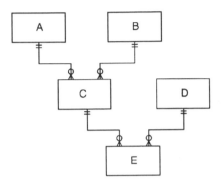

3.   How many times can "A 184 TGW" appear in the Vehicle table as a registrationNumber?

4.   How many times can "red" appear as a colourOfPaintworkBody in the Vehicle table?

5.   How many times can "0056" appear as a loanNumber in the Export table?

6.   How many times can "12" and "14/07/95" appear together as RoomNumber and dateRoomRequired on the RoomBooking table?

7.   What is wrong with each of the diagrams below?

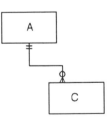

(a)

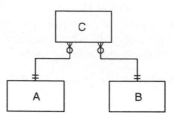

(b)

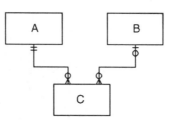

(c)

8.   What are the two possible referential integrity policies governing the deletion of a mandatory owner?

9.   Under what circumstances could the insertion of an owner occurrence violate the integrity of a relationship?

10.   What are the advantages and disadvantages of making the relationship between Customer and Order transferable?

4

Subtype and supertype entities

Introduction

This chapter introduces the notion of entity subtypes and supertypes and demonstrates how the expressive power of a data model can be enhanced significantly through the use of entity generalizations and specializations.

4.1 Subtype entities

4.1.1 Jointly optional attributes

Consider the Vehicle entity shown in figure 4.1 which stores details of cars and lorries. A few extra attributes have been added to it recently to record information about the lorries tachographs and tail lifts. A tail lift may be fitted to the back of a lorry with an enclosed cargo area to allow goods to be raised and lowered between ground level and the cargo area's doors. A tachograph records distances and speeds driven to ensure compliance with legal restrictions.

Vehicle
    registrationNumber
    manufacturerName
    modelName
    colourOfPaintworkBody
    colourOfPaintworkRoof
    colourOfUpholstery
    yearOfManufacture
    dateRoadFundLicenceRenewable
(o)   serialNumberTachograph
(o)   manufacturerNameTailLift
(o)   quantityMaximumWeightTailLift
Foreign: manufacturerName, modelName → VehicleModel
Foreign: yearOfManufacture → Year
Foreign: dateRoadFundLicenceRenewable → Date
Foreign: manufacturerNameTailLift → Manufacturer
Foreign: quantityMaximumWeightTailLift → Quantity

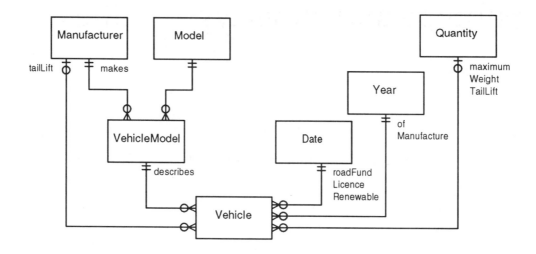

Figure 4.1: *Entity diagram for Vehicle*

The attributes serialNumberTachograph, manufacturerNameTailLift and quantityMaximumWeightTailLift are all optional because they apply only to lorries. In any occurrence of the entity which represents a car, all of them will be null. The attributes are therefore **jointly optional**.

Since these attributes describe lorries but not cars they can be moved to a new specialist entity, or subtype entity, called Lorry. The general attributes, such as manufacturerName, which hold true for every vehicle remain in the

Vehicle entity - the supertype entity. This means that for every vehicle which is a lorry there must be an occurrence of both Vehicle and Lorry, but only one of each. This data structure is represented by the following attribute list:

Vehicle
  <u>registrationNumber</u>
  manufacturerName
  modelName
  colourOfPaintworkBody
  colourOfPaintworkRoof
  colourOfUpholstery
  yearOfManufacture
  dateRoadFundLicenceRenewable

Foreign: manufacturerName, modelName → VehicleModel
Foreign: yearOfManufacture → Year
Foreign: dateRoadFundLicenceRenewable → Date

Lorry
  <u>registrationNumber</u>
  serialNumberTachograph
(o)   manufacturerNameTailLift
(o)   quantityMaximumWeightTailLift

Foreign: registrationNumber → Vehicle
Foreign: quantityMaximumWeightTailLift → Quantity
Foreign: manufacturerNameTailLift → Manufacturer

Lorry, like Vehicle, has a key of registrationNumber. Because the key of one entity appears among the attributes of the other, the two entities must be related. The key of one entity appears in the key of the other, which means there is a primary key relationship. However, since there are no other attributes in the key of the subtype entity it would be impossible for more than one occurrence of the subtype entity to correspond to an occurrence of the supertype entity.

A **subtype entity** is therefore a group of jointly optional attributes taken from one entity to form another entity. Both entities have the same primary key. The subtype entity is related to the supertype entity by a 1:1 primary key relationship.

The relationship between a supertype entity and its subtypes is represented by a line without crow's feet. The supertype entity is shown above the subtype entity and as a mandatory owner (as is the case with all primary key owners). The subtype entity has a minimum cardinality of nought and a maximum of one. In other words, for each occurrence of the supertype entity there may be either no occurrences of the subtype entity or one (figure 4.2).

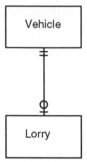

Figure 4.2: *Diagramming convention for a subtype entity*

The subtype relationship also differs from the 1:1 foreign key (crow's foot) relationship in that the subtype relationship must refer to the same occurrence of the supertype entity and the subtype entity. For example, an occurrence of Vehicle, TIN 500X, if it is a lorry can only be associated with one occurrence of Lorry, and that occurrence must also be TIN 500X. It is not appropriate, for example, to link vehicle TIN 500X with lorry K529 DMV. This is an essential difference between a 1:1 foreign key relationship and a supertype/subtype relationship.

The attribute of Lorry, serialNumberTachograph, which was optional when part of the supertype entity Vehicle, has now become mandatory. This reflects our understanding that tachographs must be installed in all lorries and their serial numbers must be recorded. When all attributes were lumped together in the supertype entity this attribute had to be optional because it was not relevant to cars.

The introduction of the subtype entity has therefore allowed extra business understanding to be captured in the data model. The entity diagram for Vehicle introduced in figure 4.1 can now be redrawn as shown in figure 4.3 to demonstrate that only occurrences of Lorry, a subtype of Vehicle, may have a tail lift fitted.

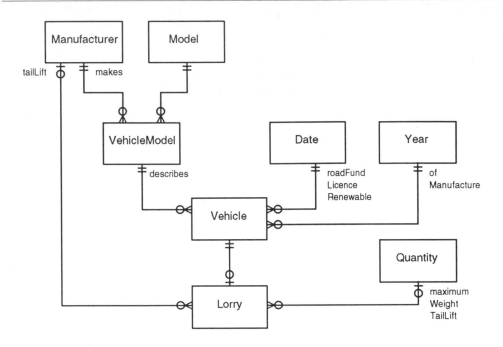

Figure 4.3: *Entity diagram for Vehicle with subtype*

4.1.2   Subtypes of subtype entities

Even though they are now part of Lorry, the two attributes manufacturerNameTailLift and quantityMaximumWeightTailLift remain optional. These attributes are only relevant for lorries that have tail lifts fitted, making the attributes jointly optional. Such attributes, as we have seen above in the case of Vehicle and Lorry, can be moved into a subtype entity of Lorry called LorryWithTailLift (represented diagramatically in figure 4.4).

Vehicle
     <u>registrationNumber</u>
     manufacturerName
     modelName
     colourOfPaintworkBody
     colourOfPaintworkRoof
     colourOfUpholstery
     yearOfManufacture
     dateRoadFundLicenceRenewable
Foreign: manufacturerName, modelName → VehicleModel
Foreign: yearOfManufacture → Year
Foreign: dateRoadFundLicenceRenewable → Date

Lorry
>   registrationNumber
>   serialNumberTachograph

Foreign: registrationNumber → Vehicle

LorryWithTailLift
>   registrationNumber
>   manufacturerNameTailLift
>   quantityMaximumWeightTailLift

Foreign: registrationNumber → Lorry

Foreign: manufacturerNameTailLift → Manufacturer

Foreign: quantityMaximumWeightTailLift → Quantity

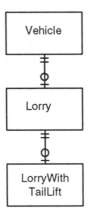

Figure 4.4: *Subtype of a subtype*

By adding the LorryWithTailLift subtype we have removed all optional attributes from Lorry. This means that the Vehicle entity diagram is now as in figure 4.5, in which the tailLift relationship is no longer optional for occurrences of LorryWithTailLift.

Further subtype entities can be added to provide more specialization to meet whatever degree of differentiation is required. There could be subtype entities of LorryWithTailLift, for example, such as LorryWithManualTailLift and LorryWithAutomaticTailLift. Similarly, supertype entities can be added to provide a greater degree of generalization. For example, we may wish to generalize Vehicle into Transporter which has, in addition to LandVehicle, the subtype entities AirVehicle and WaterVehicle.

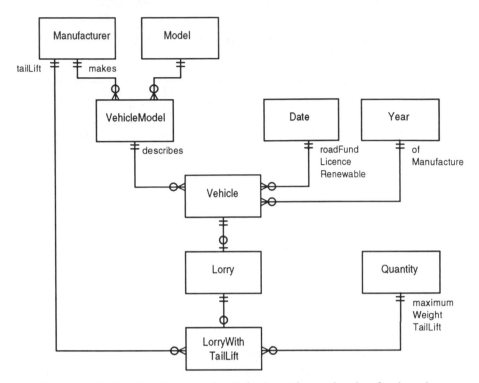

Figure 4.5: *Entity diagram for Vehicle with two levels of subtyping*

4.2   Subtype groups

In the Lorry example we have considered a single subtype entity where vehicles may be subtyped as lorries and lorries may be subtyped as lorries with tail lifts. Now imagine a letting agency that rents out residential properties and maintains those properties on behalf of their owners. The agency stores details of properties available for rent as follows:

```
Property
        address
        partyOwns
(o)     companyCodeServiceBoiler
(o)     dateNextBoilerService
(o)     companyCodeServiceGarden
(o)     quantitySquareMetreGarden
Foreign:        partyOwns → Party
Foreign:        companyCodeServiceBoiler → Company
Foreign:        dateNextBoilerService → Date
Foreign:        companyCodeServiceGarden → Company
Foreign:        quantitySquareMetreGarden → Quantity
```

The Property entity is represented in figure 4.6.

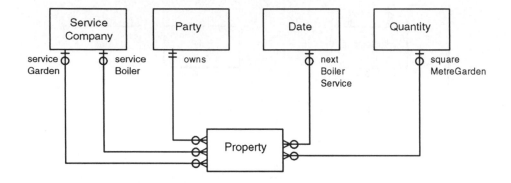

Figure 4.6: *Entity diagram for Property entity*

Those properties that have central heating require that the boiler be serviced (optional attributes companyCodeServiceBoiler and dateNextBoilerService) and those properties that have gardens need to have those gardens maintained by a service company (companyCodeServiceGarden). The Property entity also contains an attribute to record how large the garden is in square metres (quantitySquareMetreGarden). Some properties will have gardens, some will have central heating, some will have both and some will have neither. For the Property entity two subtypes can be introduced:

Property
    <u>address</u>
    partyOwns
Foreign: partyOwns → Party

CentrallyHeatedProperty
    <u>address</u>
    companyCodeServiceBoiler
    dateNextBoilerService
Foreign: address → Property
Foreign: companyCodeServiceBoiler → Company
Foreign: dateNextBoilerService → Date

PropertyWithGarden
    <u>address</u>
    companyCodeServiceGarden
    quantitySquareMetreGarden
Foreign: address → Property

Foreign: companyCodeServiceGarden $\rightarrow$ Company
Foreign: quantitySquareMetreGarden $\rightarrow$ Quantity

The entity diagram for Property is as in figure 4.7.

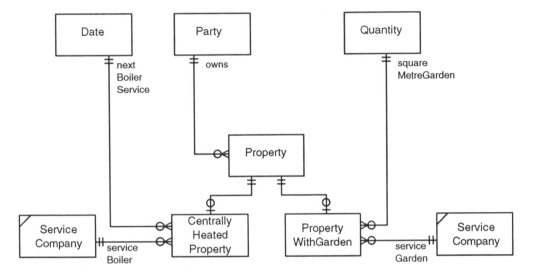

Figure 4.7: *Entity diagram for Property entity with multiple subtypes*

Figure 4.7[*] shows that centrally heated properties must have a service company for the boiler and must have a next service date. Properties with gardens must have the size of the garden recorded and must have a service company to maintain the garden. Since a particular property could have both subtypes (because it is centrally heated and it has a garden) these subtypes are referred to as **overlapping** or **independent**.

So far we have looked at subtype groups that contain a single subtype. In the next section we consider subtype groups that contain multiple subtypes.

4.2.1   Mutually exclusive subtypes

In figure 4.8, the entity ITStaff has two subtypes, SupportStaff and DevelopmentStaff. IT staff may be members of the support staff or members of the development staff, but they cannot be members of both. That is, the categories SupportStaff and DevelopmentStaff are mutually exclusive. The subtypes are grouped together by an arc, on which the cardinality of the

---

[*] Where an entity is repeated on a diagram, all appearances of that entity are marked with a diagonal in the top left hand corner.

grouping has been specified. The minimum cardinality of zero means that it is possible to have occurrences of ITStaff that exist without an associated subtype. The maximum cardinality of one means that no more than one subtype is allowed, thus representing mutually exclusive subtypes.

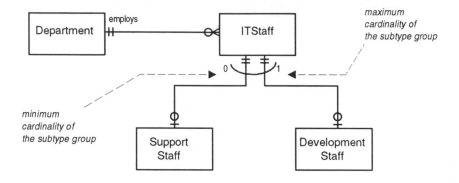

Figure 4.8: *Mutually exclusive, optional subtypes of ITStaff*

The rules can be changed so that IT staff *must* be categorized as either support staff or development staff by changing the minimum cardinality on the arc to one. The maximum cardinality remains at one, indicating that one, and only one, subtype entity must be associated with an occurrence of the ITStaff entity.

4.2.2   Independent subtypes

The data model in figure 4.8 is now extended to include Analyst and Programmer, two subtype entities of DevelopmentStaff. Analyst and Programmer are independent - that is, they are allowed to overlap - since an individual member of the development staff can be both an analyst and a programmer (the ubiquitous analyst/programmer). This is shown in figure 4.9 by a minimum cardinality of zero and a maximum cardinality of many (m) on the arc. Subtyping of DevelopmentStaff is optional - it is possible for occurrences of DevelopmentStaff to exist without any associated subtypes. (These IT staff might be involved in project administration or database design). The dotted line has been introduced to delineate the supertype/subtype structure and to make the model easier to interpret.

The subtype entities of DevelopmentStaff have been introduced because the representation of Analyst and Programmer further specializes the representation of DevelopmentStaff. Let us now assume that analysts must have aquired SSADM certification and that programmers must have attended a Jackson Structured Programming (JSP) course. The analyst/programmer is someone who has achieved SSADM certification and attended a JSP course.

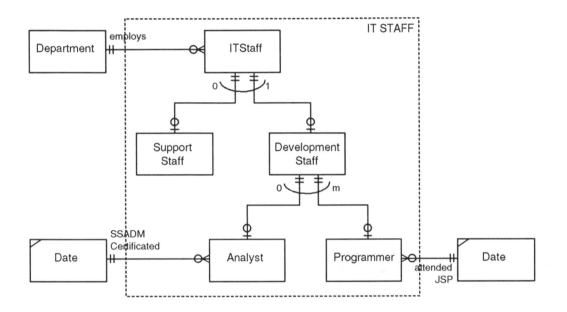

Figure 4.9: *Independent, optional subtypes of DevelopmentStaff*

The corresponding attribute list for the entity diagram in figure 4.9 is:

        ITStaff
                <u>employeeNumber</u>
                name
                address
                departmentNumberEmploys
        Foreign: departmentNumberEmploys → Department

        SupportStaff
                <u>employeeNumber</u>
                mobileTelNumber
        Foreign: employeeNumber → ITStaff

        DevelopmentStaff
                <u>employeeNumber</u>
        Foreign: employeeNumber → ITStaff

Analyst
    employeeNumber
    certNumberSSADM
    dateSSADMCertificated
Foreign: employeeNumber → DevelopmentStaff
Foreign: dateSSADMCertificated → Date

Programmer
    employeeNumber
    dateAttendedJSP
Foreign: employeeNumber → DevelopmentStaff
Foreign: dateAttendedJSP → Date

In this example, the entity DevelopmentStaff has no attributes; it is simply a list of those employees who have been designated as developers. It may help to visualize the classification structure in figure 4.9 in terms of set membership (figure 4.10).

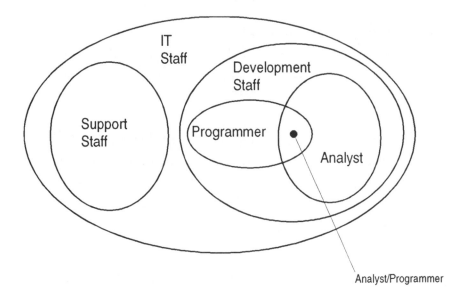

Figure 4.10: *IT staff - set membership*

The intersection of analyst and programmer represents those development staff who have skills in both systems analysis and programming. The subtype AnalystProgrammer is not shown on the model explicitly unless the representation of analyst/programmer requires attributes other than those already defined for the programmer and analyst subtypes.

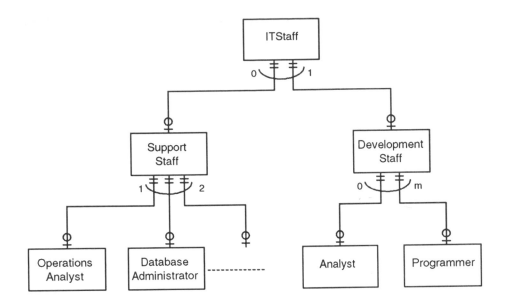

Figure 4.11: *Mandatory and independent SupportStaff subtypes with incomplete enumeration*

As we have already seen, where the subtypes are independent and the subtype group is mandatory then the minimum cardinality on the arc is set to one.   In figure 4.11, the entity SupportStaff has been subtyped into OperationsAnalyst and DatabaseAdministrator.   The dotted line extending from DatabaseAdministrator indicates that the subtypes of SupportStaff are not fully enumerated.   More subtype entities may exist but have yet to be identified.   The minimum cardinality of one indicates that an occurrence of SupportStaff must have at least one subtype present; the maximum cardinality of two indicates that an occurrence of SupportStaff cannot have more than two associated subtypes.   This constraint may reflect a business rule that seeks to avoid members of the support staff becoming 'Jacks of all trades' by limiting them to a maximum of two support roles.

Note that in figure 4.11 only the supertype/subtype structure is shown - all the entities and relationships external to ITStaff have been suppressed on the entity subtype diagram.   It should also be apparent that a subtype arc with a cardinality of 0..m is not strictly necessary and can be removed without loss of meaning to the diagram.   However, the arc does provide a visual cue when interpreting the diagram.   There was no arc on the Property subtypes in figure 4.7 and the addition of an arc with a cardinality of 0..m adds no further information. In other words, figures 4.12 (a) and 4.12 (b) are equivalent.

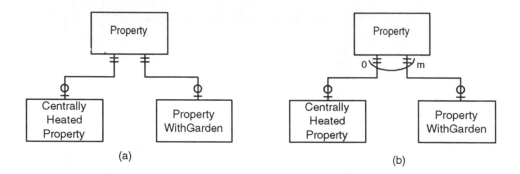

Figure 4.12: *Property subtypes - redundant 0..m arc cardinality*

4.2.3   Identifying a need for subtypes

Optional attributes provide a strong clue that the analyst should consider the introduction of subtypes - this is usually reflected by the presence of mutually exclusive relationships. In figure 4.13 a record shop may purchase stock from record companies and from wholesalers. Supplier invoices must be either from a record company or from a wholesaler, as indicated by the lower and upper cardinality constraints on the exclusivity arc.

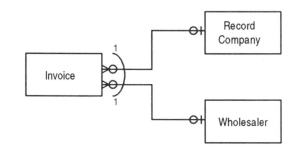

Figure 4.13: *Entity diagram for Invoice and mutually exclusive suppliers*

The keys of RecordCompany and Wholesaler have to be shown as optional foreign keys of Invoice - neither can be mandatory. The exclusivity arc cardinality indicates that an invoice must be related to one record company or to one wholesaler but not to both. Recognizing that RecordCompany and

Wholesaler are specialized forms of the more general entity Supplier allows us to remodel the data as shown in figure 4.14.

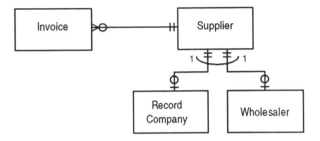

Figure 4.14: *Entity diagram for Invoice with Supplier subtypes*

In figure 4.14 it is now evident that all invoices must have a supplier and that record companies and wholesalers are types of the same thing, namely suppliers. As a general rule, wherever mutually exclusive owners are found the analyst should expect the exclusivity construct to be replaced by a subtype structure.

4.3   Multiple inheritance

4.3.1   Multiple inheritance within a subtype group

In some situations it will be necessary to represent development staff who are both analysts and programmers explicitly as a subtype entity. Let us assume that for analyst/programmers it is necessary to know which hardware platforms they have experience of. The new subtype entity, AnalystProgrammer, will need to inherit the representation of two supertype entities, namely Analyst and Programmer. This situation, where a subtype entity requires more than one supertype, is known as **multiple inheritance** and, although the solution is perhaps inelegant, it is possible to model multiple inheritance using the techniques introduced so far.

However, the relational model does not allow the subtype entity AnalystProgrammer to have two supertypes - we must select either Analyst or Programmer to be the supertype of AnalystProgrammer. This choice is largely arbitrary, but let us assume that Analyst is chosen to be the supertype as it is perceived to be the more natural owner of AnalystProgrammer. How are we to deal with the relationship between AnalystProgrammer and Programmer ? For occurrences of AnalystProgrammer there is a constraint that the employeeNumber inherited from Analyst through a 1:1 primary key relationship must be one that exists as a key to an occurrence of the programmer entity. Whether or not this inter-relationship constraint is shown on the entity diagram it should be captured in the underlying dictionary. The data model is shown in figure 4.15

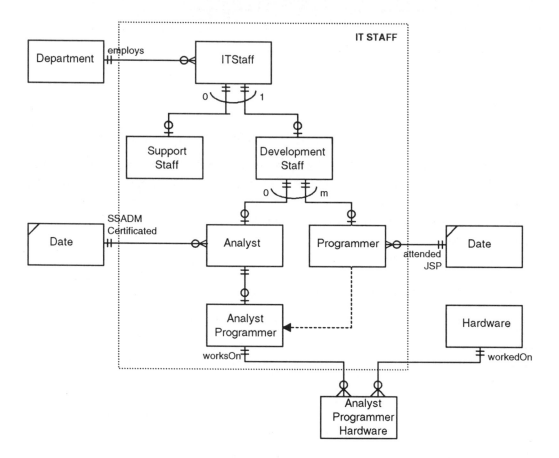

Figure 4.15: *Multiple inheritance within a subtype group*

In figure 4.15 multiple inheritance has taken place within the DevelopmentStaff segment of the ITStaff supertype/subtype structure. Multiple inheritance within a supertype/subtype structure requires that the supertypes that are being inherited from are overlapping, as is the case with Analyst and Programmer. To implement the model in figure 4.15, an additional subtype entity, AnalystProgrammer, is needed:

AnalystProgrammer
      <u>employeeNumber</u>
Foreign: employeeNumber → Analyst
Constraint: AnalystProgrammer.employeeNumber in
               Programmer.employeeNumber

A Constraint clause has been added to specify that the value of AnalystProgrammer.employeeNumber must have a corresponding Programmer.employeeNumber. Such a Constraint needs to be captured and included in the system design.

You might be wondering why we did not model multiple inheritance using two subtype relationships (figure 4.16 (a)) or indeed using a combination of a subtype relationship and a 1:1 foreign key relationship (figure 4.16 (b)).

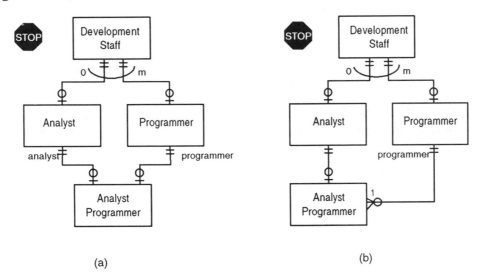

(a)   (b)

Figure 4.16: *Multiple inheritance within a subtype group - redundant data*

Both of these structures, although visually appealing, involve redundant data. In the case of figure 4.16 (a), the AnalystProgrammer table is:

AnalystProgrammer
      <u>employeeNumberAnalyst</u>
      <u>employeeNumberProgrammer</u>
Foreign: employeeNumberAnalyst → Analyst
Foreign: employeeNumberProgrammer → Programmer
Constraint: employeeNumberAnalyst = employeeNumberProgrammer

In the above list it was necessary to rolename the attributes employeeNumberAnalyst and employeeNumberProgrammer in order to be able to distinguish the different parts played by each. As with other rolenames this is achieved by concatenating the owner's key attribute name and the relationship name. A constraint is needed to ensure that the same occurrences of Analyst and Programmer are referred to. However, the employeeNumberAnalyst could have been derived from the employeeNumberProgrammer and vice versa. This form of the model has introduced redundant data - something we most certainly do not want to do in a logical data model.

What about figure 4.16 (b)? The table definition for this scenario is as follows:

```
AnalystProgrammer
        employeeNumber
        employeeNumberProgrammer
Foreign:       employeeNumber → Analyst
Foreign:       employeeNumberProgrammer → Programmer
Unique:        employeeNumberProgrammer
Constraint:    employeeNumber = employeeNumberProgrammer
```

Once again, derivable data has been introduced into the model. It is better to model the data without redundancy and then to introduce a constraint that says that for an occurrence of AnalystProgrammer to be created then there must already exist an occurrence of Programmer with the same employeeNumber. This was achieved using a constraint. By definition, the occurrence of Analyst must already exist since the owner of a subtype entity is never optional.

4.3.2   Multiple inheritance from different subtype groups

It is also possible to inherit from more than one subtype group. In figure 4.17 there are two entity types, Treasure and Weapon[1], where each has its own independent subtype/supertype structure. Now imagine that there is an entity named JewelledSword that requires the attributes of Jewellery (a type of Treasure) and Sword (a type of Weapon). To model the new entity JewelledSword can we now show it as a subtype of Jewellery and Sword? If we do model it this way then the JewelledSword will be identified uniquely by a combination of treasureNumber and weaponNumber, when in fact one will suffice with the other acting as a foreign key. Also, since a subtype has been defined as consisting of a group of jointly optional attributes from a supertype it should not be a subtype of more than one entity.

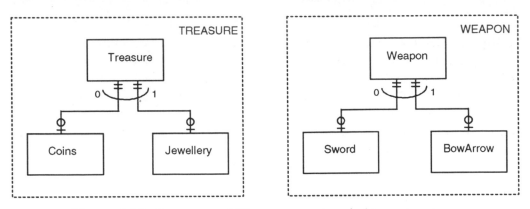

Figure 4.17: *Treasure and Weapon supertype/subtype structures*

Although it was not admissible to model multiple inheritance using a foreign key where the supertypes are from the same subtype structure, where the supertypes are from different subtype structures then we can use a foreign key since there should not be a danger of introducing redundant data. However, we will need to decide whether Jewellery or Sword will own the JewelledSword subtype. In this case, it is decided that jewelled swords are more decorative than functional and consequently JewelledSword has been made a subtype of Treasure (figure 4.18).

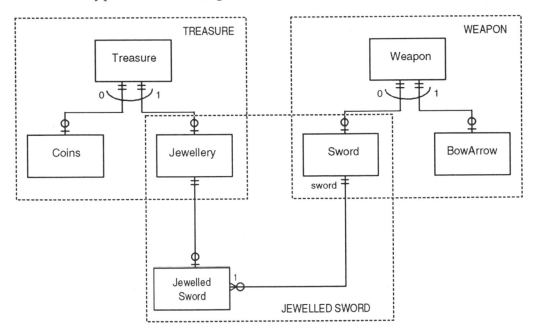

Figure 4.18: *Multiple inheritance from different supertype/subtype structures*

In figure 4.18 the entity Sword has a 1:1 foreign key relationship with JewelledSword. The attribute list might be:

JewelledSword
      treasureNumber
      weaponNumber
Foreign: treasureNumber → Jewellery
Foreign: weaponNumber → Sword
Unique: weaponNumber

As JewelledSword inherits from different subtype structures the constraint specified for the AnalystProgrammer subtype entity in section 4.3.1 is not required.

4.4   Multiple subtype groups

In figure 4.19 DevelopmentStaff has been categorized using two subtype groups (or partitionings).

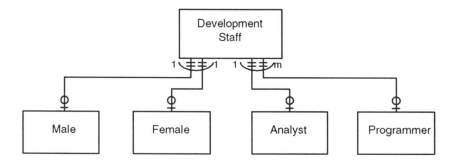

Figure 4.19: *Multiple subtype groups (mandatory subtypes)*

Developers must be categorized as Male or Female and must be categorized as Analyst and/or Programmer. The valid types of development staff that can exist are as follows:

	Neither	Analyst	Programmer	Analyst/ Programmer
Neither	No	No	No	No
Male	No	Yes	Yes	Yes
Female	No	Yes	Yes	Yes

The above table shows that occurrences of DevelopmentStaff by themselves are not allowed. An occurrence of DevelopmentStaff must have a {Male or Female} subtype and an {Analyst and/or Programmer} subtype.

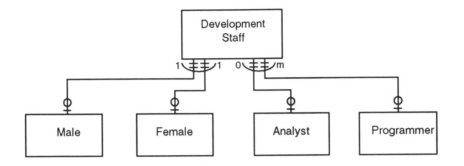

Figure 4.20: *Multiple subtype groups (mandatory and optional subtypes)*

In figure 4.20 the rules have been changed so that the subtyping of Analyst and Programmer is now optional. The valid types of DevelopmentStaff are now shown below:

	Neither	Analyst	Programmer	Analyst/ Programmer
Neither	No	No	No	No
Male	Yes	Yes	Yes	Yes
Female	Yes	Yes	Yes	Yes

4.5   Subtypes and alternate keys

With the exception of multiple inheritance from different subtype structures (the JewelledSword example) it has been assumed that the primary key of the subtype is the same as the primary key of the supertype. For example, all of the subtypes of ITStaff use employeeNumber as their primary key. Consider the structure in figure 4.21, where InvolvedParty is subtyped into Employee, Customer, and Suppplier, all of which are independent. It is important to the organization to be able to identify where the same involved party has a number of roles. For example it may wish to be able to identify which of the customers are also suppliers, as this could affect the way relationships with customers and suppliers are managed, or which of the employees are also customers, as this information may help the organization in targetting one particular market segment - its employees.

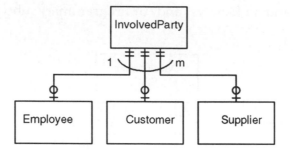

Figure 4.21: *True subtypes of InvolvedParty*

We would normally model this situation by making Employee, Customer, and Supplier subtypes of InvolvedParty (figure 4.21). The representation of the involved parties as a subtype structure allows the similarities and differences between involved parties to be captured. For example, every InvolvedParty has an address but only an Employee has a staff grade.

In this model all involved parties, whether they be employees, customers, or suppliers must have an involvedPartyNumber as primary key. Suppose the organization already uniquely identifies employees by an employee number and suppliers by a supplier number. The codes from the existing systems can be stored alongside the new identifier in the relevant subtype tables. EmployeeNumber and supplierNumber are optional and need not be assigned to new employees or suppliers.

The attribute lists for this solution would be as follows.

```
        InvolvedParty
                involvedPartyNumber
                partyName
                partyAddress

        Employee
                involvedPartyNumber
        (o)     employeeNumber
                staffGrade
        Foreign:        involvedPartyNumber → InvolvedParty
        Unique:         employeeNumber

        Supplier
                involvedPartyNumber
                paymentTerms
```

(o)   supplierNumber
Foreign: involvedPartyNumber → InvolvedParty
Unique: supplierNumber

Customer
          <u>involvedPartyNumber</u>
          quantityCreditLimit
Foreign: involvedPartyNumber → InvolvedParty

An alternative way of modelling these requirements is to use the technique introduced for multiple inheritance - that is, the alternate key. This solution is shown in figure 4.22. The Employee entity is identified by its existing primary key employeeNumber, but has involvedPartyNumber as a mandatory foreign key. Similarly, the entity Supplier retains the primary key supplierNumber and has as a foreign key involvedPartyNumber. The Customer entity is new and will use the involvedPartyNumber as its primary key.

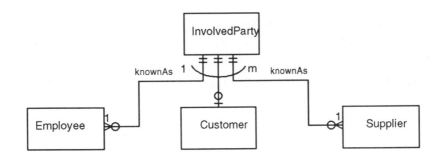

Figure 4.22: *Subtypes and alternate keys*

The attribute list for this implementation might be as shown.

InvolvedParty
          <u>involvedPartyNumber</u>
          partyName
          partyAddress

Employee
          <u>employeeNumber</u>
          staffGrade
          involvedPartyNumber
Foreign: involvedPartyNumber → InvolvedParty
Unique: involvedPartyNumber

Supplier
> supplierNumber
> paymentTerms
> involvedPartyNumber

Foreign: involvedPartyNumber → InvolvedParty
Unique: involvedPartyNumber

Customer
> involvedPartyNumber
> quantityCreditLimit

Foreign: involvedPartyNumber → InvolvedParty
Foreign: quantityCreditLimit → Quantity

The involvedPartyNumber is an alternate key in the Employee and Supplier tables and has been flagged as unique.

Both approaches allow the new involvedPartyNumber to be held alongside the legacy systems' identifiers. Either would overcome difficulties of merging data structures with incompatible values and formats. Either would allow existing interface programs that copy data from one system to another to continue using references to employeeNumber and supplierNumber.

Implementation techniques which take account of legacy systems are the province of the physical database designer. However the logical data modeller will need to be aware of such considerations.

4.6   How generalized/specialized should the model be?

The over-generalized model, where all entities are seen as subtypes of 'thing', and the under-generalized model, where similarities between entities are lost, are situations we should like to avoid. But how does the analyst find the appropriate level of generalization/specialization? As with most aspects of the analysis task there is no definitive answer to this question - it depends upon the situation in which the model is being developed. In some situations generalization may be resisted if it requires people to change the way they picture the organization. For example, the organization may not yet be ready to see customers and employees as kinds of the same thing (InvolvedParty). In other situations the fashion for Object-Orientation may lead analysts to see everything as 'a kind of thing'.

Over-generalization can lead to grandiose models where everything is perceived to be connected and an attempt to capture all the aspects of an organization in a single unifying model, possibly to the detriment of projects where scope and focus is needed if local business objectives are to be achieved. The analyst should be aware of cultural impediments to data modelling and the pragmatic considerations of project scope and focus. For reasons that are discussed in chapter 15, data modelling should not be seen as an objective exercise where a 'good' model is produced by following a set of rules. We may be able to develop guidelines for the modelling of supertype/subtype structures, but the success of the model depends also upon the abilities and perceptions of the analyst and whether the resulting generalization/specialization structure is considered to be meaningful by business and other users.

Chapter summary

The introduction of subtype entities and supertype entities gives a data model considerable expressive power. Relationships that were previously optional often become mandatory following the introduction of subtypes. Generalization (the creation of supertypes) allows us to see the similarities between different types of entities and specialization (the creation of subtypes) allows us to differentiate between entities. An approach to the modelling of subtypes has been introduced that caters for mutually exclusive and independent subtypes, optional and mandatory subtypes, multiple inheritance from within a subtype structure and from different structures, and multiple subtype groups.

NOTES

1. This example is taken from:
       Graham, I., (1994). *Object-Oriented Methods*. Second edition. Addison Wesley.

Questions

1.   What is wrong with the following diagram?

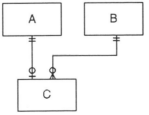

2.   Suggest which of the attributes of Student, listed below, could be used to form subtypes. Diagram the supertype and subtype structure.

> Student
> > studentNumber
> > nameFamily
> > nameGiven
> > addressTermtime
> > addressVacation
> > (o)   grantGivingAuthority
> > (o)   quantityGrant
> > (o)   NUSMembershipNumber
> > gender

3.   When might a subtype with no non-key attributes be introduced into a data model?

4.   The entity Transporter has four subtypes: LandVehicle, AirVehicle, WaterVehicle and SpaceVehicle. Draw up a set membership diagram (like the one in figure 3.10) to represent all five entities.

5.   From your set membership diagram, deduce the maximum and minimum cardinality of the subtype group which contains LandVehicle, AirVehicle, WaterVehicle and SpaceVehicle.

6.   What is the cardinality of a subtype group representing mutually exclusive subtypes?

7.   How should a subtype group with a cardinality of 0..m be interpreted?

8.   AmphibiousVehicle is a type of Transporter that has the characteristics of a LandVehicle and a WaterVehicle, but with additional characteristics of its own. Modify your entity diagram for Transporter and create an attribute list for Transporter and its subtypes.

9.   Separate entities exist for human resources (Consultant) and for machines (Robot). A new type of resource has been developed that is part human and part robot (Android). Develop an entity diagram and attribute lists for Consultant, Robot and Android.

10.   Two insurance companies are about to merge. Each has its own way of identifying policyholders. Some people have policies with both companies. Suggest two alternative data structures for the new company's policy administration system.

5

Resolving difficult relationships

Introduction

The two previous chapters dealt with the 1:n relationship between an owner and a detail entity and the 1:1 relationship between a supertype and one of its subtypes. These are the only permissible relationships in a relational data model. This chapter looks at some of the difficulties which modellers encounter in real life in modelling and diagramming entity relationships. It proposes a coherent set of standardized solutions to help express complex situations in terms of the permitted constructs.

5.1   Implicit relationships

Changes in data structures can result in existing relationships being superseded by new ones which convey the same information. The potential duplication of information must be avoided.

5.1.1   Replacing explicit relationships

For example, imagine that the personnel function in a group of companies keeps track of which employee works for which of its companies. Inspecting the existing entity's attribute lists below it can be seen that Company is a mandatory owner of Employee.

```
Company
        companyName
        address
        telephoneNumber

Employee
        employeeNumber
        givenName
        familyName
        dateOfBirth
        companyName
Foreign:        dateOfBirth → Date
Foreign:        companyName → Company
```

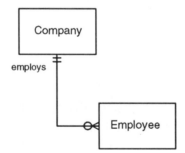

Figure 5.1

This structure works well until the head of personnel needs to show which department of the employing company each employee works for. A new entity, Department, is created which sits between Company and Employee.

```
Department
        companyName
        departmentName
Foreign:        companyName → Company
Foreign:        departmentName → DepartmentName
```

Company is now an owner of Department and Department of Employee. Since these two new relationships represent exactly the same fact as the direct one between Company and Employee - the fact that employees work for the company - the old relationship is said to be **implicit** in the new relationships.

In diagramming the relationships, there is no longer any need to link Company and Employee except through Department. Departments are not unique across the group and so the key of Company contributes to the key of Department.

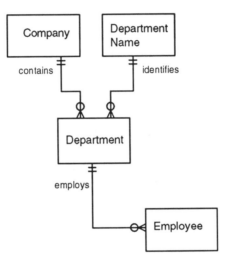

Figure 5.2

The Employee entity is revised as follows.

```
Employee
        employeeNumber
        givenName
        familyName
        dateOfBirth
        companyName
        departmentName
Foreign:        dateOfBirth → Date
Foreign:        companyName, departmentName → Department
```

5.1.2   Maintaining explicit relationships

The old relationship between Company and Employee becomes implicit in the two new ones only so long as they are both mandatory. If Department became an optional owner of Employee or if Company became an optional owner of Department then an employee could no longer be guaranteed to be associated with a company. The new relationships would no longer adequately subsume the original one.

For example, imagine that new graduates joining the company are not to be allocated to departments until the end of their four week induction programme. Under these circumstances Department would become an optional owner of Employee and the direct relationship between Company and Employee would have to be restored. Established employees would have Departments as owners and newly recruited graduates would have Companies as owners.

One implementation-time solution would be to introduce a dummy department, such as "Graduates". This device is covered in chapter 8, section 8.2.6, as a denormalisation technique. The logical model, however, needs to describe the existing rules fully without relying on dummy data. Once again the solution is to create mutually exclusive subtypes, this time of the Employee entity.

Company
    <u>companyName</u>
    address
    telephoneNumber

Department
    <u>companyName</u>
    <u>departmentName</u>
Foreign: companyName → Company
Foreign: departmentName → DepartmentName

Employee
    <u>employeeNumber</u>
    givenName
    familyName
    dateOfBirth
Foreign: dateOfBirth → Date

EstablishedEmployee
    <u>employeeNumber</u>
    companyName

departmentName
Foreign: employeeNumber → Employee
Foreign: companyName, departmentName → Department

GraduateTrainee
<u>employeeNumber</u>
companyName
Foreign: employeeNumber → Employee
Foreign: companyName → Company

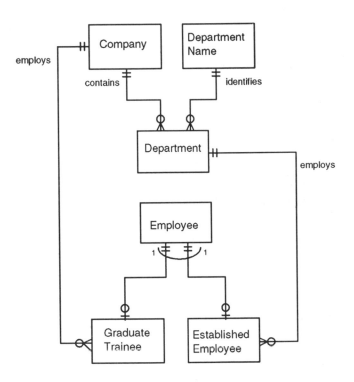

Figure 5.3

5.2   Resolving many-to-many relationships

Chapter 2 suggested that entities usually represent objects of business significance. This was something of a simplification because many entities are created in order to satisfy the technical needs of the relational database. The only legitimate relationships in the relational data model are 1:n primary key, 1:n foreign key relationships and 1:1 links between supertype and subtype entities. Any relationships which appear to be more complex than this need to be restated in terms of these simpler components.

5.2.1   The many-to-many resolver

Imagine a supermarket chain that sells a range of items in stores throughout the UK. It recognizes both store and item as entities.

Store
      <u>storeCode</u>
      storeName
      address
      telephoneNumber

Item
      <u>itemCode</u>
      description
(o)   quantityWeight
(o)   unitsWeight
(o)   quantityVolume
(o)   unitsVolume
      quantityPrice
      ifOwnBrand

Foreign: quantityWeight $\rightarrow$ Quantity
Foreign: quantityVolume $\rightarrow$ Quantity
Foreign: quantityPrice $\rightarrow$ Quantity

There are some items that are sold in every store and other items that are stocked to cater for local tastes. For example, only the Edinburgh store sells Irn Bru and garlic butter can only be found in the store in Finchley. Suppose the supermarket's head office wants a list of all the products which are sold at the Blackpool store.

In making the enquiry, head office expects to be sent a list of values of the attribute itemCode. Therefore we know we are starting the enquiry at the owner end of a relationship, with the value of one attribute in the owner entity - in this case the value Blackpool for storeName in Store. The key of the owner, storeCode, must appear among the attributes of the detail entity. It may even be among the key attributes of the detail but, because it needs to occur many times, it could not form the key on its own.

While we are studying the nature of Store's detail, head office contacts us again, this time to request a list of all the stores that stock 1 kg packets of own brand Italian brown rice. Once more the required answer is a list of values, so again the enquiry needs to start with a particular occurrence of an owner. In this case the owner is Item and the occurrence is identified by 97441355, the code for rice of the specified quality and pack size.

By definition, the detail contains the key of the owner, itemCode. This may form part of the primary key of the detail.

In fact the detail of Store and the detail of Item are one and the same. Each occurrence of the detail has a key consisting of storeCode and itemCode. It provides a look-up table between the two original entities.

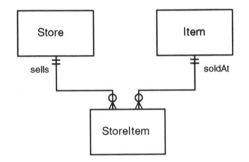

Figure 5.4

Each occurrence of StoreItem contains a pairing of a store and an item which is sold there. It is therefore capable of providing the anwers to both enquiries from head office. To find all the stores which sell the rice pack it is necessary to go through all the pairings and find those with an itemCode of 97441355. Since this item is sold in most of the chain's stores, there could be a hundred or more such pairings. To find all the items on sale in the Blackpool store it is necessary to find every pairing with a storeCode of BCP, the code for Blackpool. This time there will probably be thousands.

The tables below show just a few occurrences of each entity.

Store

storeCode	storeName	address	telephoneNumber
EBG	Edinburgh	48 Lothian Road	031 409 8717
BCP	Blackpool	17-45 Coronation Road	0445 309188
FLY	Finchley	14 Hendon Hall Road	081 654 1154
HSH	Haywards Heath	Unit 7, 14 Rycart Way	0444 464481

Item

itemCode	description	qWeight(o)	uWeight(o)	qVol(o)	uVol(o)	qPrice	
97441355	Italian brown rice	1.000	kg			0.84	...
74661904	Irn Bru			0.375	litre	0.35	
33314478	Skimmed milk			1	pint	0.39	
59080034	Taramasalata	0.200	kg			0.88	
40045473	Garlic butter	0.250	kg			1.55	

StoreItem

storeCode	itemCode
EBG	97441355
HSH	59080034
BCP	59080034
EBG	33314478
BCP	33314478
BCP	97441355
FLY	40045473

The fact that a store does not stock a particular item can only be deduced from the absence of the relevant pairing. So if head office asks for a list of all stores which do not stock taramasalata, our enquiry will have to scour StoreItem to compile a list of all those stores which do stock it and then subtract that from another list of all Stores. Fortunately database query languages have wrapped up this type of enquiry into a single command.

5.2.2   The key of the many-to-many resolver

A shared detail is the most efficient way to represent the relationship between Store and Item. Because one store sells many items and one item is sold in many stores, the direct relationship between the two is a many-to-many (n:m)[*] link. N:m relationships cannot be represented relationally until they are broken down into two 1:n relationships with a newly created entity called a **resolution entity** or **resolver**.

Figure 5.4 shows a resolver whose key is made up entirely of the keys of its two owners: in other words both owners are primary key owners of the resolver. This is the classic way to resolve a n:m relationship. However there are two other possibilities.

---

[*] Many methodologies use the notation M:M as an abbreviation for a many-to-many relationship. We have chosen m:n to show that counts of the two entities need not produce the same answer.

- Both owners are foreign key owners.

- One owner is primary key owner, the other is a foreign key owner.

In the first case, the resolution entity will need an artificial key, since the owners' keys will be foreign keys of the detail.

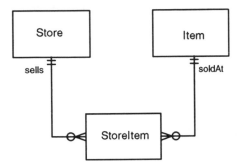

Figure 5.5

In the second case it will still need an artificial key component so that the owner's contribution to the primary key can take on the same value many times.

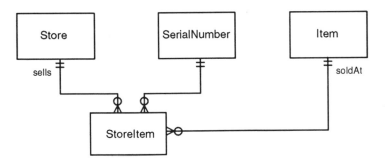

Figure 5.6

The need to invent an artificial key when a natural one would have sufficed is one drawback of these solutions. The other is that they give too much freedom in that they allow each pairing of owner entities' keys to be repeated.

5.2.3   Non-key attributes of the many-to-many resolver

Many n:m resolvers are created simply to provide a cross-reference between two other entities. To achieve this they need have as attributes only the keys of the other two. However, further analysis sometimes results in an n:m resolver acquiring non-key attributes of its own, as we shall see.

Head office is on the 'phone again. The caller needs to know how many tins of black treacle are in stock at the Haywards Heath store. Stock level depends on both item and store so it is to be found in an entity whose key contains the key of Store and the key of Item. Fortunately StoreItem fits the bill.

StoreItem

storeCode	itemCode	quantityStockLevel(d)
EBG	97441355	37
HSH	59080034	141
BCP	59080034	8
EBG	33314478	15
BCP	33314478	7
BCP	97441355	11
FLY	40045473	0

Note that had either of the other key options been chosen for the resolver, then it would have been unsuitable for the quantityStockLevel attribute. This is because only one stock level value can be allowed for each combination of store and item.

5.2.4   The many-to-many resolver as owner

The supermarket also keeps track of deliveries of items into stock at each store. It uses the term delivery to include returns of unsold or faulty goods from the store to the manufacturer: these are regarded as negative deliveries. The attribute lists for a delivery looks like this:

> Delivery
> > storeCode
> > itemCode
> > dateOfDelivery
> > timeOfDelivery
> > manufacturerName
> > quantityDelivered

Foreign: storeCode, itemCode → StoreItem
Foreign: dateOfDelivery → Date
Foreign: timeOfDelivery → Time
Foreign: manufacturerName → Manufacturer
Foreign: quantityDelivered → Quantity

A delivery involves a given item being delivered to, or removed from, a particular store, but neither Store nor Item is a foreign key owner of Delivery. Instead the attributes storeCode and itemCode are both inherited from the resolver entity StoreItem. The direct relationships between Store and Delivery and between Item and Delivery are implicit in the relationships shown below.

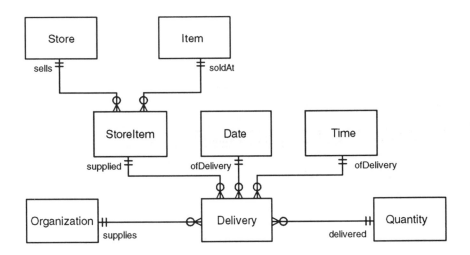

Figure 5.7

The implication of making StoreItem the owner of Delivery is this: no store can accept a delivery of any item it does not already stock or plan to stock. By modelling the data in this way we show that this constraint is required.

The stock level attribute is a kind of balance. It could be calculated from historical delivery data and should be marked as derivable data on the attribute list.

StoreItem
        storeCode
        itemCode
(d)   quantityStockLevel

5.2.5   Resolving more than two entities

A resolver entity can provide a look-up between more than two entities. Suppose several archaelogists can each decipher one or more of the runes found on buildings in a recently excavated site.   Each archaeologist is allocated to interpret a particular rune on a given building.

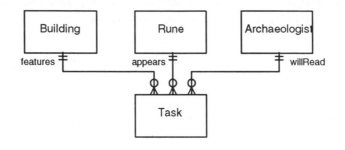

Figure 5.8

Task

buildingName	runeName	archaeologistNameWillRead
Pyramid	Squiggly	Vladimir
Pyramid	Squiggly	Maria
Pyramid	Upright	Helen
Temple	Squiggly	Maria
Temple	Upright	Helen
Temple	Angular	Siobhan
Temple	Pictogram	Miles
Ball court	Angular	Siobhan
Obelisk	Squiggly	Vladimir
Obelisk	Pictogram	Miles

The three-way resolver is an admirable record of the tasks allocated to each archaeologist. However, it would be impossible to tell from this table that Miles is regarded as an expert interpreter of the upright rune, since he has his hands full on this particular site making sense of pictograms.   The relationship between archaeologists and the runes they can interpret is also a n:m connection, since one archaeologist may read many runes and one rune may be understood by many archaeologists. It needs to be stored separately in its own resolver. The resolver might have non-key attributes, such as level of expertise. Here Miles can be given full credit.

ArchaeologistRuneCompetence

runeName	archaeologistNameCanRead	expertise
Squiggly	Vladimir	Competent
Squiggly	Maria	Learner
Upright	Helen	Expert
Upright	Miles	Expert
Angular	Siobhan	Competent
Pictogram	Miles	Expert

Note that the existence of a record in the table above implies that the archaeologist has some competence in the interpretation of the rune; the last attribute just qualifies that ability.

The three-way resolver also fails to tell us that there is another rune on the ball court, so obscure that no archaeologist has yet managed to make sense of it. Another resolver is needed, this time between building and rune.

BuildingRune

buildingName	runeName
Pyramid	Squiggly
Pyramid	Upright
Temple	Squiggly
Temple	Upright
Temple	Angular
Temple	Pictogram
Ball court	Angular
Ball court	Dotty
Obelisk	Squiggly
Obelisk	Pictogram

The data modeller should never be afraid of creating extra resolver entities where they seem to be needed. Those who try to force too much information into too few tables are the most likely to violate the normal forms of relational theory, which are explained in chapter 7.

5.3   Relational constraints

The relational constraint, introduced in the previous chapter to address multiple inheritance within a subtype entity group, can be used to ensure that attribute combinations created in one table are a subset of those which exist in another.

For instance, it is important to ensure that archaeologists are never sent off to particular buildings to decipher runes which do not appear on those buildings. In other words, for every record in the Task table there should be a record in the BuildingRune table with the same buildingName and runeName. The attribute list is annotated to show the need for a check.

BuildingRune
  buildingName
  runeName
Foreign: buildingName → Building
Foreign: runeName → Rune

Task
  buildingName
  runeName
  archaeologistNameWillRead
Foreign: buildingName → Building
Foreign: runeName → Rune
Foreign: archaeologistNameWillRead → Archaeologist
Constraint: buildingName, runeName in
    BuildingRune.buildingName, runeName

Likewise, we want to ensure that the staff are only allocated to tasks they are capable of discharging so we need to check on the existence of a suitable record in the ArchaeologistRuneCompetence table before inserting a new Task record.

ArchaeologistRuneCompetence
  runeName
  archaeologistNameCanRead
  expertise
Foreign: runeName → Rune
Foreign: archaeologistNameCanRead → Archaeologist

Task
  buildingName
  runeName
  archaeologistNameWillRead
Foreign: buildingName → Building
Foreign: runeName → Rune
Foreign: archaeologistNameWillRead → Archaeologist

Constraint:	buildingName, runeName in
	BuildingRune.buildingName, runeName
Constraint:	runeName, archaeologistNameWillRead in
	ArchaeologistRuneCompetence.runeName,
	archaeologistNameCanRead

The need for such checks is diagrammed using relationship constraint symbols as shown below.

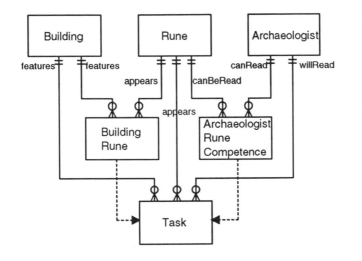

Figure 5.9

5.4   Avoiding duplicate inheritance

The reader may ask at this point, "Why do we need to use relational constraints? When we wanted to ensure that a Delivery related to an existing StoreItem we just made it into a detail of StoreItem. If Task were a detail of BuildingRune and ArchaeologistRuneCompetence then the constraints would arise automatically."

This is a fair point. It is true that if Task had had to be constrained by one or the other of the other tables, the solution used in section 5.2.4 would have worked well: the problem arises only because it must be constrained by both. If Task were a detail of both the other two tables it would feature the keys of both among its attributes. The key of BuildingRune includes runeName, as does the key of ArchaeologistRuneCompetence. Task would thus inherit runeName twice.

Since a task can only involve one rune at a time this would clearly be wrong. Other than the chosen solution, there were two possible devices we could have adopted.

- We could have permitted the duplicate inheritance but made a rule that both runeNames should be the same and should never be allowed to be set to different values.

The solution chosen in section 5.3, by ensuring there is only one runeName attribute in the Task entity, achieves the same thing rather more neatly.

- We could have said that runeName appeared only once among the attributes of Task but was required to support relationships with both BuildingRune and ArchaeologistRuneCompetence - in other words, that the key contributions of the two tables had overlapped.

The chosen solution implies that an attribute is never required to support more than one direct relationship with an owner and is therefore sound from a relational point of view. It means that there are no such things as overlapping keys.

5.5   Avoiding mixed primary and foreign key relationships

Constraints can also be used to ensure that an owner entity is always either a primary key owner or a foreign key owner. In other words, a relationship with an owner is supported by one or more primary key attributes **or** one or more foreign key attributes, but never with a mixture of primary and foreign keys. If diagrams are to remain meaningful, mixed primary/foreign key owners are unacceptable[*].

As an illustration, consider an entity which stores information about cities worldwide. Each city is identified by its name and the key of the country it is in - so that, for example, Birmingham, UK is distinguished from Birmingham, US.

The entity also shows which time zone each city is in. A time zone is a subdivision of country, though only large countries such as the United States and Australia need to have such divisions. Time zones are broadly based on geographical bands of longitude which may cover several countries, but

---

[*] In the physical relational environment this is unimportant: table joins can be made on any combination of columns, regardless of their origins or even their names, if their data values are compatible.

since it is up to individual governments to decide precise boundaries and to enforce the daylight saving schedules within each zone, the time zone is perceived as that part of a country where the geographical band is enforced.

Country
    <u>countryCode</u>
    countryName

TimeZone
    <u>countryCode</u>
    <u>quantityHoursAheadGMT</u>
(o)   quantityHoursAheadGMTDaylightSaving
(o)   monthDaylightSavingStarts
(o)   dayDaylightSavingStarts
(o)   monthDaylightSavingEnds
(o)   dayDaylightSavingEnds
Foreign: countryCode → Country
Foreign: quantityHoursAheadGMT → Quantity
Foreign: quantityHoursAheadGMTDaylightSaving → Quantity
Foreign: monthDaylightSavingStarts → Month
Foreign: dayDaylightSavingStarts → DayOfMonth
Foreign: monthDaylightSavingEnds → Month
Foreign: dayDaylightSavingEnds → DayOfMonth

City
    <u>countryCode</u>
    <u>cityName</u>
(o)   countPopulation
(o)   yearOfLastCensus
    quantityHoursAheadGMT
Foreign   countryCode → Country
Foreign   cityName → cityName
Foreign   countPopulation → Count
Foreign   yearOfLastCensus → Year
Foreign   quantityHoursAheadGMT → Quantity
Constraint: countryCode, quantityHoursAheadGMT in
            TimeZone.countryCode,
            TimeZone.quantityHoursAheadGMT

If TimeZone were to be a direct owner of City, it would contribute one attribute to its primary key and one to its collection of non-key attributes. Instead, the key-only owner of TimeZone, Quantity, also owns City. A relational constraint ensures that a city is only placed in a time zone which already exists. The structure is illustrated in figure 5.10.

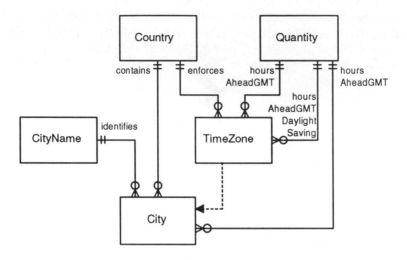

Figure 5.10

5.6   Multiple relationships

On some occasions it is vital to allow a detail entity to inherit its parent's keys more than once. This is true where there are multiple relationships between owner and detail, each relationship representing a different fact.

For example, an airline wishes to keep records of the routes it flies. Each route is characterised by its airport of origin and its airport of destination. The entity Airport therefore has two separate 1:n relationships with the Route entity. In each case Airport is the owner.

    Airport
        airportCode
        airportName
        altitude
        latitude
        longitude

    Route
        routeCode
        airportCodeOfOrigin
        airportCodeOfDestination
    Foreign: airportCodeOfOrigin → Airport
    Foreign: airportCodeOfDestination → Airport

Both airportCodeOfOrigin and airportCodeOfDestination are roles of airportCode, their rolenames inherited from the relationships which link Airport and Route. Although it is not always necessary for relationship labels to become rolenames of foreign key attributes of the detail entity, where multiple relationships link two entities their rolenames must be propagated.

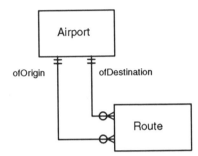

Figure 5.11

We have in fact come across several examples of multiple relationships before. Colour was the owner of Vehicle three times, describing its body, roof and upholstery. Month is twice the owner of TimeZone and so is DayOfMonth.

A recurring difficulty for practising data modellers is to decide whether two entities have many distinct 1:n relationships between them or are related by a n:m relationship which needs to be resolved in the usual way. For example, imagine that a scientist in a genetic engineering company proposes to spend £300,000 on a piece of laboratory equipment. The scientist originates the proposal which must then be countersigned by his line manager, endorsed by her boss and authorized by two directors of the company. If it survives this ordeal the proposed expenditure will be converted into an order by a clerk in the purchasing department.

The relationships between Employee and CapitalExpenditure could be modelled as shown in figure 5.12. This model shows that the existing rules governing capital spending have been fully understood and analysed. However it is susceptible to any changes in procedure which might occur. Were one signature more or less to be required the data structure would have to change.

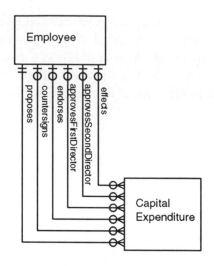

Figure 5.12

A modeller under pressure of project deadlines and fearing that a required relationship might already have been overlooked might be tempted to revert to a resolution entity.

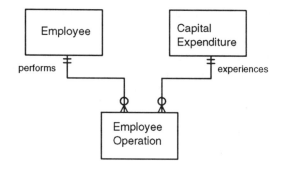

Figure 5.13

The primary key of EmployeeOperation assumes that an employee will not perform more than one operation on the same expenditure proposal. If this were unrealistic then the attribute typeOfOperation would have to be introduced into the identifier. TypeOfOperation is a key-only entity that holds the domain of acceptable values for the attribute typeOfOperation, such as "propose", "endorse" and "effect".

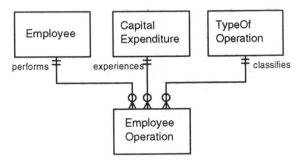

Figure 5.14

This structure allows flexibility but fails to exert the same control as that shown in figure 5.12. The program code would have to work harder to ensure that the correct number of operations had been performed on the expenditure proposal. The program code would take on some of the duties that should be undertaken by the due rigour of the data model.

Use of a resolver in these circumstances is the top of a slippery slope whereby incomplete analysis is disguised by introducing what is effectively meta-data (data about data - see chapter 14) into the business data model. Look at the permissible values of typeOfOperation: "propose", "endorse", "effect" and so on. They are the names of what should have been relationships.

A compromise solution might be a structure which allowed a variable number of authorizations but recognized the proposing and the effecting of capital expenditure as separate activities.

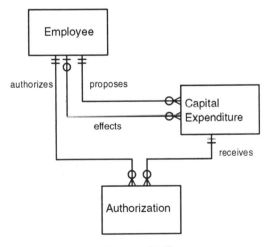

Figure 5.15

5.7   Reverse multiple relationships

So far all the multiple relationships we have investigated have been in the same direction. Sometimes two entities can be related such that one is the owner of the other and vice versa.

Let us say that the supermarket chain we investigated earlier wants to record the names of all the staff who work in each of its stores and also to indicate which member of staff is the manager. The entity Store now has employeeNumberManager among its attributes to show who manages it. The entity Employee holds storeCodeLocates among its attributes to show where the employee is currently posted. Therefore Store is the owner of Employee and Employee the owner of Store.

```
Store
        storeCode
        storeName
        address
        telephoneNumber
(o)     employeeNumberManager
Foreign:        employeeNumberManager → Employee


Employee
        employeeNumber
        familyName
        givenName
        dateOfBirth
        storeCodeLocates
Foreign:        dateOfBirth → Date
Foreign:        storeCodeLocates → Store
```

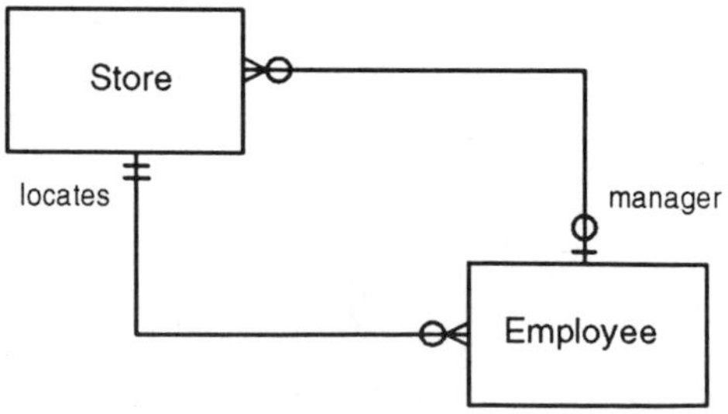

Figure 5.16

This is a general solution for relationships between an owner and many foreign key detail occurrences where one of the details has to be picked out as the chief, the default, the main or the representative occurrence.

Note that each store is likely to have many employees in post and each employee can be the manager of several stores at once. By implication, an employee could manage a store without being posted to it at the time.

Suppose we are asked to impose a further control through the data model to ensure that an employee manages only one store at a time. We must prevent any value of employeeNumberManager occurring in more than one Store record. This can be achieved by making employeeNumberManager into an alternate key of Store. In effect this reduces the relationship of which Store is the detail from a 1:n to a 1:1.

```
Store
        storeCode
        storeName
        address
        telephoneNumber
(o)     employeeNumberManager
Foreign:        employeeNumberManager → Employee
Unique:         employeeNumberManager

Employee
        employeeNumber
        familyName
        givenName
        dateOfBirth
        storeCodeLocates
Foreign:        dateOfBirth → Date
Foreign:        storeCodeLocates → Store
```

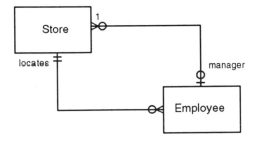

Figure 5.17

This construction, while preventing one employee from managing more than one store, still allows the manager to manage a store other than the one to which he or she is currently posted. If the data model is to preclude this possibility too it must place a relational constraint between the two tables.

Store
>   storeCode
>   storeName
>   address
>   telephoneNumber
>   employeeNumberManager

Foreign:	employeeNumberManager → Employee
Unique:	employeeNumberManager
Constraint:	storeCode, employeeNumberManager in Employee.storeCodeLocates, employeeNumber

Employee
>   employeeNumber
>   familyName
>   givenName
>   dateOfBirth
>   storeCodeLocates

Foreign:	dateOfBirth → Date
Foreign:	storeCodeLocates → Store

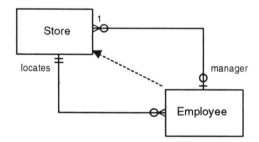

Figure 5.18

Note also that each relationship is a 1:n so we are assuming that an employee is posted to one store at a time and that a store has at most one manager at a time. Suppose a store is now allowed to have two job-sharing managers. The relationship indicating management becomes a many-to-many and needs to be resolved as shown below.

Store

    <u>storeCode</u>
    storeName
    address
    telephoneNumber

Employee

    <u>employeeNumber</u>
    familyName
    givenName
    dateOfBirth
    storeCodeLocates

Foreign: dateOfBirth $\rightarrow$ Date
Foreign: storeCodeLocates $\rightarrow$ Store

StoreManager

    <u>storeCode</u>
    <u>employeeNumberManager</u>

Foreign: storeCode $\rightarrow$ Store
Foreign: employeeNumberManager $\rightarrow$ Employee
Unique: employeeNumberManager
Constraint: storeCode, employeeNumberManager in
            Employee.storeCodeLocates, employeeNumber

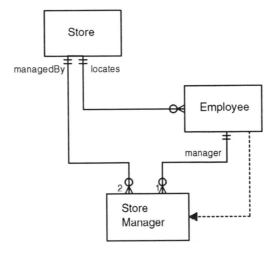

Figure 5.19

As the diagram indicates, the existing constraints have been built into the new model: it is still true to say that neither manager may manage any other stores and that both must be posted to the store they manage jointly.

An alternative construction for showing leadership or representative status is shown below.

```
Store
        storeCode
        storeName
        address
        telephoneNumber

Employee
        employeeNumber
        familyName
        givenName
        dateOfBirth
        storeCodeLocates
        ifManager
Foreign:        dateOfBirth → Date
Foreign:        storeCodeLocates → Store
```

This structure is deemed less elegant because it introduces a new attribute, ifManager, where a new relationship would have sufficed. In every case where an employee is not a manager the new attribute will be set to N. Code will be required to ensure that for any store no more than one record of Employee (or two if job-sharing is permitted) has the ifManager attribute set to Y. The structure also prevents an employee managing a store unless he or she is physically based there. In other words the relationship "manager" can never be anything more than a glorified version of the relationship "works in".

5.8   Historical data

A data structure which reflects only the current situation will normally be simpler than one which is required to hold a record of past and future values too. There are two types of histories: those which record alterations to the values of attributes which change discretely and those which record snapshots of continuously changing data at regular or irregular time intervals.

5.8.1   Histories of mandatory attributes

Imagine that a slimming club holds records of its members. Two of the attributes are a member's current address (a discretely changing variable) and his or her current weight (whose value changes continuously). At any time, a member has one weight and one address but over time either may change - indeed, in the case of the weight attribute, the hope is that it will change. The club decides that in order to log its members' progress it needs to keep a history of their weights. It also wants to hold a history of addresses - perhaps because its well-organized members tend to notify it of planned moves so far in advance that it needs to hold future addresses alongside current ones.

The existing Member entity holds the latest values of weight and address but doesn't give any indication of what the situation has been in the past or what it will be in the future.

```
Member
        membershipNumber
        familyName
        givenName
        address
        quantityHeight
        quantityWeight
Foreign:        quantityHeight → Quantity
Foreign:        quantityWeight → Quantity
```

The members are weighed when they first join and every week when they attend classes. The club now wants to be able to compile charts of members' weight loss over time. For each member, it requires a list of dates and corresponding weight values to be returned. This kind of enquiry demands that the weights are held in a detail entity of Member. The detail will inherit part of its key from Member. If membershipNumber is part of the detail's key, what is the rest? A history detail will always have one or more time-related key attributes such as a date or a time within a date, depending on the degree of time sensitivity required.

In this case a date is adequate: members are normally weighed weekly. Weighings may be less frequent if members miss classes, but will never be more frequent than once a day.

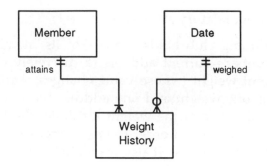

Figure 5.20

Note that the weight attribute whose history is recorded in the detail now disappears from the main entity Member.

Member
    <u>membershipNumber</u>
    familyName
    givenName
    address
    quantityHeight
Foreign: quantityHeight $\rightarrow$ Quantity

WeightHistory
    <u>membershipNumber</u>
    <u>dateWeighed</u>
    quantityWeight
Foreign: dateWeighed $\rightarrow$ Date
Foreign: quantityWeight $\rightarrow$ Quantity

When the AddressHistory entity is created the same thing happens.

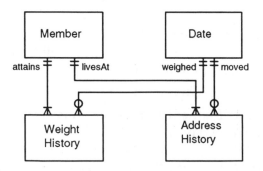

Figure 5.21

Member
     <u>membershipNumber</u>
     familyName
     givenName
     quantityHeight
Foreign: quantityHeight → Quantity

WeightHistory
     <u>membershipNumber</u>
     <u>dateWeighed</u>
     quantityWeight
Foreign: dateWeighed → Date
Foreign: quantityWeight → Quantity

AddressHistory
     <u>membershipNumber</u>
     <u>dateMoved</u>
     address
Foreign: dateMoved → Date

Occasionally the time-related component of a history detail's key is a time period rather than a date or datetime. This is only the case when the history detail has been established to hold future plans. Imagine that a large project has been given a spending budget for each quarter of its projected duration. The history detail might look like this.

Project
     <u>projectName</u>
     employeeNumberManager
Foreign: employeeNumberManager → Employee

ProjectBudgetHistory
     <u>projectName</u>
     <u>yearBudget</u>
     <u>quarterBudget</u>
     quantityBudget
Foreign: projectName → Project
Foreign: yearBudget → Year
Foreign: quarterBudget → Quarter
Foreign: quantityBudget → Quantity

In an occurrence whose year and quarter attributes had past values, such as the 3rd quarter of 1979, the budget value would still show the amount that was budgeted for spending in that quarter, an amount proposed when the quarter was still in the future. The quantityBudget attribute would never be used to show the sum of actual expenditure in the period.

The total actual spend could be calculated once the period was over from the records of individual items of spending. Because it is derived data total actual spend has no place in the logical data model. However, summaries of the events of a past time period are often useful in the physical data model and we shall return to them in chapter 8.

5.8.2   Histories of mandatory 1:n relationships

So far, the examples in this section have concentrated on non-key attributes whose histories are required. The same technique is used to store histories of foreign key attributes - and thus, effectively, to store the histories of the foreign key relationships themselves. If a history of a foreign key attribute is required, the relationship with the owner is by implication transient.

For example, recall that Colour is an owner of Vehicle. At any one time, a vehicle must have exactly one body paintwork colour, but over time that colour may change. Suppose that it proves necessary to log the history of the attribute colourOfPaintworkBody in the Vehicle entity. The existing attribute holds the current colour of a Vehicle's bodywork but doesn't give any indication of what colour it was when first registered or indeed what colour it will be next week when it is due for a respray.

```
Vehicle
        registrationNumber
        manufacturerName
        modelName
        colourOfPaintworkBody
        colourOfPaintworkRoof
        colourOfUpholstery
        yearOfManufacture
        dateRoadFundLicenceRenewable
Foreign:        manufacturerName, modelName → VehicleModel
Foreign:        colourOfPaintworkBody → Colour
Foreign:        colurOfPaintworkRoof → Colour
Foreign:        colourOfUpholstery → Colour
Foreign:        yearOfManufacture → Year
Foreign:        dateRoadFundLicenceRenewable → Date
```

We should like to enquire what colour a Vehicle's body is, or has been, or will be at any time in its life - in other words, we are asking for a list of values to be returned. This kind of enquiry demands that the colours are held in a detail entity of Vehicle. The detail will inherit part of its key from Vehicle and the rest will be made up of a date or time within a date. In this case a date is adequate: it is safe to assume a Vehicle doesn't change colour more than once a day because spray paint takes two or three days to dry.

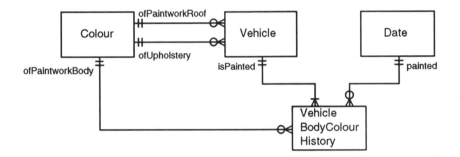

Figure 5.22

The attribute whose history is recorded in the detail now disappears from the main entity Vehicle.

        Vehicle
                registrationNumber
                manufacturerName
                modelName
                colourOfPaintworkRoof
                colourOfUpholstery
                yearOfManufacture
                dateRoadFundLicenceRenewable
        Foreign: manufacturerName, modelName → VehicleModel
        Foreign: colurOfPaintworkRoof → Colour
        Foreign: colourOfUpholstery → Colour
        Foreign: yearOfManufacture → Year
        Foreign: dateRoadFundLicenceRenewable → Date

        VehicleBodyColourHistory
                registrationNumber
                datePainted
                colourOfPaintworkBody
        Foreign: registrationNumber → Vehicle
        Foreign: datePainted → Date
        Foreign: colourOfPaintworkBody → Colour

Vehicle

registrationNumber	manufacturerName	modelName	...
A 184 TGW	Vauxhall	Astra	
E 358 OLL	Vauxhall	Astra	
NRK 156 P	Ford	Cortina	
J 166 CHM	Volkswagen	Polo	
OAL 50 W	Vauxhall	Astra	
B 292 APN	Toyota	Carina	

VehicleBodyColourHistory

registrationNumber	datePainted	colourOfPaintworkBody
A 184 TGW	04.05.87	burgundy
A 184 TGW	14.01.91	turquoise

It is worth noting that the new entity, VehicleBodyColourHistory is a many-to-many resolver between Vehicle and Colour. The effect of time is to turn a 1:n relationship into a m:n. It was always true that a colour could be the body colour of many vehicles; now it is also necessary to record the fact that a vehicle can have many body colours during its lifetime. VehicleBodyColourHistory resolves two entities of which one is its primary key owner and the other its foreign key owner. This key structure was discussed in chapter 3 and rejected as unsuitable for the StoreItem resolver because it allowed many occurrences with the same Item and Store. In this situation, however, the key structure is ideal: we want to allow many occurrences of the same Vehicle and Colour in case the car is eventually resprayed back to its original colour.

5.8.3   Histories of optional attributes

At any time in its life a Vehicle's body must be a particular colour. It is possible to assume that A 184 TGW stopped being burgundy on 14th January 1991 when it was sprayed turquoise. This is often a fair assumption. For example, the price of a 1kg packet of Italian brown rice in a store in the chain we visited earlier will be charged right up until the date the new price comes into effect. In essence this is because the attribute whose history is being recorded would have been mandatory had it remained on the original entity. A car must always have a current colour. An item must always have a price. Where histories of optional owners are required the picture changes.

For example, the local chamber of commerce is a club for self-employed business people. Some of its members are registered for VAT and others are not. Those who are VAT registered one year may not meet the criteria for

VAT registration the next and conversely some who were not registered when they first set up their businesses may be able to register after a period of time because of an increase in turnover or profit. Someone who has been registered once then re-registers after a break is allocated a new registration number by Customs and Excise.

To keep a history of members' VAT registration numbers over time, the chamber would have to set up a detail entity with the starting date of each registration in the key. But how would it know when a registration ceased? Because it cannot deduce the finish date of one registration from the start of the next it must store a finish date on each registration record. DateFinish is a foreign key in the registration history entity.

Member
        memberCode
        nameFamily
        nameGiven
        nameOfBusiness
        addressHome
        addressBusiness
        dateOfBirth
Foreign: dateOfBirth → Date

VATRegistrationHistory
        memberCode
        dateStart
        VATRegistrationNumber
        dateFinish
Foreign: memberCode → Member
Foreign: dateStart → Date
Foreign: dateFinish → Date

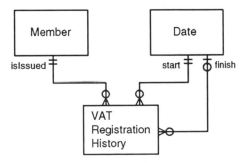

Figure 5.23

The histories of foreign key attributes supporting relationships with optional masters are stored in exactly the same way.

5.8.4   Histories of subtypes

Often a subtype entity is created to hold a particular optional attribute. If it becomes necessary to hold the history of the attribute then the attribute must be removed to a history detail of the subtype. This exercise may render the subtype useless and in these circumstances it is preferable to hang the history detail directly from the supertype.

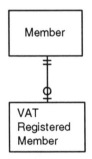

Figure 5.24

Say for example that the Chamber of Commerce had decided to create a subtype of Member to acknowledge its members who were currently VAT registered (figure 5.24).

```
Member
        memberCode
        nameFamily
        nameGiven
        nameOfBusiness
        addressHome
        addressBusiness
        dateOfBirth
Foreign:        dateOfBirth → Date


VATRegisteredMember
        memberCode
        VATRegistrationNumber
Foreign:        memberCode → Member
```

When the history of VAT registration numbers was called for, the chamber might have created a history detail of the subtype.

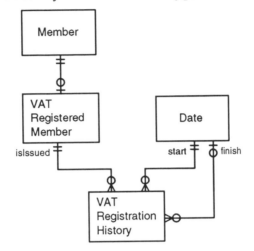

Figure 5.25

However, once the attribute VATRegistrationNumber moved to the VATRegistrationHistory detail the subtype would have been left with no non-key attributes. The chamber would probably wish to revert to the solution of figure 5.23.

Where the subtype still performs a useful function even without its attributes then the history entity must become a detail of the subtype itself. Say for example that it became necessary to hold a history of the serial numbers of tachographs which were fitted to lorries.

Vehicle
        <u>registrationNumber</u>
        manufacturerName
        modelName
        colourOfPaintworkBody
        colourOfPaintworkRoof
        colourOfUpholstery
        yearOfManufacture
        dateRoadFundLicenceRenewable
Foreign: manufacturerName, modelName → VehicleModel
Foreign: colourOfPaintworkBody → Colour
Foreign: colourOfPaintworkRoof → Colour
Foreign: colourOfUpholstery → Colour
Foreign: yearOfManufacture → Year
Foreign: dateRoadFundLicenceRenewable → Date

Lorry
    <u>registrationNumber</u>
Foreign: registrationNumber → Vehicle

LorryTachographHistory
    <u>registrationNumber</u>
    <u>dateFitted</u>
    serialNumberTachograph
Foreign: registrationNumber → Lorry
Foreign: dateFitted → Date

LorryWithTailLift
    <u>registrationNumber</u>
    manufacturerNameTailLift
    quantityMaximumWeightTailLift
Foreign: registrationNumber → Lorry
Foreign: manufacturerNameTailLift → Manufacturer
Foreign: quantityMaximumWeightTailLift → Quantity

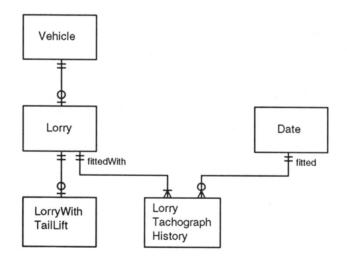

Figure 5.26

The subtype Lorry continues to exist because it has a role as the supertype of LorryWithTailLift, even though it no longer has any non-key attributes. LorryTachographHistory is its detail.

5.8.5   Histories of many-to-many relationships

The data model diagram in figure 5.27 shows a many-to-many relationship between projects and employees. At any one time an employee may be assigned to many projects.

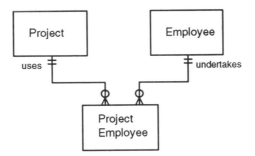

Figure 5.27

It is also true to say that over time an employee may be assigned to many projects. In this case we do not need to create a new detail entity for the history of project assignments: the existing resolution entity ProjectEmployee already stores pairings of employees and their current projects. It is necessary only to add the start date to its primary key to allow historical pairings to occupy the entity as well as current ones.

It is also necessary to include finish date as a foreign key attribute. Because an employee may be engaged on none, one or many projects at a particular moment in time it is impossible to deduce when his or her engagement on one project finished by looking at the start date of any other particular assignment.

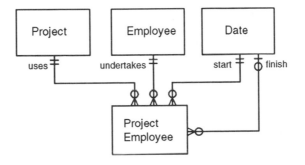

Figure 5.28

Chapter summary

The only relationships allowed in a relational data model are the 1:n primary key relationship, the 1:n foreign key relationship and the 1:1 relationship between a supertype entity and one of its subtypes. All other relationships must be restated in terms of these basic components.

Although two entities are not directly related, a connection between them may be implicit in other relationships. If any of the other relationships is optional the implicit relationship cannot be relied upon.

Many-to-many relationships must always be resolved into 1:n relationships. The resolver entity, whose key is normally composed of those of the original entities, may have non-key attributes of its own.

Overlapping foreign keys and mixed primary/foreign keys can be avoided by using owner entities with single attribute keys instead of those with concatenated keys. In some cases this means that key-only entities become foreign key owners. Relational constraints allow the data model to indicate some of the inter-entity verification work which process code will undertake.

Where two or more different relationships exist between the same two entities, they must be shown separately. Each relationship obliges the detail entity to inherit the owner's key. If several relationships between the two entities run in the same direction, the detail entity will inherit several copies of the owner's key attributes. These must be rolenamed to distinguish them.

To show that one particular occurrence of a detail is the chief, a new relationship from detail to master can be used. Often the maximum cardinality of the detail will be restricted to 1.

Histories of attributes, foreign key relationships and many-to-many relationships can be created. A history detail will always have a timestamp attribute as part of its primary key. Continuously changing attributes are subject to regular or irregular snapshots. Discretely changing attributes can have gaps between them - in which case a foreign key finish date and, if necessary, time must be specified as well.

Questions

1. A disc jockey has various recordings each consisting of a number of tracks. Some of the recordings are on cassette (in which case she notes the cassette recorder's counter number at the start of each track) and some on compact disc (in which case she notes the track numbers of each track). In each case she notes the duration of a track. Model the situation.

2. Is the relationship between a Vehicle and its Manufacturer explicit or implicit? What change in our business understanding would cause this to alter?

3. A Student may enrol on many courses. A Course has many Students. Model this situation.

4. A building firm employs several workers. Each worker has one or more skills, such as plumbing, carpentry, electrical wiring, brick-laying and roofing. The firm is working on a number of sites, each of which requires a different combination of skills. It assigns particular workers to use their skills on the various sites. Model this situation.

5. A cricket team consists of eleven players, one of whom is designated as the captain and one as the wicketkeeper. Model this situation.

6. The minimum cardinality of a history detail is always 1 with respect to the previous owner of the attribute whose history is required. Why?

7. In each case, model the required solution:

    (a)   Entity A has a mandatory attribute. The history of the attribute now needs to be held.

    (b)   Entity B has an optional attribute. The history of the attribute now needs to be held.

    (c)   Entity C has a subtype D with one non-key attribute. The history of this attribute now needs to be held. Show two different ways of modelling the new situation and discuss the merits of both.

8. What can you say about a history detail whose timestamp key component is financialYear?

9. The following information is available:

    Wayne is interested in movies and wants to catalogue his collection of video-cassettes. He wants to record the director's name, date of birth and date died.

For each movie, Wayne wants to record the title, year made, a critical rating (this is Wayne's opinion of the movie on a scale from 1 to 10), and the number of Oscars the movie won. Each of the movies must have one director. For each star, details to be stored are the name, birth-place, date of birth and date died. Stars may appear in many movies and some movies may cast many stars. Wayne is not interested in producers at all as he considers them to have little creative ability. Wayne keeps copies of the movies on video-cassettes, and although he only records one film on a given cassette, he does keep multiple copies of some movies so that he can lend them to friends. He would like to record to whom he has lent any particular copy, the date he lent it and the date it was returned. Wayne needs to record the name and telephone number of any friend to whom he lends a tape. Video-cassette copies are uniquely identified by a combination of the movie identifier and a copy number.

Using the above information create an entity diagram and attribute lists to meet the requirements as specified

10.   The ABC Software Company has been retained by a television production company, Weezle Productions, to create a management information database. After having conducted a number of interviews with Weezle personnel the ABC systems analyst has prepared the following specification:

Weezle Productions makes television programmes. Some television programmes are commissioned by a television company, other programmes are made speculatively in the hope of finding a television company interested in screening it once it has been made. A programme is known by its name (for example, Brideshead Revisited) and must be produced by one person. Details that must be held about producers include producer number, producer name, address, mobile telephone number (all producers are issued with a mobile telephone by Weezle Productions) and the maximum amount that the producer can sign off against a programme budget. For each television company, Weezle Productions records the company name, address, and the name of a contact person. A programme comprises a number of episodes which are identified by the programme name and an episode sequence number. Each episode must have a title and a director. Although there is only one producer for a program (and therefore for all episodes), each episode could have a different director. For directors, it is necessary to know a director number, director name, address, and telephone number (if they are on the telephone). Each episode requires a number of actors (the cast), and each actor may appear in a number of episodes. Weezle needs to know how many minutes of dialogue any particular actor has in any given episode. For each actor Weezle needs to know an actor number, name and the date the actor joined Equity (all actors must be members of Equity to appear in a programme episode). Weezle gives television companies permission to screen programme episodes and need to record the date and time that a television company screened a particular episode and how much they were charged. An episode may be screened by many television companies and a television company may screen the same episode more than once.

You are a database designer working for ABC - it is your task to design and implement a database to meet the above requirements. As a first step you should:

(a)   Draw an entity diagram and compile attribute lists to satisfy the above requirements.

(b)   Create test data in relational table format (maximum of 14 entries per entity) for four programmes made by Weezle Productions. Pick your favourite soaps/dramas as the basis for test data.

6

Recursion

Introduction

Large fleas have little fleas
upon their backs to bite 'em,
And little fleas have lesser fleas,
and so ad infinitum[1].

A recursive relationship is one that links a data entity to itself. The need to model recursion efficiently becomes more pronounced when generalization entities are used. Because supertype entities embrace concepts that were traditionally regarded as separate, recursive relationships are replacing links that used to exist between different entities. Where once teachers taught pupils and reports contained tables, people may now teach other people and documents consist of other documents.

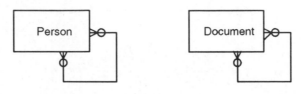

Figure 6.1

Recursion need hold no terrors for the data modeller. There are standard techniques for handling recursive relationships that are entirely derived from the methods covered in earlier chapters.

In the relational model all relationships other than that between a supertype and its subtype have a cardinality of 1:n. Where m:n relationships appear to exist they must be resolved; apparent 1:1 foreign key relationships must be expressed as constrained 1:ns. Recursive relationships can also appear to be m:n, 1:n or 1:1 relationships. Again, the m:n is illegal and must be resolved.

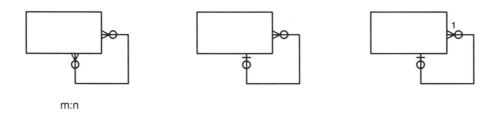

Figure 6.2

6.1   Many-to-many recursion: the bill of materials

The standard way to resolve an m:n relationship between two different entities is to introduce a new entity. The new entity is a detail of both the original ones and it acts as a cross-reference between them. An occurrence of the cross-reference entity, for example StoreItem, pairs off occurrences of the original entities, Store and Item, by holding the key of each among its attributes, as shown in figure 6.3.

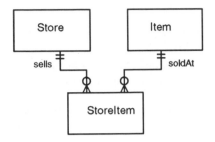

Figure 6.3

An m:n recursive relationship is resolved in exactly the same way: with a new cross-reference entity that pairs off occurrences of the original entity. It is a detail of both occurrences of the original entity, so it has to hold the key of each occurrence among its attributes. The new entity now has two 1:n relationships with the original entity.

6.1.1   Restricted networks

To resolve the Person to Person recursion which links pupils with their teachers, a new entity is introduced which inherits the keys of both teacher and pupil. The data structure is shown in entity diagram, attribute list and table form below.

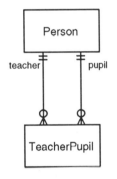

Figure 6.4

Person
> personName
> dateOfBirth
> address
> telephoneNumber

Foreign: dateOfBirth → Date

TeacherPupil
       <u>personNameTeacher</u>
       <u>personNamePupil</u>
Foreign: personNameTeacher → Person
Foreign: personNamePupil → Person

The resolver entity TeacherPupil has two relationships with its owner, Person, and therefore inherits the attribute personName twice. TeacherPupil cannot have two attributes with the same name and in order to distinguish them we have propagated the relationship name into the attribute name giving personNameTeacher and personName Pupil. This is the standard treatment for multiple relationships as described in chapter 5.

Person

personName	dateOfBirth	address	telephoneNumber
Brenda Bridges	09.03.58	18 High Street	0727 459104
James Ford	16.02.80	The Haven, Mill Lane	0727 320085
Harish Shah	12.11.79	76 Byward Street	0727 033452
Clive Brown	28.06.71	3 Rutter Road	0727 171668

TeacherPupil

personNameTeacher	personNamePupil
Brenda Bridges	Harish Shah
Clive Brown	James Ford
Brenda Bridges	Sarah Kidd
Clive Brown	Harish Shah

To find out which pupils are taught by Brenda Bridges, look down the column that features the person as teacher. Whenever her name appears, look across for the name of the pupil and note it down. To find out who teaches Harish Shah, trawl the column that features the person as pupil, and glance to the left to pick up a teacher's name when necessary.

This example shows that we can acknowledge both teachers and pupils as people and in a Person entity we can store attributes they have in common, such as their ages or addresses. The resolver entity stores details of the relationship between people; in this case it shows that a teacher teaches many pupils and that a pupil is taught by many teachers.

An occurrence of the resolver can be thought of as a pairing of nodes from different levels in a network. Each node is an occurrence of the original entity and each occurrence is represented by a single node in the network.

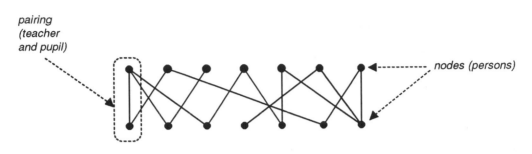

Figure 6.5

In considering the straightforward example of the school we would not expect to see anyone who features as a teacher turning up in the pupil layer, or vice versa. Each node knows whether it is on the top level or the bottom level of the network.

Figure 6.6

But not all networks are restricted to two levels. The full power of the m:n recursive resolver is demonstrated when this restriction is removed.

6.1.2   Infinite networks

Let us return to the recursive relationship between documents. A newsletter contains a certain article. The article is so well received that it is also featured in the annual report. The article contains, among other things, a table and a quotation from the chairman.

Document

documentRef	documentDescription	creator
Q17629	annual report 1993	Mork & Wellard Ltd
NL92665	factory newsletter Jun 1992	Poh Loon Lee
326	article on production capacity	Sophie Burns
412005	quotation to Channel 4	Sir Cuthbert Hedges
67D444	table of production 1982-1992	Irene Dwek

DocumentNetwork

docRefFramework	docRefContent
Q17629	326
NL92665	326
326	412005CH
326	67D444

The document network diagram can be extended upwards and downwards ad infinitum. Each level represents a different degree of complexity of document, but each node is a document in its own right. An occurrence of the resolver entity pairs two documents - a framework document with one of its contents - but a document could be a framework in one pairing yet a content in another. Apart from the top and bottom layers, no layer could be labelled FRAMEWORK or CONTENT. Looking upward to the layer above, a document will act as a content; looking down to the layer below, the same document will seem to be a framework.

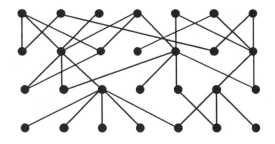

Figure 6.7

The resolver of an m:n recursion is often called a **bill of materials** structure. This reflects its heritage in the engineering industry. An engineering workshop making assemblies of any degree of complexity will maintain a bill of materials, showing which parts make up which sub-assemblies and how the sub-assemblies fit together as finished products. It is a clear example of generalization: all components, whether basic parts, assemblies or end products, are seen as having a common structure. Apart from the simplest components, each component will be made up of other components. Apart from the final saleable creation, each component will go to make up other components. By recognizing them all as components, there is no need to think up different names for each level of complexity and there is no need to set a limit on the number of levels that there are.

A well-used example of the engineering bill of materials is the bicycle factory. Its components include primitive parts such as nuts and bolts and spokes; assemblies such as wheels, saddles and handlebars and finished goods including men's, women's and children's bikes.

6.1.3   Non-key attributes of the bill of materials resolver

A study of the bill of materials for a bicycle workshop reveals not only which components go to make up which others, but also the quantity of each component required. This crucial piece of information belongs naturally in the resolver entity as it depends on knowing both occurrences of component: the parent and the child. Six nuts may be required in the construction of a saddle, but only two in a bell. Just as the m:n resolver between Store and Item in chapter 5, originally created to satisfy the rules of relational modelling, turned out to be the home for the item's stock level, so the m:n recursive resolver may hold attributes of its own.

Component

componentNumber	description	drawingNumber (o)
A4567	0.5 cm steel nut	HRW22300/1
L7712	luxury gents sadddle	G55899/2
M9802	gents racing frame	
Q6669	gents racing bike	
U7119	large chrome bell	REC3000

BillOfMaterials

componentNumberParent	componentNumberChild	quantityOfChild
L7712	A4567	6
U7119	A4567	2
Q6669	M9802	1
Q6669	L7712	1
Q6669	A4567	2

6.1.4   Non-adjacent pairings

Close inspection of the bill of materials reveals also that parent and child components in different but non-adjacent levels can be paired, so long as this is not a duplication of information stored implicitly in other pairings. For example, six nuts go to make up a particular saddle. The saddle itself is part of a finished racing bike and so are two more nuts used to hold the saddle onto the frame. These are different nuts so the pairing of the nut and the racing bike is not a repetition of information already stored.

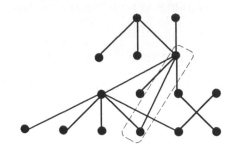

Figure 6.8

6.1.5   The key of the bill of materials resolver

Until now we have assumed that the key of the resolution entity will be composed of the two keys it inherits from the original entity, and nothing else. Very often this is the case but it is not the only solution, as the following examples illustrate.

Investors can buy a piece of paper known as a warrant which gives them the right to exchange one financial asset for another at a predetermined rate. The relationship between the two assets is represented by the warrant. The warrant entity will specify both assets by having their keys among its attributes but it may have a unique key of its own. The data model diagram would look something like figure 6.9[*].

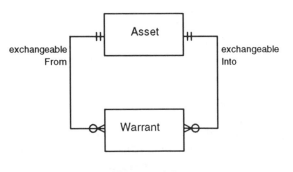

Figure 6.9

[*] One way of modelling a warrant would be to make it a subtype of asset. This relationship would be additional to those shown on the diagram.

This structure is reminiscent of that which related Airports and Routes in chapter 5 to exemplify multiple 1:n relationships. Does this mean that every detail of such a multiple relationship is acting as a many-to-many resolver? It does: there is no difference between the Warrant which pairs Assets, or the Route which pairs Airports. The many-to-many resolver with its own key allows repeated pairings of its owner entity - for example, a producer and director may make many films together - and is a widely used construction.

It is also possible for one occurrence of the main entity to contribute to the key of the resolver but not the other. This is a solution which will become useful later on when the effect of time on recursive structures is considered. Again one or both sets of the main entity's key attributes would be rolenamed on appearing in the resolver. The diagram would look like this.

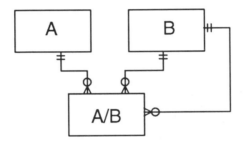

Figure 6.10

6.1.6   The absence of roles

The rolenames of the foreign key attributes within a bill of materials resolver indicate that the two occurrences of the original entity do have distinct roles. One person is the teacher, the other the pupil. One document is the framework, the other the content. One component is the parent assembly, the other the child part.

It is nearly always possible to distinguish the roles played by the main entity's occurrences but just occasionally they prove elusive. Consider an entity which seeks to resolve the m:n relationship between countries on a map: that one country is adjacent to many others and itself has many neighbours. The pairing which tells you that Belgium borders on France is the same as the one which tells you that France abuts Belgium. There is no clue to let you know which country should be in which column in the resolver table.

If each pairing is held once with the countries in an arbitrary sequence then the question, "Who are Belgium's neighbours?" can only be answered by a trawl of both columns.

NeighbouringCountries

countryName1	countryName2
Belgium	Luxembourg
France	Belgium
Belgium	The Netherlands
Germany	Belgium

To answer the question by scouring only one column requires each pairing to be held twice, once with France first and once with Belgium.

NeighbouringCountries

countryName1	countryName2
Belgium	Luxembourg
France	Belgium
Belgium	The Netherlands
Germany	Belgium
Luxembourg	Belgium
Belgium	France
The Netherlands	Belgium
Belgium	Germany

Although this solution contravenes one of the fundamental tenets of relational thought - that data should not be duplicated - it is considered the more satisfactory of the two. But it does reveal a limitation of the relational world.

6.2   One-to-many recursion: the hierarchy

6.2.1   Restricted hierarchies

In the school example we modelled an m:n relationship between people: that one person teaches many others and one is taught by many others. This was a useful model for a senior school where pupils have a different teacher for each subject they study. However in an infants' school a pupil's form teacher is usually his or her only teacher for the year.

Figure 6.11

In these circumstances the recursive relationship between the people in the school can be reduced from an m:n to a 1:n. One person teaches many others, but is taught by only one other. Because it is not an m:n this relationship does not have to be resolved.

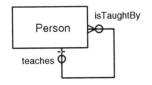

Figure 6.12

Unresolved, the Person entity looks like this.

```
        Person
                personName
                dateOfBirth
                address
                telephoneNumber
        (o)     personNameTeaches
        Foreign:        dateOfBirth → Date
        Foreign:        personNameTeaches → Person
```

Each occurrence of the person as pupil has an attribute which identifies his or her teacher. It is the teacher's key attribute, suitably rolenamed to distinguish it from that of the pupil. The key of the teacher is a foreign key of the pupil.

This is a simpler proposition than m:n recursion. The bicycle factory could not have stored its data in this form. Each nut, when asked to specify its parent, would have responded with a list: saddles, bells, whole bikes... in other words, a repeating group of unknown length. So that the information could be stored in rectangular tables, the bill of materials resolver was introduced. There are no such problems here. The infants' school pupil has just one teacher who is named succinctly in the attribute personNameTeaches.

There will also be an occurrence of Person for each teacher but these occurrences will have a null value for the attribute personNameTeaches. Because the foreign key attribute is sometimes null it is an optional attribute and has been marked as such with the (o) sign.

From chapter 4 we know that any group of jointly optional attributes of an entity may be split out to form a subtype. A single attribute is a special case of an attribute group and may also form a valid subtype: by definition an attribute must be jointly optional with itself. Let us suppose the attribute personNameTeaches is used to form a subtype entity. Like any other subtype, it is identified by the key of its supertype. In this case the key of the main entity is the name of the pupil.

```
Person
        personName
        dateOfBirth
        address
        telephoneNumber
Foreign:        dateOfBirth → Date


TeacherPupil
        personName
        personNameTeaches
Foreign:        personName → Person
Foreign:        personNameTeaches → Person
```

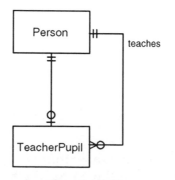

Figure 6.13

The data model diagram shows that there are two relationships between the supertype and the subtype: the 1:1 which is implicit in their identical keys, and the 1:n foreign key relationship which specifies a person's form teacher. Notice that the foreign key attribute is no longer optional, as it was when it was part of the supertype. This is because the subtype as a whole is optional. Occurrences of Person which represent teachers will not have a related subtype occurrence.

6.2.2   Infinite hierarchies

The 1:n recursive relationship typically describes a hierarchy, in which each occurrence of the entity may be subdivided into many others, but can only be part of one other. It is at its most powerful when there is no limit to the number of levels in the hierarchy. For example, a textile manufacturing firm wants to group its products for sales reporting purposes.

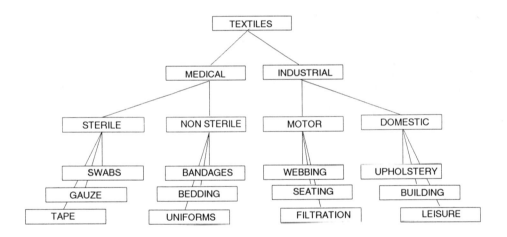

Figure 6.14

The firm's data modeller has recommended that every node of the hierarchy should be an occurrence of the same entity, ProductCategory. Unresolved, the ProductCategory entity will be a master of itself.

ProductCategory
      <u>categoryCode</u>
      categoryName
(o)   categoryCodeParent
Foreign: categoryCodeParent → ProductCategory

Each category will specify its parent in a rolenamed foreign key attribute. Since at the top of the hierarchy there will be a product category without a parent, the entity will be an optional master of itself and the foreign key which specifies the parent will be optional. The optional attribute can be moved into a subtype entity.

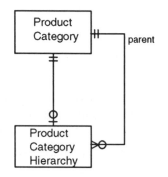

Figure 6.15

The multi-level product category hierarchy is therefore no more complex in structure than the two-layered instance of the infants' school. But it is far more important to the flexibility of the data structure that generalization and recursion are used to describe a hierarchy when it does have an unlimited number of possible layers. If the data modeller at the infants' school had missed the opportunity to generalize teachers and pupils as Persons, it wouldn't have mattered too much: each Pupil would have ended up with a foreign key naming his or her Teacher. The textile manufacturer could find itself in greater difficulties.

Let us suppose that the firm rejects the advice of its data specialist. Instead of adopting the ProductCategory generalization, it decides to implement the product breakdown as three entities: ProductSector, ProductGroup and ProductClass. Each sector is composed of many groups and each group comprises many classes. At the lowest level each product is assigned to one class. In order to get the results for the company as a whole the sales for the two sectors are added together.

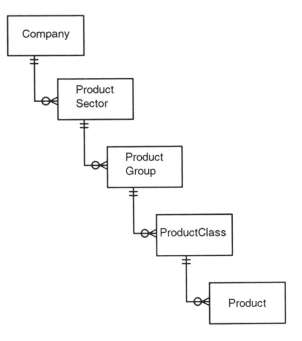

Figure 6.16

All goes well for a year until the market for leisure goods suddenly expands and the sales director requires a more detailed breakdown of this class. Meanwhile, underfunding of the domestic health service has depressed the medical sector and less detail is needed on this side.

In order to insert the extra level into the right hand side of the hierarchy a completely new ProductSubClass entity has to be invented. Every Product record is changed to refer to a ProductSubClass instead of a ProductClass. On the left hand side, where products really should have been assigned directly to groups, artificial ProductClasses and ProductSubClasses are created, each with only one detail occurrence. After working all weekend to implement the changes the systems manager realises that the data modeller was right. All the changes could have been accommodated by the recursive structure without any new tables and without the need for artificial entity occurrences. Only the products aimed at the burgeoning leisure market would have needed recategorization.

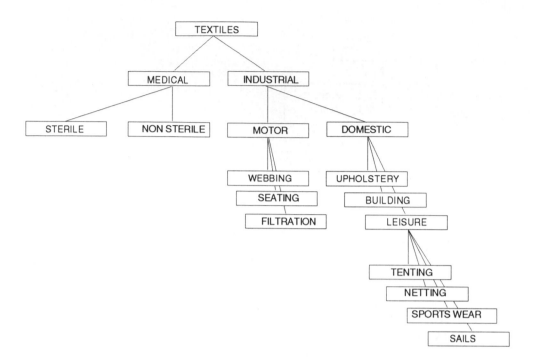

Figure 6.17

6.2.3   Hierarchies versus bills of materials

Although it is not compulsory to resolve 1:n recursive relationships it is useful to see how it can be done and to compare the results with the m:n resolver. The similarities are clear: in both cases the new entity exists to pair off occurrences of the main entity in order to describe a two-dimensional network of linked nodes[*].

Where occurrences of an entity are truly hierarchical the bill of materials structure is too loose a description. Consider the product categories. By drawing up a sample table for the subtype we can see that a product category will feature several times in the second column, as a parent, but only ever once in the first column, as a child. As a child it can only be paired with one parent. Each pairing can be identified by the key of the child alone, since a category will only act as the child in one occurrence of the subtype.

---

[*] Perhaps this is why many data analysis courses will mistakenly suggest that all recursive relationships should be resolved by a bill of materials structure.

ProductCategory

categoryCode	categoryName
45	Industrial
83	Motor
7	Bandages
26	Webbing
15	Seating
2	Filtration
97	Domestic

ProductCategoryHierarchy

catCodeChild	catCodeParent
83	45
97	45
26	83
15	83
2	83

In contrast the bicycle component needed the freedom to appear many times in both columns. As a parent it could be paired with many children; as a child it contributed to several parents. The attribute that told the engineers how many of each component to use needed a key consisting of both parent and child components.

6.3   One-to-one recursion: the pair and the chain

6.3.1   Pairs

Imagine that instead of a senior or infants' school we are confronted with a tutor service. In this establishment each pupil has just one teacher and each teacher is devoted entirely to one pupil.

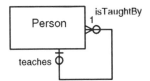

Figure 6.18

Person
      <u>personName</u>
      dateOfBirth
      address
      telephoneNumber
(o)   personNameTeaches
Foreign: dateOfBirth → Date
Foreign: personNameTeaches → Person
Unique: personNameTeaches

Each occurrence of the person as pupil has an attribute which identifies his or her tutor. The key of the tutor is a foreign key of the pupil. To ensure that a tutor only takes on one pupil, the foreign key becomes an alternate key of the unresolved entity.

Once more the foreign key attribute is optional: Person occurrences representing the tutors themselves will have a null value here; and so, incidentally, will those of any pupils not yet allocated to tutors.

The optional attribute can become a subtype entity with the following effect.

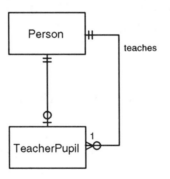

Figure 6.19

Person
      <u>personName</u>
      dateOfBirth
      address
      telephoneNumber
Foreign: dateOfBirth → Date

TeacherPupil
      <u>personName</u>
      personNameTeaches

Foreign:	personName → Person
Foreign:	personNameTeaches → Person
Unique:	personNameTeaches

The tutor's name is no longer optional because the sub-entity as a whole is optional. Tutors and unallocated pupils will have no related subtype occurrence. Where the subtype does exist it **pairs** a pupil and a tutor: it has no other function. The subtype can be uniquely identified by the pupil's name because the pupil is only paired with one tutor. Since in this case a tutor is only paired with one pupil, the teacher's name would also provide a unique identifier for the pairing, and in recognition of this it retains its status as an alternate key.

Just as in the other schools examples, the resolver pairs nodes in a limited level network: each node is either on the teacher level or on the pupil level.

Figure 6.20

The limited, two level, 1:1 recursion is used to record entity occurrences paired so as to exclude any other pairings involving either of the partners. Consider the following example. A ballroom dancing club keeps records of its members. The dancers form partnerships, each of which is expected to consist of a male and a female dancer. A dancer can only have one partner at a time and newer members may not yet have partners.

Male and female dancers have many attributes in common and are represented by one entity, Dancer. The recursive relationship between Dancers, by which one is the partner of at most one other, is represented by a foreign key on the unresolved entity.

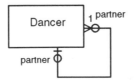

Figure 6.21

The following attribute list for the unresolved entity is an obvious solution.

        Dancer
                dancerName
                address
                dateOfBirth
                yearStartedDancing
        (o)   countOfSequinsOnDress
        (o)   dancerNamePartner
        Foreign: dateOfBirth → Date
        Foreign: yearStartedDancing → Year
        Foreign: countOfSequinsOnDress → Count
        Foreign: dancerNamePartner → Dancer
        Unique: dancerNamePartner

However it is fundamentally flawed. If every dancer who had a partner stored their partner's name, and the foreign key was only optional in recognition of the newer members who hadn't yet fixed themselves up, then each partnership would be held twice. It is in fact the solution that was forced upon us as a way of storing the map of the world because the roles of the individual countries could not be distinguished.

In this instance the roles of the partners are clearly delineated: one is male and the other is female. It is no bad thing if these days most people have difficulty in recognising the sexes as two levels in a restricted hierarchy. However, in data terms it is helpful to consider them thus. The only consolation is that each modeller can choose whether the male or the female is superior.

Let us assume that this arbitrary decision has been made and that the women are on top. This means that every male dancer (as the "child" in this hierarchy) must specify his female partner. Female dancers, as well as those without partners, have a null value in the foreign key attribute.

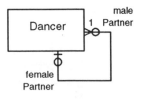

Figure 6.22

Dancer
      dancerName
      address
      dateOfBirth
      yearStartedDancing
(o)   countOfSequinsOnDress
(o)   dancerNameFemalePartner
Foreign: dateOfBirth → Date
Foreign: yearStartedDancing → Year
Foreign: countOfSequinsOnDress → Count
Foreign: dancerNameFemalePartner → Dancer
Unique: dancerNameFemalePartner

Introduction of the subtype entity results in the following structures.

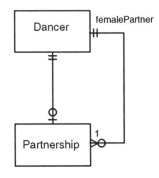

Figure 6.23

Dancer
      dancerName
      address
      dateOfBirth
      yearStartedDancing
(o)   countOfSequinsOnDress
Foreign: dateOfBirth → Date
Foreign: yearStartedDancing → Year
Foreign: countOfSequinsOnDress → Count

Partnership
      dancerName
      dancerNameFemalePartner
Foreign: dancerName → Dancer
Foreign: dancerNameFemalePartner → Dancer
Unique: dancerNameFemalePartner

6.3.2   Infinite chains

The tutor service and the ballroom dancers represented pairings in networks restricted to two levels. If this limitation is lifted the 1:1 recursion represents a chain, in which one node leads on to at most one more node and is preceded by at most one other node.

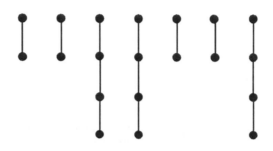

Figure 6.24

The personnel department of a large company recruits staff for the other departments. It keeps records of all the interviews granted to applicants. As a result of a first interview a candidate may be offered a job on the spot (unusual), rejected outright or invited to a further interview. A decision is normally made after a second interview but sometimes a candidate is seen for a third or even fourth time. This is most likely to happen when someone who applied for one job is identified as being more suitable for another job and returns to see a different set of line managers.

Each set of interview notes is marked with the interview number of the one that led up to it, unless it was the first in the sequence. An interview can lead directly on to at most one other.

```
Interview
        interviewCode
        roomNumber
        dateRoomRequired
        timeRoomRequired
        applicantCode
        vacancyNumber
(o)     result
(o)     interviewCodePreceding
Foreign:        roomNumber, dateRoomRequired, timeRoomRequired →
                RoomBooking
```

Foreign: applicantCode → Applicant
Foreign: vacancyNumber → Vacancy
Foreign: interviewCodePreceding → Interview
Unique: interviewCodePreceding

The subtype may be introduced with the following result.

Interview
    <u>interviewCode</u>
    roomNumber
    dateRoomRequired
    timeRoomRequired
    applicantCode
    vacancyNumber
(o)   result
Foreign: roomNumber, dateRoomRequired, timeRoomRequired →
                RoomBooking
Foreign: applicantCode → Applicant
Foreign: vacancyNumber → Vacancy

InterviewSequence
    <u>interviewCode</u>
    interviewCodePreceding
Foreign: interviewCode → Interview
Foreign: interviewCodePreceding → Interview
Unique: interviewCodePreceding

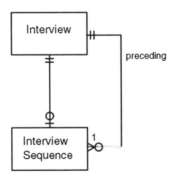

Figure 6.25

6.4   Multiple recursive relationships

Just as two separate entities may be linked by more than one relationship, so one entity may be related to itself by several different recursive relationships. The only difficulty is in recognising how many relationships there are. Each different link is then resolved using the techniques described in the earlier part of this chapter.

For example, an international bank maintains details of all major currencies and the latest exchange rates between them. One of the currencies it deals in is the ECU. The ECU is a basket currency - that is to say, it is made up of other currencies, each weighted according to its significance in European trade. The bank likes to record how the basket currency is composed and the weighting of each of its components. The bank also deals in the International Monetary Fund's basket currency, the SDR, and anticipates others arising in future.

A recursive relationship represents pairings of currency occurrences in which the roles of basket and component are played by different currencies. The ECU will appear many times as a basket - once with each of its components. The French franc is a component of more than one basket and will therefore recur in the component column. Since both columns in the resolver table could feature many appearances by the same currency, both will be needed to identify a pairing. In other words, the recursive relationship is an m:n which must be resolved.

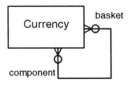

Figure 6.26

This relationship is a restricted bill of materials structure: a network with with only two levels. Assuming a basket currency will never be composed of other baskets, a currency is either a basket currency or an ordinary one, and never both.

Enquiring further of the bank's requirements we find we need to store the exchange rate of every currency against every other currency - in other words, the bank wants cross rates. We have to represent a matrix of rates with currencies on each axis. Note that the rate for US dollars against

Deutschemarks is not simply a mathematical inverse of the Deutschemark/dollar rate: if it were, the bank would not make any profit on its foreign exchange transactions.

		SELL		
		US Dollar	£ Sterling	...
B	US Dollar	-	1.7595	
U	£ Sterling	0.5681	-	
Y	Deutschemark	1.65	2.9155	
	Yen	123.10	234.37	
	French Franc	5.601	9.85	

Every exchange rate is associated with two currencies: the one being bought and the one being sold. A currency which features as a sell currency in some rates will turn up as a buy currency in other rates. Knowing that each currency can play each role more than once, we immediately suspect another m:n recursion. In fact this relationship is another restricted bill of materials structure with only two levels. To ensure completeness there is a rule that every currency must appear on each level and must be linked to every currency on the other level.

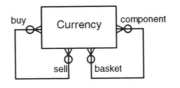

Figure 6.27

The relationships must be separately resolved.

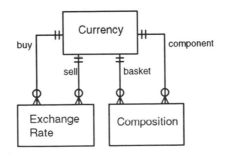

Figure 6.28

Currency
    codeCurrency
    nameCurrency

ExchangeRate
    codeCurrencyBuy
    codeCurrencySell
    quantityExchangeRate
Foreign: codeCurrencyBuy → Currency
Foreign: codeCurrencySell → Currency
Foreign: quantityExchangeRate → Quantity

Composition
    codeCurrencyBasket
    codeCurrencyComponent
    quantityWeighting
Foreign: codeCurrencyBasket → Currency
Foreign: codeCurrencyComponent → Currency
Foreign: quantityWeighting → Quantity

Consider the lists which would have arisen if we had mistakenly tried to resolve both relationships with one new entity.

Currency
    codeCurrency
    nameCurrency

CurrencyRelationship
    codeCurrencyA
    codeCurrencyB
    quantityExchangeRate
(o)   quantityWeighting
Foreign: codeCurrencyA → Currency
Foreign: codeCurrencyB → Currency
Foreign: quantityExchangeRate → Quantity
Foreign: quantityWeighting → Quantity

Since a complete set of cross exchange rates is required the exchange rate attribute is mandatory. Some of the time a weighting would be completed too, but in the majority of occurrences it would be blank. This structure in fact violates the fourth normal form of relational theory (multi-valued dependencies), which is explained in the next chapter.

An entity may have many recursive relationships with itself. The data modeller should not be surprised to discover ten or more recursions of a high order generalization entity. Not all will be m:n: a mix of m:n, 1:n and 1:1 relationships should be expected.

6.5   Occurrences with extra attributes

A recursion describes a network, a hierarchy or a chain in which each node, at whatever level, has the same characteristics. Occasionally some nodes may require additional attributes.

Consider a company's hierarchical chart of accounts. At the lowest level of the hierarchy are accounts which can accept postings (accounting transactions that represent business events such as deliveries and withdrawals of cash or cash values). All other accounts are non-postable summary accounts. The hierarchy is held in a subtype in the usual way. Additionally, every postable account has an extra attribute linking it to a cost centre. This optional attribute is held in a further subtype of the account entity. The two subtypes are independent of each other: occurrences without children will have the subtype PostableAccount and occurrences with parents will have the subtype AccountHierarchy; some accounts will therefore have both, some will have neither, and some will have one subtype.

```
Account
      accountCode
      accountDescription

AccountHierarchy
      accountCode
      accountCodeParent
Foreign:         accountCode → Account
Foreign:         accountCodeParent → Account

PostableAccount
      accountCode
      costCentreCodeResponsible
Foreign:         accountCode → Account
Foreign:         costCentreCodeResponsible → CostCentre
```

Occurrences without children are sometimes called **leaf nodes** because a hierarchy could be thought of as an inverted tree. In many structures, including the example above, it is the leaf nodes which have more attributes than the other occurrences, but extra attributes can be required at any level of a hierarchy.

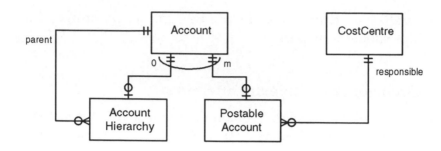

Figure 6.29

The subtype arc with a cardinality of 0..m does not add to the meaning of the above entity diagram but does provide a useful visual clue concerning the presence of a subtype group and makes the cardinality of the group explicit.

6.6   Time and the recursive relationship

6.6.1   History of the bill of materials resolver

The history of the bill of materials resolver is constructed in the same way as the history of any other m:n resolver. The history is created by adding a timestamp attribute to the primary key of the existing resolver. It is also necessary to add a finish date and perhaps time to the entity.

The weightings of currencies within baskets is adjusted every few years to reflect changed levels of trade activity. Suppose the international bank wanted to keep a history of the weightings of different currencies within baskets.

```
Currency
        codeCurrency
        nameCurrency

CompositionHistory
        codeCurrencyBasket
        codeCurrencyComponent
        dateWeightingStarts
        quantityWeighting
        dateWeightingFinishes
Foreign:        codeCurrencyBasket → Currency
Foreign:        codeCurrencyComponent → Currency
Foreign:        dateWeightingStarts → Date
```

Foreign: dateWeightingFinishes → Date
Foreign: quantityWeighting → Quantity

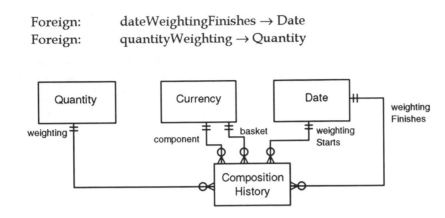

Figure 6.30

As well as keeping the history of the weightings, the resolver must continue to perform its original function: that of recording which currencies are in which baskets. If a currency is newly introduced into a basket the start date will indicate more than just a change in weighting; likewise an end date could signal that a currency has been dropped from the basket altogether.

6.6.2   History of the hierarchy

The history of a hierarchy is kept in the same way that the history of an optional attribute is always held - whether the attribute is in a subtype or not. Suppose that a group of companies records its hierarchical reporting structure by the resolved recursion below.

OrganizationUnit
    <u>organizationUnitCode</u>
    name
    address

OrganizationHierarchy
    <u>organizationUnitCode</u>
    organizationUnitCodeParent
Foreign: organizationUnitCode → OrganizationUnit
Foreign: organizationUnitCodeParent → OrganizationUnit

The OrganizationUnit entity holds the group as a whole, each of its companies, their divisions and departments, sections and teams. Each OrganizationUnit reports to just one other. This strict hierarchy is used to report all financial data.

The company faces a major restructuring, which will change the reporting lines for most of its OrganizationUnits. But in a year's time the finance director wants to be able to restate the returns as though the organization structure had not changed, so as to be able to make year on year comparisons at all levels of the hierarchy. This request will entail a change to the data model. From now on, the future organizational structure must be held without overwriting the current one. For example, the Travel department has always reported to Group Personnel. On its OrganizationHierarchy subtype it specifies the Group Personnel office as its parent. In future it will be a part of the International Finance division and it will need to specify not just its new parent but its old one too.

The modeller faces the usual choices when holding the history of the subtype. In this case the subtype exists for the sole purpose of recording an organizational unit's parent. With the attribute OrganizationUnitCodeParent destined for a history detail the subtype is probably not worth preserving. The history will be held in a detail of the supertype, as shown in figure 6.31.

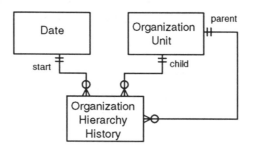

Figure 6.31

OrganizationUnit
    organizationUnitCode
    name
    address

OrganizationHierarchyHistory
    oganizationUnitCode
    dateStart
    organizationUnitCodeParent
Foreign: organizationUnitCode → OrganizationUnit
Foreign: dateStart → Date
Foreign: organizationUnitCodeParent → OrganizationUnit

At any moment in time an OrganizationUnit reports to only one other. In its foreign key attribute the history detail still holds a lone parent for each child from any given date. It can be assumed that the child continues reporting to that parent until another occurrence of OrganizationHierarchyHistory mentions in its key the same child but a later date. This assumption means that no foreign key for finish date is required.

Over the course of time, however, a child may report to several parents. It may even report to one and then to another and eventually return to the embrace of the first. For this reason the history detail is also a many-to-many resolver between organization units. Because only the child unit features in the resolver's key, it is possible for the same two units to be paired as parent and child on separate occasions.

6.6.3   History of the pair and chain

Suppose the ballroom dancing club decided to record past partnerships. The relationship between dancers would effectively become a many-to-many link.

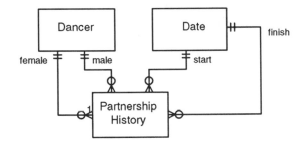

Figure 6.32

Its resolver would need to be structured so as to allow a couple to be reunited after a time spent dancing apart. The foreign key relationship between Dancer and PartnershipHistory is still constrained to be in effect a 1:1 link: this ensures that from any one start date a man may have at most one female partner. There is a finish date foreign key too in case we need to reflect the break up of a partnership which is not immediately followed by another pairing for the man.

Chapter summary

All forms of recursion involve the pairing off of two occurrences of the same entity. By recognising the precise nature of the recursive relationship and resolving it accordingly, the modeller is providing freedom where it is needed and specifying constraints wherever possible. The more restrictions that can be held in the data structures, the less processing code[2] has to be written.

Many-to-many recursions describe the relationships between nodes in a network. They are illegal in relational terms and must be resolved by a bill of materials structure. The bill of materials usually has both occurrences of the entity as its primary key owners. This key construct permits only one pairing of each parent and child. Such a key construct is often useful, especially when the bill of materials resolver has non-key attributes of its own. The bill of materials may have a key structure which only involves one occurrence of the main entity. This structure is used to describe a relationship which has changed from a 1:n to a m:n because its history has been requested.

One-to-many recursions describe the relationships between nodes in a strict hierarchy. If the recursion is constrained to a 1:1 by a unique clause then it describes the link between two nodes in a chain. Such recursions can be resolved with a subtype of the child node, though they need not be.

NOTES

1. De Morgan, Augustus, (1806-1871). *A Budget of Paradoxes.*

2. It is not necessary to process recursive data structures by recursive programs. A recursive program is elegant, but if your programming language does not support recursive calls (some 4GLs do not) then to process up the chain of command in a hierarchy all you need is a module that executes an SQL statement with a WHERE juniorOrgUnit = tempJuniorOrgUnit. Call this model using a DO...UNTIL statement that replaces the current tempJuniorOrgUnit with the next seniorOrgUnit until seniorOrgUnit = NULL (or the subtype holding the senior does not exist). The non-recursive routine will be easier to understand (and therefore easier to maintain by somebody else) and might well run faster than the recursive version. These are physical design issues but we wanted to show that program code is simpler for recursive data structures than it is for the equivalent non-recursive data structures where levels of a hierarchy are established explicitly. Also, with recursive data structures the program code will not need to be changed if you add or remove levels from the hierarchy - it will work for any number of levels.

Questions

1. Different shades of paint are made by mixing basic shades together. Model the situation as a recursive structure. What are the attributes of the resolver entity?

2. Discuss whether the model you have just drawn represents a limited or an infinite network.

3. Model the food chain as a recursive structure, showing which species eat which other species.

4. In the army a lieutenant reports to a captain, a captain to a major, a major to a colonel, a colonel to a brigadier, and a brigadier to a general. Model the chain of command as a recursive structure.

5. A security firm supplies bodyguards to well-known personalities. At any one time a bodyguard is assigned to one personality, but over time a bodyguard may have many assignments and a personality might ask for a change of guard. Model the situation showing both bodyguards and personalities as occurrences of Person.

6. A person is friendly with many other people. What problem can you envisage in modelling this situation relationally?

7. In a group of companies, each company is divided into divisions, each division into departments, each department into sections and each section into production teams. Model the situation as a recursive structure. The companies are legally constituted bodies, each one registered in a particular country. Show how registration details can be catered for in your model.

8. Do generalization and specialization structures always make recursive structures more likely to occur?

9. In SQL or structured English, write code which finds the ultimate parent of a given leaf occurrence in a 1:n hierarchy. Do the same for a leaf occurrence in a m:n network.

10. Given that a bill of materials structure describes a series of linked nodes, discuss the applicability of the construct in modelling a roadmap of Europe.

7

The relational model and normal forms

Introduction

Earlier chapters have described a data modelling technique which will result in normalized data structures: that is, stuctures which store data in the most efficient and unambiguous way. We find that successful modellers are those who have acquired a feel for fifth normal form that has become second nature - tacit knowledge gained through practical experience. However, every student should have an understanding of the formal theory underlying **the relational model** and an appreciation of how an unstructured collection of data items can be modelled through the successive stages of **normalization**. This chapter describes the relational model and the process of data normalization.

Data modelling as described in preceding chapters and the formal technique of normalization described in this chapter should result in similar data structures. However, the two approaches sometimes bring to light quite different aspects of the business situation. In this chapter data modelling and normalization are compared and contrasted to show how they can be used jointly in practice.

7.1   The relational model

The relational model, as proposed by EF Codd[1], stressed the need to separate the user view of the data from the physical implementation of that data involving file access mechanisms, hashing, and so on. The user should perceive a database as a collection of tables, in which a table comprises columns and rows. When referring to data modelling we use the terms entity, attribute, and occurrence; in relational databases the corresponding terms are table, column, and row, while in the relational model we refer to relation, attribute, and tuple respectively. Although we can interchange these terms we will tend to use the terminology appropriate to the subject matter: entities are identified in the data modelling process; relations are produced as a result of the normalization process.

The basic requirements of a relation are:

- each relation must have a unique name, such as Employee;

- each of the attributes of the relation must also have a unique name. For example, the Employee relation has the attributes emp number*, gender, salary, dept number, and start date (see figure 7.1);

- the entries in a column such as gender are homogeneous; that is to say, they are of the same type for each row;

- each row must be uniquely identifiable. One or more of the attributes must ensure that each row is distinct. There must be no duplicate rows;

- the order of the rows and the columns is not significant;

---

* We name attributes using all lower case letters and with spaces between the words comprising the name (for example, emp number. rather than empNumber which would be used in data modelling). Relations will be referred to using capitals but with spaces between the words comprising the relation name (for example, Order Line rather than OrderLine). This will help us to distinguish the data structures derived from a data model (entity diagram) and the data structures produced by normalization.

- all the entries in the relation are single-valued. For any intersection of a row and column there must be a single value. Multi-valued entries, known as **repeating groups**, are not allowed.

The range of possible values that the entries in a particular column can take is known as the **domain**. For example, the domain of gender has only two values: male and female. The domain of start date could be defined to be any valid date, whilst the domain of salary might be restricted to numbers in the range +2,000.00 to +80,000.00.

emp number	gender	salary	dept number	start date
2031	male	20,000	10	01/01/88
3024	female	15,000	10	01/05/93
1039	female	22,000	20	01/08/82

Figure 7.1: *A populated Employee relation*

Domains are particularly important since relations with columns that draw their values from the same domain can be joined. For example, to find out the location of the department in which an employee works would require a join, or comparison, of the dept number column in the Employee relation with the dept number column in the Department relation. It is not necessary for the columns in the different relations to have the same name, but it is necessary for them to take their values from the same domain.

Organizing the data so that they appear as a set of relations will give some flexibility, but does not guarantee that a database will be free from redundancy and update anomalies. Redundancy is introduced if the same attribute is held more than once. For example, the Invoice relation illustrated in figure 7.2 contains customer number, customer name and customer address. Holding a customer's name and address many times - once for each of the customer's invoices - has introduced redundancy into the database. This redundancy can lead to update anomalies. If the customer changes address, and the customer has a number of invoices open at that time, then it will be necessary to update all the invoices for that customer. Unless all the invoices are modified, the database will be in an inconsistent state - who is to say which of the customer addresses is the correct one?

There is also a potential for losing data that is of interest to the organization. If invoices are purged periodically and if a customer has no open invoices then all trace of that customer could be lost.

invoice number	invoice date	invoice total	customer number	customer name	customer address
18724	01/01/94	200.12	102	Smith	1 Ash Gardens
20392	12/01/94	500.00	102	Smith	1 Ash Gardens
39201	18/12/93	1,403.45	167	Jones	5 Beech Rd
72053	19/12/93	32.65	201	Davies	12 Elm Lane
92012	15/01/94	89.65	102	Smith	1 Ash Gardens

Figure 7.2: *A populated Invoice relation*

To remove redundant data and to guard against update anomalies where valuable data might become inconsistent or be lost altogether, the relations should be normalized. Normalization is a process of decomposing complex structures into simpler relations. However, before describing the normalization process it is necessary to introduce the concept of functional dependency.

7.2   Functional dependency

Consider the relation of film titles and directors illustrated in figure 7.3. It can be seen that any given film title is associated with only one director, whilst any given director could be associated with a number of film titles. For example, Charles Crichton has directed two of the films in the relation.

film title	director
The Titfield Thunderbolt	Charles Crichton
Night of the Demon	Jacques Tourneur
Withnail and I	Bruce Robinson
The Wizard of Oz	Victor Fleming
Whisky Galore	Alexander MacKendrick
The Lavender Hill Mob	Charles Crichton
The Night Porter	Liliana Cavani

Figure 7.3: *Film titles and directors*

For any given film title it is possible to determine a single director. However, for any given director it is not possible to determine a single film title. Thus, film title is said to determine director, or, to say exactly the same thing the other way round, director is functionally dependent upon film title.

Definition: Attribute B is functionally dependent upon attribute A (or a collection of attributes) if a value of A determines a single value of attribute B at any one time.

The fact that film title functionally determines director can be represented as:

film title $\rightarrow$ director

The same fact can be restated to say that director is a function of film title and can be represented as:

director = f(film title)

But what of the inverse? For a given director it is not always possible to determine a single film title and therefore director cannot be said to functionally determine film title:

director $\nrightarrow$ film title

and film title is not functionally dependent upon director:

film title $\neq$ f(director)

Functional dependencies are not cast in concrete and may change over time and with the context in which they are used. Many of the dependencies will derive from business rules, such as the rule that a customer may only have one account manager. A change in policy to allow a customer to have many account managers means that the functional dependencies between the attributes customer number and account mgr number will also change.

By inspection of the data in figure 7.3 we might draw the conclusion that film title determines director. Inspection of further data reveals an entry for "My Learned Friend", a film that has two directors: Will Hay and Basil Dearden (figure 7.4). We only have to find one such instance in the data for the assertion that film title functionally determines director to be invalidated.

film title	director
The Titfield Thunderbolt	Charles Crichton
Night of the Demon	Jacques Tourneur
My Learned Friend	Will Hay
My Learned Friend	Basil Dearden
Withnail and I	Bruce Robinson
The Wizard of Oz	Victor Fleming
Whisky Galore	Alexander MacKendrick
The Lavender Hill Mob	Charles Crichton
The Night Porter	Liliana Cavani

Figure 7.4: *Film titles and directors*

We can never prove that a functional dependency exists purely by inspection of data as there may be more data in existence that we have yet to inspect or data that has yet to be created that will invalidate our assumption of functional dependency. This is the notion of falsificationism. Regardless of the number and completeness of the items found that support a functional dependency the best one can say is that we will assume that the functional dependency probably holds true. However, it only takes one occurrence of the data that contradicts the premise for us to say that the functional dependency definitely does not hold. Therefore, we need to refer to business rules and policies when identifying functional dependencies - and if these policies do not exist then they need to be created.

Functional dependency is not an intrinsic and unchanging characteristic of the data; functional dependency arises from the assumptions we make about the data and the meaning, or semantics, that we assign to the data in a specific situation at a specific time.

7.2.1   Testing for functional dependency

The test for functional dependency between two items, A and B is to ask[2]:

1. For a given value of attribute A, is there just one possible value for attribute B?

2. For a given value of attribute B, is there just one possible value for attribute A?

If the answer to 1. is yes and the answer to 2. is no, then A determines B. Similarly if the answer to 2. is yes and the answer to 1. is no, then B determines A. If the answers to 1. and 2. are both yes, then A and B are logical synonyms. For example, if for any given customer name there is only one possible customer number, and for any given customer number there is only one possible customer name, then customer number and customer name are logically equivalent. If the answers to both 1. and 2. are no then there is no functional dependency between A and B.

This notion of functional dependency is fundamental to the process of normalization, which is now described.

7.3   Normalization

The aim of normalization is to eliminate data redundancy and to remove potential update anomalies which arise from inserting, modifying and deleting data. It is easier to maintain consistent data if the circumstances where update anomalies can arise have been removed. The normal forms in figure 7.5 have been defined in relational theory.

Form	Abbrev.	basis
First normal form	1NF	functional dependency
Second normal form	2NF	functional dependency
Third normal form	3NF	functional dependency
Fourth normal form	4NF	multi-valued dependency
Fifth normal form	5NF	join dependency
Domain key normal form	DKNF	superset of 1NF through 5NF plus domain constraints

Figure 7.5: *Summary of normal forms*

The third normal form to be described here is a strong form that includes Boyce-Codd normal form (BCNF). The process of normalization to 3NF is described in detail although not in formal terms. Fourth, fifth and domain key normal forms are described in overview only[3].

7.3.1   Unnormalized form

Different sources can be used to provide data items[*] for normalization: including computer screen layouts, reports, computer programs and user manuals. In broad terms, normalization, as used in systems analysis, is characterized as a bottom-up approach, whereas data modelling is a top-down approach. When applying normalization we hope that the relevant entities will emerge from the morass of detail. With data modelling we begin by looking for "things of significance" and fill in the detail as the model is refined. See chapter 13, section 13.1.2, for a discussion of how these techniques are used together in practice. To illustrate the process of normalization the order form in figure 7.6 will be used.

---

[*] Strictly speaking, we cannot refer to the raw data items collected in unnormalized form as attributes until they have been organized into relations.

ORDER

customer number:	1489	order number:	0057435
name:	Arthur Smith	order date:	11–Jan-94
address:	1 Lime Avenue		
	Anytown		
	ZZ52 5QA		

product number:	product description:	unit price:	order quantity:	line total:
T5060	Widget	5.00	5	25.00
PT42	Didget	20.00	10	200.00
QZE248	Fidget	2.50	1	2.50

order total: 227.50

Figure 7.6: *Source data*

The data items are listed out and a key is chosen. The choice of data items that will act as the key may affect the final outcome of the normalization. The key chosen should be natural; for example, customer number is intuitively more appealing than order quantity.

> order number
> order date
> customer number
> customer name
> customer address
> product number
> product desc
> unit price
> order quantity
> order line total
> order total

Total Price

Figure 7.7: *Unnormalized form (UNF)*

Guidelines for the choice of key include:

- the key should identify uniquely each of the occurrences of the data source;

- the key should comprise the smallest number of data items (customer number is preferable to a combination of customer name and customer address);

- where there is a choice of a textual identifier and a non-textual identifier the non-textual identifier should be chosen. For example, customer number is preferred to customer name.

For the source document in figure 7.6, a suitable starting point would be to choose order number as the key of the data in unnormalized form (figure 7.7). The selected data item(s) is underlined, indicating that it forms part of the key.

The equivalent entity diagram for the UNF of the order form is shown in figure 7.8.

Figure 7.8: *UNF entity diagram*

7.3.2   First normal form

To create a set of 1NF relations, repeating groups are removed to separate relations. In the order form source data, the data items product number through order line total are repeating within the relation Order. The relational model requires the rows (tuples) of a relation to be single-valued. 1NF can be achieved by removing the repeating data to a separate relation. The new relation retains the key chosen for the unnormalized data and extends it as necessary to ensure that the rows of the new relation can be uniquely identified.

Definition: A relation is in first normal form (1NF) if it does not contain repeating groups of data items.

In the case of the order form, product number is combined with the order number (a compound key) to form a unique identifier for the individual rows of the Order Line relation.

order number	order number
order date	product number
customer number	product desc
customer name	unit price
customer address	order quantity
order total	order line total

Figure 7.9: *First normal form (1NF)*

In the order form example, we arrive at two relations: Order and Order Line (figure 7.9). The equivalent entity diagram for the 1NF relations has two entities (figure 7.10) between which a primary key relationship exists (the identifier of Order is contributing to the identifier of Order Line).

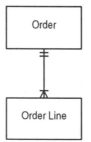

Figure 7.10: *1NF equivalent entity diagram*

Although we know that the relationship is of the type 1:n, it is not possible to define the minimum cardinality of Order Line with respect to Order. In this instance we have made it 1, reflecting a business rule that all orders must have at least one line. However, the relational model requires that the primary key of Order Line be defined and as order number comes from Order we know that the minimum cardinality of Order with respect to OrderLine must be one. This can be inferred without reference to business rules and is a requirement of primary key relationships.

7.3.3   Second normal form

Second normal form requires that functional dependencies be identified. Those attributes that depend on only part of the key of the relation are removed to separate relations.

Definition: A relation is in second normal form (2NF) if it is in 1NF and no non-key attribute is dependent upon only part of the key.

The Order relation must be in 2NF since it only has one attribute in its key. However, the Order Line relation has a compound key of order number and product number requiring that each of the attributes be checked to see whether it depends upon (is determined by) the whole key or only part of the key.

While order quantity and order line total appear to be dependent upon the key of Order Line, it seems that product desc and unit price are dependent upon only part of the key of Order Line; that is, they are determined by product number It can be seen that a functional dependency can only be identified in the context of the business rules since it would not be unreasonable to have a situation where the unit price is determined by a combination of product, customer status and even the time of year. Our 2NF relations explicitly state that the price of the product is determined wholly by the product - the implication is that each type of product must be sold for the same price to all customers (figure 7.11).

order number	order number	product number
order date	product number	product desc
customer number	order quantity	unit price
customer name	order line total	
customer address		
order total		

Figure 7.11: *Second normal form (2NF)*

The equivalent entity diagram (figure 7.12) now has a new entity, Product, which has a primary key relationship with the Order Line entity.

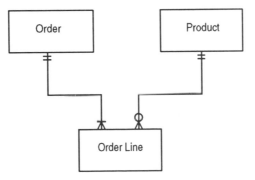

Figure 7.12: *2NF equivalent entity diagram*

7.3.4   Third normal form

The strong form of third normal form includes Boyce-Codd normal form and is:

Definition: A relation is in third normal form (3NF) if it is in 2NF and every determinant in the relation is a candidate key for that relation.

An attribute or collection of attributes that determine another attribute is called a **determinant** - this is the idea of functional dependency discussed above. A candidate key is one or more attributes that uniquely identify the rows of the relation. For example, in the Employee relation the attributes employee number and social security number might be candidate keys. In the Order relation, although order number determines customer number, it determines customer name indirectly. There is a functional dependency between customer number and customer name and between customer number and customer address. That is, customer number is a determinant since it determines customer name and customer address. However, it is not a candidate key of the Order relation, as occurrences of Order cannot be identified uniquely by customer number (a given customer may have many orders). If the relation is left in this form then there will be potential update anomalies: deleting an order may lead to the loss of customer details and changing a customer address requires all the orders for that customer to be updated.

In the order form example, the items customer number, customer name, and customer address are removed to a separate relation, the key of which is customer number The attribute customer number is left in the Order Line relation, where it plays the role of a foreign key, as signified by an asterisk (figure 7.13). As order number and product number are also foreign keys (they are special cases in that they are primary foreign) they have been marked with asterisks also - this will help us when we engineer the relations into an entity diagram.

order number	customer number	order number*	product number
order date	customer name	product number*	product desc
customer number*	customer address	order quantity	unit price
order total		order line total	

Figure 7.13: *Third normal form (3NF)*

Figure 7.14 shows the third normal form equivalent entity diagram. The Customer entity was identified during 3NF **analysis** and has a foreign key relationship to the Order entity.

The complete process of normalization to 3NF for the order form is shown in figure 7.15. There are two items of derived data present in the 3NF relations, order line total and order total, and it is recommended that these attributes are flagged with a (d) since they will not necessarily form part of the logical data model.

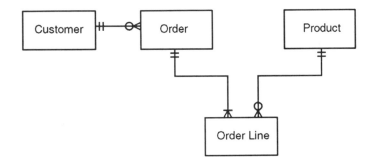

Figure 7.14: *3NF equivalent entity diagram*

The normalization process is performed on the different sources of data, usually resulting in a large number of relations, many of which will overlap and have duplicate attributes. For example, the customer relation would be expected to arise as a result of the normalization of a number of different source documents. Combining these relations into a single and coherent set is known as optimization. This is not covered here in detail but, briefly, optimization involves combining relations with the same key[*]. Particular care must be given to identifying synonyms (attributes that are the same but have different names) and homonyms (attributes with the same name, e.g., order number, but with different meanings). Also, because it is possible that the optimization process will reintroduce denormalization, the final set of relations should be checked to ensure that they are (collectively) in third normal form.

---

[*] It is not always appropriate to combine relations with the same key and indeed to do so can lead to violations of higher normal forms. Optimization might also lead to the identification of useful generalizations and specializations.

Invoice

UNF	1NF	2NF	3NF
order number	order number	order number	order number
order date	order date	order date	order date
customer number	customer number	customer number	customer number*
customer name	customer name	customer name	order total (d)
customer address	customer address	customer address	
product number	order total	order total	customer number
product desc			customer name
unit price			customer address
order quantity	order number	order number	
order line total	product number	product number	order number*
order total	product desc	order quantity	product number*
	unit price	order line total	order quantity
	order quantity		order line total (d)
	order line total	product number	
		product desc	product number
		unit price	product desc
			unit price

QTY
QTY

Figure 7.15: *Normalization to 3NF*

By carrying out the third normal form check on all attributes, regardless of which relations they are in and whether they are part of the key or not, we can ensure that the relations are in strong 3NF.

7.3.5   Normalization to 3NF - an illustration

A simple illustration of normalization is now given to show how assumptions about the business impact normalization and to illustrate how the bottom-up and top-down approaches can be combined. Hard Times, an estate agents, has a number of local offices. The local office record in the current system has the following format, in which repeating data items are shown in curly brackets:

office number + office location
  {property number + property address + number of rooms + selling price + vendor number + vendor name
    {purchaser number + purchaser name + amount offered + offer date}}
  {staff number + staff name + date joined agency}

Assume that, at any one time, the following statements are true:

- property number, vendor number, purchaser number, and staff number are unique across all offices;

- each property is the responsibility of a single office;
- each property is offered for sale by a single vendor;
- staff may work for more than one office.

In the above record, offer details is a repeating item within the repeating item property details. Staff details repeat at the same level as property details. This means that in going from UNF to 1NF it is necessary to copy the office number key attribute down to the property details, where property number is added to the key, and then to copy office number plus property number down to the offer details, where purchaser number is added to the key.

In the progression from 1NF to 2NF all of the non-key attributes of the relation with the key

> <u>office number</u>
> <u>property number</u>
> <u>purchaser number</u>
> <u>date offered</u>

were removed to a separate relation with the key property number, purchaser number, date offered. Note the simplifying assumption that a purchaser makes no more than one offer per day. The original key-only relation must be left as part of the 2NF relations. When considering the progression to 3NF, we find functional dependencies between the attributes of the key-only relation office number, property number, purchaser number, date offered. Property number functionally determines office number

> property number $\rightarrow$ office number

but is not a candidate key for the relation. Therefore we remove office number to a separate relation with property number as the key:

> <u>property number</u>
> office number

This relation is then merged with the property relation already identified. A key-only relation is left:

> <u>property number</u>
> <u>purchaser number</u>
> <u>date offered</u>

This relation has no functional dependencies and so is retained and merged with the property number, purchaser number, date offered relation already identified in 2NF.

UNF	1NF	2NF	3NF
office number	office number	office number	office number
office location	office location	office location	office location
property number			
address	office number	office number	property number
number of rooms	property number	property number	address
selling price	address		number of rooms
vendor number	number of rooms	property number	selling price
vendor name	selling price	address	vendor number*
purchaser number	vendor number	number of rooms	office number*
purchaser name	vendor name	selling price	
amount offered		vendor number	vendor number
date offered	office number	vendor name	vendor name
staff number	property number		
staff name	purchaser number	office number	property number*
date joined agency	date offered	property number	purchaser number*
	purchaser name	purchaser number	amount offered
	amount offered	date offered	date offered
	office number	property number	purchaser number
	staff number	purchaser number	purchaser name
	staff name	date offered	
	date joined agency	purchaser name	office number*
		amount offered	staff number*
		office number	staff number
		staff number	staff name
			date joined agency
		staff number	
		staff name	
		date joined agency	

Figure 7.16: *Normalization to 3NF - "Hard Times"*

We can represent the 3NF relations as an entity diagram by taking the following steps:

- make each relation an entity. The entity name is the relation name with spaces removed;

- create relationships to reflect the foreign and primary foreign keys. Foreign key relationships should be drawn entering the side of the entity box; primary key relationships should be drawn entering the top of the entity box;

- create suitable labels for the relationships;

- consider cardinality of the detail in each relationship. If the business rules imply that the detail is mandatory then set the minimum cardinality to 1;

- consider cardinality of the owner in each relationship. For primary key relationships the owner is always mandatory, so set the minimum and maximum cardinality to 1. For foreign key relationships, if the business rules suggest that the owner is optional, set the minimum cardinality to 0;

- consider any specific cardinalities, such as 1:n relationships that are constrained to 1:1 by particular business rules.

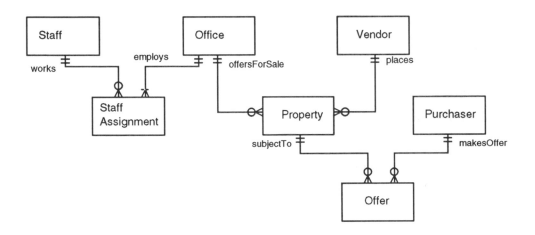

Figure 7.17: *Entity diagram for "Hard Times" 3NF relations*

After consultation with Hard Times the modeller realizes that vendors can be purchasers and that purchasers can be vendors. It is necessary that Hard Times knows if the person making an offer for a property is in fact also a vendor with the agency. Thus we would combine the vendor and purchaser entities and, if they have different attributes, would probably introduce a supertype entity, such as InvolvedParty, that has the subtypes Purchaser and Vendor. Further investigation reveals that staff may also buy and sell properties through the agency and that they qualify for special terms. Hard Times needs to be able to recognize where a member of staff is acting the role of vendor, purchaser, or both. The modeller might then introduce Staff as an independent subtype of InvolvedParty. Once the root entities Date, Quantity and Count have been introduced, the entity diagram becomes as in figure 7.18.

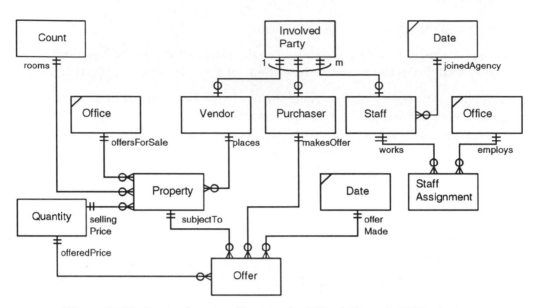

Figure 7.18: *Revised entity diagram for "Hard Times" 3NF relations*

The attribute list for the entity diagram is:

InvolvedParty
    <u>partyNumber</u>
    name

Vendor
    <u>partyNumber</u>
Foreign: partyNumber → InvolvedParty

Purchaser
    <u>partyNumber</u>
Foreign: partyNumber → InvolvedParty

Staff
    <u>partyNumber</u>
    dateJoinedAgency
Foreign: partyNumber → InvolvedParty
Foreign: dateJoinedAgency → Date

Office
    <u>officeNumber</u>
    location

StaffAssignment
    <u>officeNumber</u>
    <u>partyNumberWorks</u>

Property
    <u>propertyNumber</u>
    address
    countRooms
    quantitySellingPrice
    partyNumberPlaces
    officeNumber

Foreign:	countRooms → Count
Foreign:	quantitySellingPrice → Quantity
Foreign:	partyNumberPlaces → Vendor
Foreign:	officeNumber → Office

Offer
    <u>propertyNumber</u>
    <u>partyNumberMakesOffer</u>
    <u>dateOfferMade</u>
    quantityOfferedPrice

Foreign:	propertyNumber → Property
Foreign:	partyNumberMakeOffer → Purchaser
Foreign:	dateOfferMade → Date
Foreign:	quantityOfferedPrice → Quantity

In this section we have attempted to show the process of normalization and to align it closely with data modelling. Although normalization to 3NF is concerned with functional dependencies and keys, these can only be determined by reference to the problem domain where the meaning of the data is negotiated. The next section considers further levels of normalization.

7.4   Further normal forms

Higher levels of normalization are described in overview: fourth normal form, fifth normal form and domain key normal form.

7.4.1   Fourth normal form (multi-valued dependencies)

First, second and third normal forms address functional dependencies between attributes. Fourth normal form is concerned with multi-valued dependencies. Consider the data in the relation Employee (figure 7.19).

emp number	skill	hobby
102032	systems analysis	golf
102032	systems analysis	chess
102032	programming	golf
102032	programming	chess
123821	strategic planning	squash
123821	strategic planning	piano
123821	strategic planning	cycling
123821	management	piano
123821	management	cycling
201029	management	golf

Figure 7.19: *Multi-valued dependencies*

There are no functional dependencies between the attributes in this relation but there is clearly some kind of dependency between these attributes. A given employee is associated with the same set of skills regardless of the hobbies they pursue; similarly the set of hobbies is independent of the skills the employee possesses. To deal with this situation, we introduce the idea of multi-valued dependencies and fourth normal form. With respect to the Employee relation, emp number multi-value determines skill and emp number multi-value determines hobby, or:

emp number $\twoheadrightarrow$ skill   and

emp number $\twoheadrightarrow$ hobby

Multi-valued dependencies come in pairs. They are not properties of the information represented by a relation; rather they relate to the way in which data items have been structured into relations. It can be seen that update anomalies can occur in the Employee relation as adding (or removing) a skill or hobby to the Employee relation may involve inserting (or deleting) a number of rows. To put the Employee relation into fourth normal form requires it to be decomposed into two relations:

EmpSkills (emp number, skill)   and

EmpHobby (emp number, hobby)

If one had approached this problem from a data modelling perspective, would the Employee relation in figure 7.19 have arisen? It seems rather more likely that employees, skills and hobbies would have been recognized as entities, resulting in a data model as in figure 7.20, where employees, skills, and hobbies are all recognized as distinct things of interest.

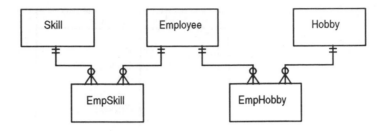

Figure 7.20: *Removing multi-valued dependencies*

Problems of multi-valued dependencies often arise from the artificial process of normalization where semantics may take second place to pedantry.

7.4.2   Fifth normal form (join dependencies)

Fifth normal form is concerned with resolving join dependencies. The populated relation Person Uses Skill On Project in figure 7.21 is in fourth normal form and cannot be partitioned into two relations without losing information.

emp number	prog lang	project
135	Cobol	X52
135	PL/1	X55
148	Cobol	X52
148	SQL	X68
187	Smalltalk	X12
193	Cobol	X52
193	Cobol	X55
193	SQL	X55

Figure 7.21: *Join dependencies*

There is a join dependency constraint that if person 135 has skill Cobol, and Cobol is used on project X52, and person 135 works on project X52, then person 135 must use Cobol on project X52. There is potential for update anomalies to occur when maintaining the relation Person Uses Skill On Project: deleting the row (193, Cobol, X55) requires that row (193, SQL, X55) is also deleted as a person must apply all their skills to a project if a project requires those skills. Thus the relation in figure 7.21 is in fact derivable. Fifth normal form requires the relation Person Uses Skill On Project, which cannot be divided into two relations, to be decomposed into three, as shown in figure 7.22.

Has Skill

emp number	prog lang
135	Cobol
135	PL/1
148	Cobol
148	SQL
187	Smalltalk
193	Cobol
193	SQL

Needs Skill

prog lang	project
Cobol	X52
PL/1	X55
SQL	X68
Smalltalk	X12
Cobol	X55
SQL	X55

Works On

emp number	project
135	X52
135	X55
148	X52
148	X68
187	X12
193	X52
193	X55

Figure 7.22: *Fifth normal form*

The equivalent data model for the fifth normal form of the Person Uses Skill On Project relation is shown in figure 7.23.

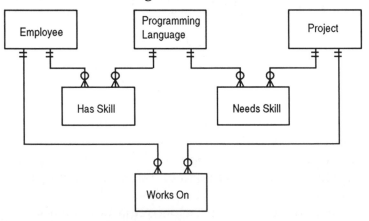

Figure 7.23: *Fifth normal form data model*

If the facts of interest are person has skill, person is assigned to project, and project requires skill, then the data model might well look like that in figure 7.23, reflecting the requirement that if a person is assigned to a project then they must use all their skills (as required by the project) on that project.

However, relaxing this assumption allows the original relation to be retained and the data to still be in fifth normal form. Assume now that some persons do not apply all their skills to a project. For example, Person 193 has skills Cobol and SQL and is assigned to projects X52 and X55, and project X55 requires the skills Cobol and SQL. But if person 193 uses only SQL on project X55, then to capture this fact it is necessary to introduce the relation Person Uses Skill On Project. It is no longer possible to decompose the original relation into three separate relations since the relation Person Uses Skill On Project is no longer derivable. Now, if we also assume that a person cannot be assigned to a project without using at least one skill on that project then the relation Works On becomes redundant since it can be derived from Person Uses Skill On Project[*]. The data model in figure 7.23 then becomes as shown in figure 7.24. If this assumption was changed (to cater for managers and consultants) the relation WorksOn would have to be reinstated.

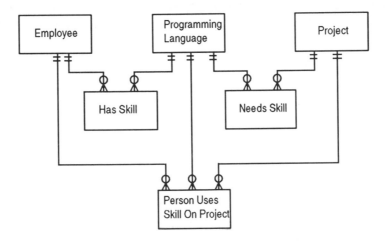

Figure 7.24

As with fourth normal form, most problems of fifth normal form arise from the artificial way in which relations are constructed, problems which arise

---

[*] The diagram would then be reminiscent of that shown in figure 5.9, where there is no resolver entity between Archaeologist and Building because we assume Archaeologists are never tasked to work on buildings unless they have been given a specific rune to decipher.

rarely when entity-relationship modelling is applied. Whereas third normal form is concerned with functional dependencies that are independent of the relations (they are concerned with dependencies between attributes), fourth and fifth normal forms are concerned with update anomalies that arise from the way in which attributes are grouped together into compound key relations. They are less likely to occur when carrying out data modelling, so long as attention is paid to the underlying semantics.

7.4.3   Domain key normal form

Relations that are in fifth normal are also in fourth normal form, and those that are in fourth normal form are also in third normal form, and so on down to first normal form. The normal forms up to and including fifth normal form address one type of constraint, whether it be functional dependency, multi-valued dependency, or join dependency. In brief, the domain key normal form is concerned with a more general type of restraint that subsumes the dependencies addressed by fifth normal form. Domain key normal form is concerned with two further types of dependency: domain dependencies and key dependencies. An example of a domain constraint is "for manager type employees salary > 40,000". This constraint leads to the need for two subtypes of the Employee relation, the Manager subtype and the NonManager subtype.

This is an area of interest for data modelling since it could provide a more rigorous basis for data modelling in general and entity sub-typing in particular[4].

Chapter summary

As we have seen, normalization, based upon the rigour of the relational model (which in turn is based upon the formal rigour of a relational calculus), is a well-defined and formalized process. The data modelling activity, by contrast, is often described as an intuitive, subjective technique. In the order form example above, we showed how the development of the normal forms can be seen pictorially through a series of entity diagrams. It should also be apparent that knowledge of the business is needed to carry out normalization - it is not possible to pump all the data items into a CASE tool and expect it to produce a logical data model that reflects the business needs (at least not unless all the business rules are specified in a formal language). Also, when attempting to put the data into 3NF, in theory it is necessary to compare each attribute with every other attribute or combination of attributes. This is usually not a tractable exercise in real-life development projects and in practice the analyst uses a mixture of experience and intuition as well as the rigour of the process of normalization.

Normalization is a bottom-up approach, concentrating on the detail available in the current environment. As such, there is a danger that the normalization approach might lead to a model of the way things are now. Such an approach may not be appropriate in situations where the objective is to instigate change.

We consider that an experienced data modeller will develop well-normalized models without needing to resort to a formal process of normalization. However, should we consign normalization to the scrap-heap? Our view is that there is a useful role to be played by normalization in the analysis phase of system development:

- normalization requires the analyst to get closer to the data and to investigate the functional dependencies between attributes - this can lead to a more detailed understanding of the problem domain;

- to perform a double-check on the completeness of the model - are there things in the domain which we have missed, such as a statutory reporting requirement?;

- to support a bottom-up approach to development which can be contrasted with the top-down technique of data modelling. Analysts need to start at a level of abstraction for which they are qualified through their knowledge of the problem domain. Beginning at too high a level is often dangerous.

NOTES

1. See:
   Codd, E., F., (1970). A Relational Model for Large Shared Data Banks. *Communications of the ACM* 13(6):

2. This approach is described in Ashworth and Goodland, and we have found it a very useful way of thinking of functional dependencies:
   Ashworth, C., & Goodland, M., (1990). *SSADM: a practical approach.* McGraw-Hill.

3. The relational model and normalization are described rather more formally in most books on database systems, for example:
   Elmasri, R., & Navathe, S., (1994). *Fundamentals of Database Systems.* Benjamin/Cummings, Redbridge, CA.
   And, more specifically:

Dutka, A., & Hanson, H., (1989). *Fundamentals of Data Normalization*. Addison-Wesley.

4. Interested readers are referred to:
Fagin, R., (1981). A Normal Form for Database That is Based on Domains and Keys. *ACM Transactions on Database Systems*, 6(Sept.): 387-415.

Questions

1.   Why is this table not a valid relation? There is a number of problems with it.

emp number	gender	salary	salary	dept number	start date
5746	male	20,000	20,000	10	01/01/88
2031	female	15,000	15,000	10, 12	01/05/93
3253	male	12,000	12,000	01/01/88	01/01/88
2031	female	15,000	15,000	10, 12	01/05/93
1039	female	22,000	22,000	20	01/08/82

2.   What is a functional dependency?

3.   Populate the following relations with sample data to demonstrate the functional dependencies as specified:

R1 (A, B) in which A $\rightarrow$ B and B $\nrightarrow$ A
R2 (C, D) in which C $\rightarrow$ D and D $\rightarrow$ C
R3 (E, F) in which E $\nrightarrow$ F and F $\nrightarrow$ E

4.   Consider the following Department relation:

department number
department name
location
telephone number (o)

The dependency department name $\rightarrow$ department number has been identified. Is this relation in 3NF and if so why?

5.   What problems might arise if a database is implemented on the basis of data structures that are not in 3NF?

6. The relation Staff has the following data showing which students a member of staff is personal tutor to and which courses the member of staff is responsible for:

staff number	student number	course number
123	4231	152
123	5362	152
234	8392	143
234	8392	167
234	8392	176
234	9283	143
234	9283	167
234	9283	176

Assuming that there are no functional dependencies between the attributes, which normal form is violated? How would you address this problem? Draw an entity diagram of your solution.

7. A train spotters' club keeps details about its members, the members' anoraks and the trains that the members have spotted. The current record format is as follows, with repeating data items shown in curly brackets:

train spotter name + spotter address + spotter phone number + date joined
    {anorak number + anorak colour}
    {train number + model number + train colour + train weight + year built
    + manufacturer name + manufacturer address}

Assume that anorak number is not unique and that each train spotter may own many anoraks. Carry out normalization of the train spotter club record, showing the progression from unnormalized form through first, second, and third normal forms. Clarify any assumptions that you make in normalizing the data.

8. Represent the 3NF relations produced for the train spotter club as an entity diagram.

9. What assumptions is it necessary to make when producing the train spotter entity diagram with a full specification of cardinality?

10. How would you go about validating the assumptions you made when normalizing the train spotter record (question 7) and producing the entity diagram (questions 8 and 9)?

8

Physical implementation

Introduction

This chapter shows how and why logical data models are denormalized before physical implementation on a relational database management system (RDBMS). It then illustrates how a physical database can be generated from a data model in a repository.

Before any denormalizations are carried out it is vital to freeze the logical model and maintain it as a representation of the business understanding compiled at the analysis stage. If any further business data comes to light at a later stage of the project it should be incorporated into the logical model before being cascaded into the developing physical version.

In this chapter we shall use the terminology of the physical relational database in which entities become tables, attributes become columns, and occurrences become rows. Relationships are traversed by joining tables using the columns they have in common - in other words, by using foreign keys.

The ideal physical database design would in many ways be one where every entity in the logical schema resulted in a table in the physical design. This is possible on small systems with few users and low data volumes. For example a system written for a single user PC rarely needs to denormalize its logical data model.

In larger systems reasons for denormalization include performance, parameterization and code simplification. These are all good reasons, as indeed they must be because denormalization carries penalties in terms of ease of maintenance and comprehensibility of the system. A user who could recognize his or her sphere of activity in a logical data model may be hard put to see the basic business concepts shining through a data model readied for implementation.

It is impossible to say whether any particular denormalization is right or wrong without considering firstly the purpose and performance requirements of the application system and secondly the chosen implementation platform. Whereas logical data modelling can - must - be done quite independently of platform considerations, physicalization cannot. It is when these considerations begin to impinge that logical design has finished and physical design has begun.

Before examining techniques of denormalization, it is worth cataloguing the reasons for which it is undertaken.

8.1   Reasons to denormalize

8.1.1   Performance

The main stimulus for data denormalization is a desire to speed up the application - that is, to reduce the time delay between an enquiry being made and the receipt of the response by the user. In order to ascertain the most effective performance-enhancing techniques a database designer must first find out:

- the average and peak volumes of data expected in each database table;

- the nature of the enquiries which will be made of the data and how many table joins each enquiry will demand of the database in its normalized form;

- the time taken by the relational database software to perform a basic join operation on two tables with known volumes;

- the number of users likely to be using the system simultaneously at average and at peak times;

- the required performance level of the system at average and at peak times.

Using this information the designer can calculate where enquiries will cause processing bottlenecks which will prevent target performance being met.

8.1.2   Rationalization

By the time logical process design has been completed it may become apparent that some parts of the data model will not be needed immediately.

8.1.3   Simplification of code

Significant advantages in terms of program simplification can sometimes be gained from altering data structures or domains. This kind of consideration can affect the code at the client end of the application - that which handles the interaction with the user - or at the server end - that which handles the interaction with the database.

In particular, Structured Query Language (SQL) is an enquiry language which is built into many database products to handle database calls. Because it is a non-procedural language, data structures may need to be augmented to facilitate certain enquiries.

8.1.4   Physical distribution

Databases may be split and data replicated in order to allow the physical distribution of a system.

8.1.5   Archiving

The logical data modeller should assume that all data will be available online in its raw form indefinitely. In practice this is unlikely to be the case but the need to archive data to improve performance and reduce storage space is the province of the physical database designer.

It is common practice when removing raw data from the users' grasp to replace it with summary information which takes up less space. This is derived data and therefore not a concern of the logical data model.

8.1.6   Interfaces

When a new system is introduced it is rarely into an ideal environment of other systems designed according to the same corporate data model. Rather than compromise the design of the new system it is sometimes necessary to encase it in an interface layer which simulates the ideal environment. Assuming the corporate IT strategy is eventually implemented, the interface layer may be allowed to melt away. The interface layer will have process as well as data components and will accommodate any transfers of information to and from existing external systems, whether manual or computerized.

8.1.7   Parameterization

To a data modeller, a system which can be parameterized is in a sense a system whose data structures are not yet complete. This is often highly desirable to the users who can then finish the design themselves according to individual tastes, varying operational requirements or different hardware provisions.

8.1.8   Security

It may be that the data has to be removed from the database to a more secure repository. Particularly sensitive business data may be hidden in this way.

8.1.9   Economy of storage

There are no data denormalizations which save attribute storage space: the logical model represents the most economical and elegant way to store data. Besides, the expense of disc storage has become much less significant as a proportion of the total expense of creating and maintaining a computer system. However in some circumstances economies will be justifiable and a few denormalization techniques will help to achieve savings on table overheads.

8.2   Techniques of denormalization

There are a variety of techniques of denormalization, each of which achieves one or more of the objectives listed above.

8.2.1   Removing redundant entities

Key-only owners which were used in the logical data model to show key structures of other entities will generally be removed in the name of rationalization. However it is important that any domain restrictions represented by the key-only entity are preserved in the system design.

For example, say that the logical model had an entity called Option. An option is a piece of paper which gives the holder the right to buy or sell a particular share, commodity or other asset for a predetermined price - the strike price - on or before a given date. In the logical model the option has been identified by these characteristics.

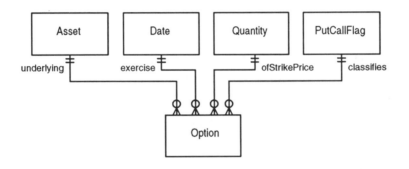

Figure 8.1

Both Date and Quantity are key-only masters of the Option entity. The entity has an attribute called quantityOfStrikePrice which can take on any value subject to the space reserved for its datatype in the database. It would be unthinkable to hold a table full of all the values which had ever been used for quantityOfStrikePrice. Likewise a table of all dates which had ever been used as option exercise dates would be a waste of space. However, a table holding the values Put and Call, the only two legitimate values of the attribute indPutCallClassifies, would be a valid way of enforcing the domain constraint on that attribute.

8.2.2   Removing redundant relationships

Most relational database systems can enforce relationships. For example, Sybase uses the trigger to enforce relationship parameters. However, relationships identified in the logical data model may also be rationalized out of existence at design time.

For example, subtypes can be detached from their supertypes. Suppose a data modeller has recognized that a LocalAuthority is a subtype of the generalized entity Organization. It is in the generalized entity that the organization's address is held. However, the application in question never needs to know the address of a local authority and will therefore never traverse the relationship.

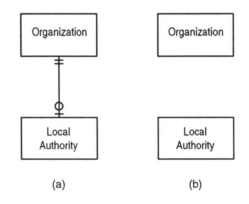

Figure 8.2

Likewise, owners can be safely detached from details if the relationship between them will never be traversed. For example, a relationship by which Country is the domicile of Organization, while perfectly valid as a reflection of reality, may not be used by any of the enquiries offered by the application.

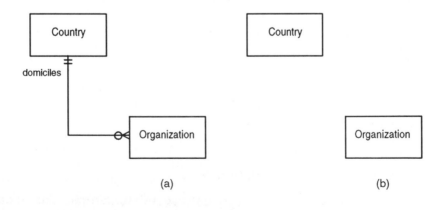

Figure 8.3

8.2.3   Adding derived attributes

As discussed in chapter 2 there is no place for derived data in the logical data model. If a derived attribute is stored in the logical model it is on the understanding that a bit of physicalization has crept in ahead of time. At physicalization time, any number of pieces of derived data may be held. The purpose is nearly always to improve performance.

Derived data at its simplest is a data attribute repeated, or replicated somewhere else. In a case like this the attribute is derived from one other attribute simply by copying it. In other cases attribute values are derived from the values of one or more other attributes by performing statistical computations. The most common statistics required are listed below with typical enquiries which generate them.

Sum	What is this customer's bank account balance?
	How many Firestone 145R13 tyres are there at the Barnstaple warehouse?
	What is the total weight of live babies born so far this month at this maternity unit?
Count	How many live babies have been born at the maternity unit this month?
Average	What is the average birthweight of live babies born in the maternity unit this month - and how does that compare with the average for this month last year?
Standard deviation	What is the smallest range of values which covers 95% of household incomes?
	What is the price volatility of this stock?
Maxima & minima	What is the salary of the lowest paid employee in the plastics division?
	What is the record number of consecutive days without an accident in the plastics division?
	What was the last order number used?

All these enquiries can be answered by looking at raw data values held in the logical data model, but two factors may cause the answers to be returned unacceptably slowly. The first is the number of table joins involved and the second is the time taken to do the calculation itself. By calculating the answers in advance and storing them as derived data both these problems are overcome. There is a penalty: every time raw data is inserted, deleted or amended the data which is derived from it must be recalculated. The recalculation is time-consuming but it will be probably be carried out at a time when no user is waiting for the answer.

There are many other statistics which can be derived from collections of raw data. The more complex the calculation involved the more likely that the result will be stored as derived data.

Derived data is held in a number of different places in the database, as the following examples show.

Owner holds attribute derived from a detail

Often the derived data is held in an owner table whose detail holds the raw data. The bank account balance in chapter 2 was just such an example: it could have been calculated from the individual account transactions but was instead held on the account entity.

```
        BankAccount
                bankSortCode
                accountNumber
                dateOpened
                customerNumberHolder
                currencyDenominates
        (d)     quantityBalance
        Foreign:        bankSortCode → Branch
        Foreign:        accountNumber → AccountNumber
        Foreign:        dateOpened → Date
        Foreign:        customerNumberHolder → Customer
        Foreign:        currencyDenominates → Currency
        Foreign:        quantityBalance → Quantity


        BankAccountTransaction
                bankSortCode
                accountNumber
                dateOfTransaction
                timeOfTransaction
                quantityOfTransaction
        Foreign:        bankSortCode, accountNumber → BankAccount
        Foreign:        dateOfTransaction → Date
        Foreign:        timeOfTransaction → Time
        Foreign:        quantityOfTransaction → Quantity
```

In data terms, the account is analagous to the warehouse or subdivision of a warehouse such as a bin. Both are locations for storing quantities of countable commodities. An account may contain a balance of £157.35; a warehouse bin may contain a stock on hand of 684 tyres. Both the account and the warehouse bin balances are replenished by deliveries, or deposits, and diminished by withdrawals. The only difference is that the physical stock in the warehouse must always be positive whereas no such constraint applies to the balance in your bank account...

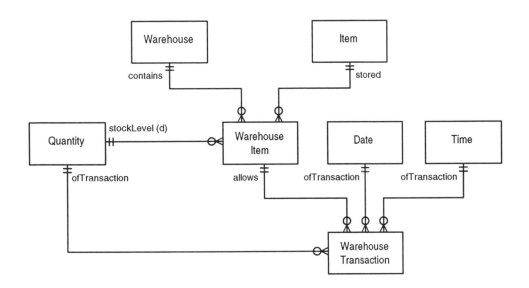

Figure 8.4

To find out how many Firestone 145R13 tyres there are in the Barnstaple warehouse it would be possible to sum all the deliveries and all the withdrawals of this particular tyre since the warehouse was built. Instead for performance reasons the physical database will hold a stockLevel attribute on the WarehouseItem entity[*].

Warehouse
    warehouseName

Item
    itemCode
    itemDescription

---

[*] Why is an Account analogous to WarehouseItem and not Warehouse? Because an account only holds one currency at a time whereas a warehouse holds many items. If a bank's customer wants to have a stock of Deutschemarks as well as a stock of sterling, the customer must open a second account.

WarehouseItem
    <u>warehouseName</u>
    <u>itemCode</u>
(d)   quantityStockLevel
Foreign: warehouseName → Warehouse
Foreign: itemCode → Item
Foreign: quantityStocklevel → Quantity

WarehouseTransaction
    <u>warehouseName</u>
    <u>itemCode</u>
    <u>dateOfTransaction</u>
    <u>timeOfTransaction</u>
    quantityOfTransaction
Foreign: warehouseName, itemCode → WarehouseItem
Foreign: dateOfTranaction → Date
Foreign: timeOfTransaction → Time
Foreign: quantityOfTransaction → Quantity

We also need to find the salary of the lowest paid worker in the plastics division. In the logical model, Employee is a detail of Division and each employee has a current salary.

Division
    <u>divisionCode</u>
    divisionName

Employee
    <u>employeeNumber</u>
    employeeNameGiven
    employeeNameFamily
    divisionCode
    quantitySalaryCurrent
Foreign: divisionCode → Division
Foreign: quantitySalaryCurrent → Quantity

The query which determines the lowest salary will need to trawl through all occurrences of employee with a divisionCode representing plastics; if this enquiry threatens to take too long a derived attribute could be added to the Division table. The attribute would need to be checked every time an employee joined or left the division and every time an employee had a change of current salary.

Division
    divisionCode
    divisionName
(d)   quantitySalaryMinimum
Foreign: quantitySalaryMinimum → Quantity

Employee
    employeeNumber
    employeeNameGiven
    employeeNameFamily
    divisionCode
    quantitySalaryCurrent
Foreign: divisionCode → Division
Foreign: quantitySalaryCurrent → Quantity

To determine how many days the plastics division has ever gone between accidents, we could trawl the records of the raw data in the Accident table, which includes the key of the division where the accident took place.

Division
    divisionCode
    divisionName
(d)   quantitySalaryMinimum
Foreign: quantitySalaryMinimum → Quantity

Accident
    accidentRef
    dateOfAccident
    timeOfAccident
    divisionCode
    employeeNumberReports
    description
Foreign: dateOfAccident → Date
Foreign: timeOfAccident → Time
Foreign: divisionCode → Division
Foreign: employeeNumberReports → Employee

However, calculating the maximum gap between the dates on different records is complex for any RDBMS that does not support direct date functions. The database designer might prefer to store the maximum as a derived item on the Division table. It would need to be updated not only if an accident took place that happened after a record-breaking interval of time, but also once sufficient time had passed since the last accident broke the record.

Division
        divisionCode
        divisionName
(d)   quantitySalaryMinimum
(d)   quantityDaysMaximumWithoutAccident
Foreign: quantitySalaryMinimum → Quantity
Foreign: quantityDaysMaximumWithoutAccident → Quantity

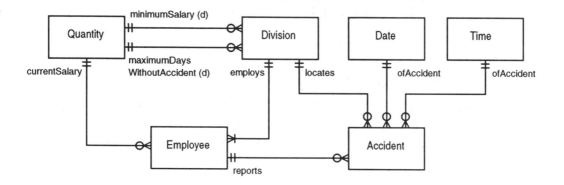

Figure 8.5

Entity holds attribute derived from itself

Creating structured codes is a legitimate denormalization. The structured attribute is usually derived from two or more attributes of the same entity.

New entity holds derived attribute

The maternity hospital's raw data will consist of details of individual births, each with a date and weight recorded. Note that date and time of birth are included in the key of the entity in case of twins or other multiple births.

Birth
        admissionNumber
        dateOfBirth
        timeOfBirth
        nameFamilyBaby
        nameGivenBaby
        ifLive
        quantityBirthweight
Foreign: admissionNumber → Admission
Foreign: dateOfBirth → Date
Foreign: timeOfBirth → Time
Foreign: quantityBirthweight → Quantity

The average birthweight in each time period is calculated from a count (number of live babies born) and a sum (total weight of live babies). In each case the data is available from the records on the Birth table whose date falls in the requisite period and whose ifLive flag is set to Y. To satisfy the enquiry two averages must be calculated - one for this month and one for the same month last year. Suppose the unit is short of disc space and needs to archive all occurrences of Birth where dateOfBirth is more than six months ago. To satisfy the enquiry it must hold summary statistics derived from the raw data before it is archived. In this case, monthly average birthweights will be held online for all months in the last five years. The key of a monthly average birthweight is month and year. Since no existing entity has this key a new one must be created.

Birth
      admissionNumber
      dateOfBirth
      timeOfBirth
      nameFamilyBaby
      nameGivenBaby
      ifLive
      quantityBirthweight
Foreign: admissionNumber → Admission
Foreign: dateOfBirth → Date
Foreign: timeOfBirth → Time
Foreign: quantityBirthweight → Quantity

MonthlyBirthStatistics
      year
      month
(d)   quantityAverageLiveBirthweight
Foreign: year → Year
Foreign: month → Month
Foreign: quantityAverageLiveBirthweight → Quantity

Note that if the derived data is being held solely so that Births can be archived after six months, the statistics need not be calculated until archiving is about to happen. Thus any enquiries about averages in the most recent time periods would still cause calculations from raw data. However for performance reasons the unit may decide to derive statistics for recent months too. There could even be an occurrence of the entity for the current month, whose attribute quantityAverageLiveBirthweight would be updated with every live birth.

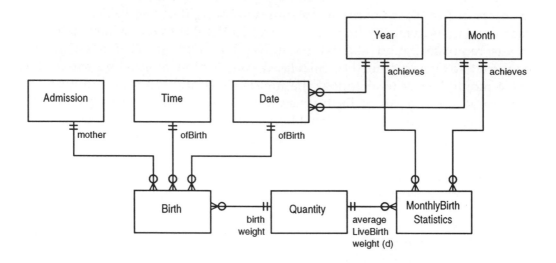

Figure 8.6

Another form of statistic is that derived by an arbitrary allocation algorithm. Suppose a firm of investment consultants records the profit figures from a range of publicly quoted companies so as to advise investors on their relative performances.

Company
    companyCode

CompanyProfit
    companyCode
    dateReporting
    quantityProfitBeforeTax
Foreign: companyCode → Company
Foreign: dateReporting → Date
Foreign: quantityProfitBeforeTax → Quantity

Making comparisons over a standard financial half-year is difficult because ICI, say, reports its profits in June whereas Fisons reports in April. To overcome the problem a month-by-month profit allocation is calculated and held in a new table.

Company
    companyCode

CompanyProfit
    <u>companyCode</u>
    <u>dateReporting</u>
    quantityProfitBeforeTax
Foreign: companyCode → Company
Foreign: dateReporting → Date
Foreign: quantityProfitBeforeTax → Quantity

CompanyProfitAllocation
    <u>companyCode</u>
    <u>dateReporting</u>
    <u>yearAllocatedTo</u>
    <u>monthAllocatedTo</u>
(d)   quantityProfitForMonth
Foreign: companyCode → Company
Foreign: dateReporting → Date
Foreign: yearAllocatedTo → Year
Foreign: monthAllocatedTo → Month
Foreign: quantityProfitForMonth → Quantity

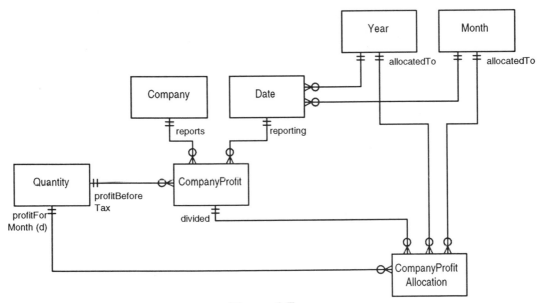

Figure 8.7

The raw data would have provided the comparison needed, but the code to extract it would have been unwieldy. The derived data allows a much simpler interrogation to come up with the same result.

An order processing system allocates order numbers automatically in sequence. The number for a newly inserted order is derived by incrementing the highest order number already allocated. This number could be derived by looking at all the existing records on the Order table.

Order
        orderNumber
        dateReceived
        organizationCode
Foreign: dateReceived → Date
Foreign: organizationCode → Customer

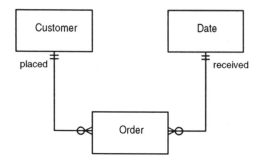

Figure 8.8

Since performance is of the essence in most order entry systems, the last number allocated is likely to be held as derived data. As the maximum value of a column in a group of detail records, the derived value would be expected to be stored on an owner entity. However, in this model Order has no primary key owner. In these circumstances it is usual to create a special table representing the system as a whole which can hold derived data such as that described. The special table has no link to any other table and its rows have no connection with each other. It can be used to hold parameters of all sorts.

Parameter

parameterName	parameterValue
lastOrderNumber	0091554
quantityDefaultCommission	2.5
percentTolerance	6

Subtype replicates attribute of supertype

Suppose that a system stores Customer as a subtype entity of Organization. The customer's full name is stored in the Organization table but it needs to be displayed every time a sales order from the customer is viewed.

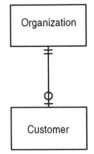

Figure 8.9

If the join between the Customer table and its supertype seemed to be slowing down the viewing of orders, the full name could be replicated on the Customer table.

       Organization
              <u>organizationCode</u>
              organizationName
              address

       Customer
              <u>organizationCode</u>
              creditRating
(d)   organizationName

Detail replicates attribute of owner

If the enquiry still wasn't considered fast enough the organizationName attribute could be moved onto the Order table. This would mean a great deal of replication - the name would be repeated on every order the customer placed and if the customer's name changed every order would need to be changed. Because this is considered a rare event the risk is taken and the derived data item moved to the Order detail.

Organization
      organizationCode
      organizationName
      address

Customer
      organizationCode
      creditRating

Order
      orderNumber
      dateReceived
      organizationCode
(d)   organizationName
Foreign: dateReceived → Date
Foreign: organizationCode → Customer

Supertype identifies which subtype exists for a record

Logically, the only way to find out which subtypes a supertype occurrence has is to search for subtype occurrences with matching keys. This can sometimes slow the application down to an unacceptable degree.

Where a supertype has a mutually exclusive subtype group then at most one of the subtypes in that group can exist. It is possible to add an indicator to the supertype showing which one of the subtypes exists.

Recall the IT department whose staff had to be classified as either DevelopmentStaff or SupportStaff or neither of these.

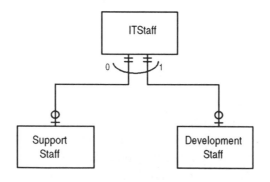

Figure 8.10

With the new indicator, the attribute lists would look like this. The indicator is marked as derived because it could have been calculated from counting the relevant instances of the respective subtypes. It is also optional because the employee need not be in development or support. The cardinality of the subtype group is 0..1.

```
ITStaff
        employeeNumber
        name
        address
        departmentNumberEmploys
(d)(o) indSupportOrDev
Foreign:        departmentNumberEmploys → Department

SupportStaff
        employeeNumber
        mobileTelNumber
Foreign:        employeeNumber → ITStaff

DevelopmentStaff
        employeeNumber
Foreign:        employeeNumber → ITStaff
```

When the rules were changed and the IT employee had to be either DevelopmentStaff or SupportStaff, the cardinality of the group changed to 1..1. In these circumstances the indicator would cease to be optional.

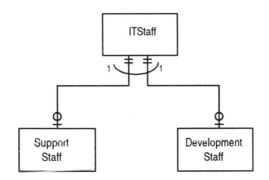

Figure 8.11

ITStaff
    <u>employeeNumber</u>
    name
    address
    departmentNumberEmploys
(d)   indSupportOrDev
Foreign: departmentNumberEmploys → Department

SupportStaff
    <u>employeeNumber</u>
    mobileTelNumber
Foreign: employeeNumber → ITStaff

DevelopmentStaff
    <u>employeeNumber</u>
Foreign: employeeNumber → ITStaff

Where subtypes are independent of each other the supertype would need an indicator per subtype to say whether or not it existed. Therefore the property letting agency may keep two markers on Property: one to say whether it has a garden and another to say whether it has central heating. Since these are there to say whether or not a specific subtype exists they are mandatory: each must take the value Y or N.

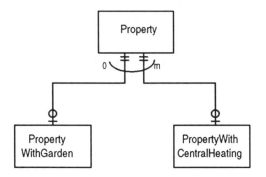

Figure 8.12

Property
    <u>address</u>
    partyOwns
(d)   ifCentrallyHeated
(d)   ifGarden
Foreign: partyOwns → Party

PropertyWithGarden
    <u>address</u>
    companyCodeServiceGarden
    quantitySquareMeterGarden
Foreign: address → Property
Foreign: companyCodeServiceGarden → Company
Foreign: quantitySquareMeterGarden → Quantity

CentrallyHeatedProperty
    <u>address</u>
    companyCodeServiceBoiler
    dateNextBoilerService
Foreign: address → Property
Foreign: companyCodeServiceBoiler → Company
Foreign: dateNextBoilerService → Date

Extra attribute replicates attribute from next row

Most table joins are performed by searching for records in a target table whose value in one column exactly matches the value retrieved from a specific cell of the original table. However, instead of aiming for a specific record or records of the target table, some queries aim for the gap between two records. For example, a building society account offers higher rates of interest on the whole of a saver's balance the higher the balance gets. The interest rates are held in a table like the one below.

InterestRateTiers

accountTypeOffers	quantityMinimumBalance	quantityInterestRate
Betterbond	0	4.5
Betterbond	10000	5.25
Betterbond	50000	5.8

Conchita Fernandez has an account balance of £11804.63. The application program which calculates how much interest she is due must find a row of the InterestRateTiers table such that the known quantity, Conchita's balance, is above its quantityMinimumBalance but not so far above it that it hits the next tier up. Note that by the "next tier up" we mean the next one in terms of the value of its quantityMinimumBalance because there is no significance to the sequence in which the rows of an ordinary (unindexed) database table are stored. A join of this kind is sometimes called a **theta join**, as opposed to the **equijoin** of matching values in common columns.

Logically, all the data is available to the application in the form shown above. However, because SQL is a set processing calculus and not an algorithmic programming language it is not ideally suited to finding "the next tier up" and prefers to check a single record for the beginning and end of a range. Physically, the table would probably be implemented like this.

InterestRateTiers

accountTypeOffers	quantityMinBalance	quantityMaxBalance(o)(d)	qtyInterestRate
Betterbond	0	9999.99	4.5
Betterbond	10000	49999.99	5.25
Betterbond	50000		5.8

The new column is derived data: it replicates the quantityMinimumBalance on the next record up, minus a minimum currency unit. It must be optional because there will not always be a next record to derive it from. Its presence speeds up the interest calculation routine.

Table holds non-occurrence rows

Some applications need to determine which occurrences are missing from a table. For example, a hire purchase company might wish to write to all customers who had *not* paid the last instalment owed. Instead of requiring the application to work out which rows are missing from the payment table, the database designer might choose to hold a record for each customer whether they have paid or not. Although the records for non-payers do not form part of the logical data model, they help to simplify and to speed up the application.

Indices are added

Physical design includes the introduction 'of indices onto database tables. The purpose of a non-unique index is to speed up searches of a table. Because speed of searching is a physical characteristic of the system it is not the concern of the logical designer. An index is effectively an extra table in the database - one which holds derived data. It has the following characteristics.

- The index table replicates one or more of the columns on a related (target) table.

- It can hold the physical addresses of records in the target table as well as matching data values.

- The index is smaller than the target table: it has less columns or less rows or (usually) both.

- Both an index and its target are physically organized in a predetermined way - for instance, sorted into primary key order.

Thus a search which begins with the values of one or more indexed columns in the target table can go to the index instead and, knowing how it is organized, quickly find the physical location of the record in the target table. Although such enquiries are speedier, insertions to and deletions from the target table take longer because they must be reflected in the index too.

There are many different ways of organizing indices and a full explanation of them is beyond the scope of this book[1]. One very basic subdivision separates indices according to whether they are dense or sparse. A **dense index** has a record corresponding to every record in the target table whereas a **sparse**, or **clustered**, **index** contains records corresponding to representative records from the target table. The physical addresses of the other records in the target table can be deduced from that of the nearest representative record, whose key value "covers" their key values. The join between a sparse index and its target table is the equivalent of a theta join. A b-tree (balanced tree) is maintained by creating a sparse index of an index table, and then a sparse index of that, and so on until the root index is small enough to fit on one block of a disc.

Indices can also be subdivided into those which are unique and those which are non-unique. Every record in a unique index relates to one and only one record in the target table. All primary key indices are unique. Primary keys are nearly always indexed because they are likely to be the entry points for very many of the enquiries of the table. However it is sometimes necessary to create indices of non-key attributes which are also heavily used for access: these are often called secondary indices and are by definition non-unique. A record in a secondary index can relate to more than one record in the target file. Secondary indices therefore have variable length records. For each value of the indexed field the secondary index holds one or many physical addresses in the target file - or alternatively, one or many primary key values for the corresponding records in the target file. If a primary key index already exists, a secondary index on the same table must be dense, because it cannot take advantage of the physical organization of the target file.

A particular example of a secondary index is one created on part of a primary key. For example, the RoomBooking entity has a key with three primary key components.

> RoomBooking
>   roomNumber
>   dateRoomRequired
>   timeRoomRequired
>   quantityDuration
>   nameBooks
> (o)   telexNumberBooks
> Foreign: roomNumber → Room
> Foreign: dateRoomRequired → Date
> Foreign: timeRoomRequired → Time
> Foreign: quantityDuration → Quantity
> Foreign: nameBooks → Employee
> Foreign: telexNumberBooks → Telex

If the room booking application has a facility to display all available rooms for a specified date, the physical database designer might decide to put a secondary index on the date field. In this way key-only owners in the logical design that were not implemented as entities in the physical implementation, such as Date, often reappear as secondary indices.

Unique indices are the only way in most relational databases to implement alternate keys. Assuming that a table is already indexed on its primary key, an alternate key must be represented by a unique, dense secondary index to the target table.

8.2.4   Combining tables

Supertypes and subtypes are merged

The concepts of generalization and specialization add a great deal of semantic richness to the logical data model. However, to reach a subtype via its supertype involves the physical system in an extra table join and could inhibit performance.

For example, consider a financial institution which likes to see all assets as the same thing in general terms. Shares, bonds, options and currencies are all means of storing wealth and all can be traded. However some assets pay dividends to their holders whereas others pay interest. Interest-bearing assets are further subdivided into those paying an unchanging interest rate and those whose rate fluctuates with a variable base rate. Logically the information is held as shown in Figure 8.13.

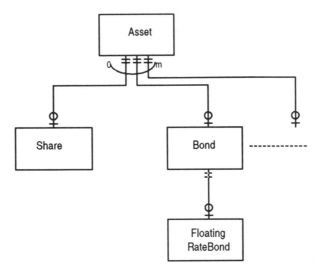

Figure 8.13

Asset
    <u>assetCode</u>
    organizationCodeIssuer
Foreign: organizationCodeIssuer → Organization

Share
    <u>assetCode</u>
    dateNextDividendPayable
    dateNextDividendRecord
    dateExDividend
    quantityDividendForecast
Foreign: assetCode → Asset
Foreign: dateNextDividendPayable → Date
Foreign: dateNextDividendRecord → Date
Foreign: dateExDividend → Date
Foreign: quantityDividendForecast → Quantity

Bond
  <u>assetCode</u>
  dateNextCoupon
  frequencyCoupon
  quantityInterestRate
Foreign: assetCode → Asset
Foreign: dateNextCoupon → Date
Foreign: quantityInterestRate → Quantity

FloatingRateBond
  <u>assetCode</u>
  baseRate
  dateNextRateChange
Foreign: assetCode → Asset
Foreign: baseRate → BaseRate
Foreign: dateNextRateChange → Date

However the physical database design could roll all the subtypes back into the ultimate supertype and produce an Asset entity as shown below. In any row of the table most of the cells will be empty, whereas there were no optional attributes in the logical model. This is a strategy which always uses more storage space for attributes, but the benefits in terms of performance could outweigh this consideration.

Asset
  <u>assetCode</u>
  organizationCodeIssuer
(o) dateNextDividendPayable
(o) dateNextDividendRecord
(o) dateExDividend
(o) quantityDividendForecast
(o) dateNextCoupon
(o) frequencyCoupon
(o) interestRate
(o) baseRate
(o) dateNextRateChange
Foreign: orgIdentIssuer → Organization
Foreign: dateNextDividendPayable → Date
Foreign: dateNextDividendRecord → Date
Foreign: dateExDividend → Date
Foreign: quantityDividendForecast → Quantity
Foreign: dateNextCoupon → Date
Foreign: quantityInterestRate → Quantity

Foreign: baseRate → BaseRate

Foreign: dateNextRateChange → Date

The technique works just as well where the subtype is the resolver of a 1:n recursion - that is, a hierarchy, chain or pair.

Entities and details are combined

Enhanced performance is also the motive for combining entities and their details. The technique is by no means as painless as the combining of supertypes and subtypes. Depending on how the denormalization is carried out, it will result in one of the following:

- variable length records

- restrictions on the maximum number of details

- duplication of data.

To illustrate how variable length records arise we shall consider the example of the bulk chemical factory. The logical model of the business includes two entities as shown in figure 8.14. For each chemical many batches are made.

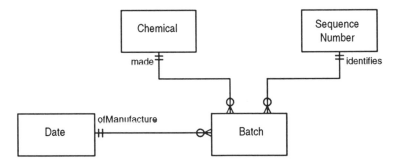

Figure 8.14

At implementation time the two entities might be merged into a single table holding details of the chemical's properties and of all the batches available. Each record of the Chemical table has a different length depending on how many batches are in existence.

Chemical

chemicalCode	chemicalName	quantity FreezingPoint	batch Number	dateOf Manufacture	quantity Made
XDP234	x-diethylprolin	12.00	3954	12.08.93	1200
			3955	13.09.93	1200
			3956	04.01.94	1000
			3957	17.03.94	1500

Merging owner and detail in this way is a denormalization of fundamental significance: it contravenes first normal form which forbids repeating groups within a record.

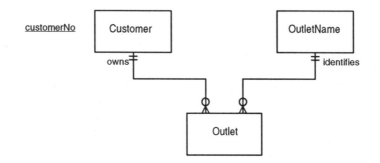

Figure 8.15

Variable length records are impossible to implement on most relational database platforms. A compromise way to merge owner and detail is to set a limit on how many of the detail records can be represented in the combined table. Say for example an organization holds details of its customers and the locations of their retail outlets. Logically the data looks like figure 8.15.

Physically the data could be held as shown. As long as no customer has more than five outlets there is no problem.

Customer

customer Number	addressHeadOffice	outlet1	outlet2	outlet3	outlet4	outlet5
RL Jones	12 High Street Wigan	Wigan	Bootle	Preston	Bolton	Bury
Sweeties	85-87 Grimsby Docks	Hull	Derby	Leeds		
Newsround	52 New Lane Exeter	Exeter	Yeovil	Bath	Dublin	
Hogan Rees	3 Rose Way Belfast	Dublin	Belfast	Formby	Cork	Paisley

To avoid both variable length records and restrictions on detail records, the combined table must duplicate the information from the owner in every record, as shown below. This format violates second normal form.

Customer

customerNumber	addressHeadOffice	outletNameIdentifies
RL Jones	12 High Street Wigan	Wigan
RL Jones	12 High Street Wigan	Bootle
RL Jones	12 High Street Wigan	Preston
RL Jones	12 High Street Wigan	Bolton
RL Jones	12 High Street Wigan	Bury
Sweeties	85-87 Grimsby Docks	Hull
Sweeties	85-87 Grimsby Docks	Derby
Sweeties	85-87 Grimsby Docks	Leeds
Newsround	52 New Lane Exeter	Exeter
Newsround	52 New Lane Exeter	Yeovil
Newsround	52 New Lane Exeter	Bath
Newsround	52 New Lane Exeter	Dublin
Hogan Rees	3 Rose Way Belfast	Dublin
Hogan Rees	3 Rose Way Belfast	Belfast
Hogan Rees	3 Rose Way Belfast	Formby
Hogan Rees	3 Rose Way Belfast	Cork
Hogan Rees	3 Rose Way Belfast	Paisley

Duplicated data, as a variety of derived data, carries with it danger of update anomaly. This would arise if, say, Newsround's head office address were changed for the Yeovil outlet but not the others. Only read-only tables can be organized in this way without any attendant update risks.

If a bill of materials resolver is merged with its owner, an entity occurrence can feature as either parent or child. Take the example of the bicycle factory. Logically its data was held like this.

Component

componentNumber	description	drawingNumber
A4567	0.5 cm steel nut	HRW22300/1
L7712	luxury gents sadddle	G55899/2
M9802	gents racing frame	
Q6669	gents racing bike	
U7119	large chrome bell	REC3000

BillOfMaterials

componentNumber Parent	componentNumber Child	quantityOfChild
L7712	A4567	6
U7119	A4567	2
Q6669	M9802	1
Q6669	L7712	1
Q6669	A4567	2

Merged, the owner and detail would appear thus. All of the owner's attributes are repeated whichever role it is playing.

BillOfMaterials

comp Number Parent	descParent	drawing Number Parent (o)	comp Number Child	descChild	drawing Number Child (o)	qtyOf Child
L7712	luxury gents sadddle	G55899/2	A4567	0.5 cm steel nut	HRW22300/1	6
U7119	large chrome bell	REC3000	A4567	0.5 cm steel nut	HRW22300/1	2
Q6669	gents racing bike		M9802	gents racing frame		1
Q6669	gents racing bike		L7712	luxury gents sadddle	G55899/2	1
Q6669	gents racing bike		A4547	0.5 cm steel nut	HRW22300/1	2

8.2.5 Splitting tables

Tables are split horizontally

Tables may be split horizontally when some of the rows need to appear in one table and some in another. For example, a manufacturing company makes organic chemicals at one site and inorganic ones at another. Each site has its own computer and once a day the computers are networked to allow updates of central records; the rest of the time they are separate. In its corporate logical data model the company has an entity called Product.

Product
    <u>productCode</u>
    productName
(o) quantityManufacturingCost
    quantityManufacturingLeadTime

Foreign: quantityManufacturingCost → Quantity
Foreign: quantityManufacturingLeadTime → Quantity

Physically, the table has to be split into two so that each site can see the records for the products it is manufacturing. Each partition has an identical column structure. Each row belongs to one or the other of the partitions but not to both.

OrganicProduct
        productCode
        productName
(o)   quantityManufacturingCost
        quantityManufacturingLeadTime
Foreign: quantityManufacturingCost → Quantity
Foreign: quantityManufacturingLeadTime → Quantity

InorganicProduct
        productCode
        productName
(o)   quantityManufacturingCost
        quantityManufacturingLeadTime
Foreign: quantityManufacturingCost → Quantity
Foreign: quantityManufacturingLeadTime → Quantity

Physical distribution is a common reason for a horizontal partition, but the technique could also be used to describe the archiving procedure. The records in one partition - those over a year old, say - could be put onto a different medium or compressed.

It is also possible to imagine circumstances in which some rows of a table were considered more sensitive than others. Imagine a system by which details of curricula vitae (cvs) received by a large company were typed into a central system so that any team manager interested in recruiting staff could interrogate it. An ApplicantExperience table stores details of the posts held by each applicant to provide a full career history.

If an applicant's career has been interrupted by a spell in prison, the prison sentence becomes a record of the table. However, such records are not released to all users of the cv system so physically the table is implemented in two horizontal parts.

ApplicantExperience

applicant Code	month Start	year Start	month Finish	year Finish	orgCodeEmployer (o)	jobTitle	...
703001	Feb	1979	Aug	1980	BBC	Tea maker	
703001	Sep	1980	Dec	1982	Ernest Anderson	Trainee accountant	
703001	Jan	1983	Aug	1986	Ball Group	Cost accountant	
703001	Aug	1986	Feb	1988	Vickery Higson	Finance manager	
703001	Jul	1992			NHS	Fundraiser	
003179	Dec	1981	May	1987	Greenaways	Draughtsman	

ApplicantExperienceCustodial

applicant Code	month Start	year Start	month Finish	year Finish	orgCodeEmployer (o)	jobTitle	...
703001	Feb	1988	Mar	1992		Serious fraud	
056662	Sep	1974	Oct	1982		Arson	

Tables are split vertically

Suppose a van rental company keeps the Vehicle details we have encountered earlier.

Vehicle
  registrationNumber
  manufacturerName
  modelName
  colourOfPaintworkBody
  colourOfPaintworkRoof
  colourOfUpholstery
  yearOfManufacture
  dateRoadFundLicenceRenewable

Foreign: manufacturerName, modelName → VehicleModel
Foreign: colourOfPaintworkBody → Colour
Foreign: colourOfPaintworkRoof → Colour
Foreign: colourOfUpholstery → Colour
Foreign: yearOfManufacture → Year
Foreign: dateRoadFundLicenceRenewable → Date

The part of the application that allows it to rent out vans requires only the first three attributes on the list. Other parts of the application, such as the part which ensures all the vans are properly licensed, need the other attributes, but they are not used so frequently and nor are they performance critical. The Vehicle entity could be split vertically in the implementation of the system. Each row appears in both partitions of the table but, other than the primary key, each column features in only one.

VehicleCoreInformation
    <u>registrationNumber</u>
    manufacturerName
    modelName
Foreign: manufacturerName, modelName $\rightarrow$ VehicleModel

VehicleSupplementaryInformation
    <u>registrationNumber</u>
    colourOfPaintworkBody
    colourOfPaintworkRoof
    colourOfUpholstery
    yearOfManufacture
    dateRoadFundLicenceRenewable
Foreign: colourOfPaintworkBody $\rightarrow$ Colour
Foreign: colourOfPaintworkRoof $\rightarrow$ Colour
Foreign: colourOfUpholstery $\rightarrow$ Colour
Foreign: yearOfManufacture $\rightarrow$ Year
Foreign: dateRoadFundLicenceRenewable $\rightarrow$ Date

Although performance enhancement is the usual motive for a vertical table split, there could be other reasons. For example, some of a logical table's columns could contain more sensitive data than others and so require separate storage. Vertical splits also allow partial archiving, whereby not all columns are kept online for the same period of time.

Note that denormalization strategies can be combined. In the above example, the VehicleCoreInformation table could be merged with its owner, VehicleModel, for even greater efficiency.

8.2.6   Changing attribute status

Program code can be significantly simplified during physical implementation by changing optional attributes into mandatory ones and extending the domain of permitted attribute values.

Recall for example the organization from chapter 3 that gave a credit rating to each of its customers. Now the firm wants to assign all its customers to an industrial sector so that at the end of each sales period it can produce a summary report showing the total value of its sales to each sector. This is easily achieved by adding an attribute called industrialSectorCode to the Customer entity. Like creditRating this attribute's value is unknown when the customer first places an order. It doesn't have to be filled until the sales summaries are due to be produced and this normally allows long enough for the correct value to be determined. In the logical model industrialSectorCode should be made optional for the same reason that creditRating was.

```
Customer
        customerNumber
        name
        address
        telephoneNumber
(o)     creditRating
(o)     industrialSectorCode
Foreign:        creditRating → CreditRating
Foreign:        industrialSectorCode → IndustrialSector
```

There will still be some customers who have not been assigned to a sector by the end of a sales period. So that the sales analysis application remembers to add in the value of their orders, it must be capable of recognizing that orders from customers with null industrialSectorCode attributes should be grouped together in a bucket section of the analysis report headed "Unknown sector".

Alternatively the industrialSectorCode attribute could be made mandatory and set to a value of "Unknown" until the customer's true sector was ascertained. This option might be chosen as a way of simplifying the sales analysis program code which could then treat a sector of "Unknown" in exactly the same way as a sector of "Chemicals". The bucket sector would need to be added to the permitted sector values in the domain entity IndustrialSector.

```
Customer
        customerNumber
        name
        address
        telephoneNumber
(o)     creditRating
        industrialSectorCode
Foreign:        creditRating → CreditRating
Foreign:        industrialSectorCode → IndustrialSector
```

Adding a bucket sector can be a dangerous thing to do. In accounting systems suspense accounts are a kind of bucket and if they are not controlled carefully then a substantial balance represented by a large number of transactions can build up, taking considerable effort to clean up the data afterwards.

8.2.7   Adding meta-data

Extra tables hold control parameters

Control parameters are data which pertain to the physical implementation of a system and have no meaning in business terms. It is convenient to hold such parameters in relational tables where they can be accessed in the same way as business data.

This information may include the following:

- Process parameters, such as the online functions of the system and how those functions are accessed by menu structures, which batch programs need to be run and when they were last run.

- Access parameters, such as the users of the system, which functions each is allowed to perform, their passwords and password expiry dates.

- Display parameters, such as the number of lines per screen and the language that text should be displayed in.

Extra tables hold meta-data

The extreme case of a parameterizable system is a report generator. Such a system allows the user to place variable business data in rows and columns on reports and to create menu systems for other users. Because the user is effectively taking over some of the role of the programmer, he or she needs access to meta-data as well as business data. For example, the user of a report generator would need to access data structures like those shown in Figure 8.16. For a fuller discussion of the meta-model, see Chapter 14.

8.3   Generating the physical database

8.3.1   Data definition

Once the database designer has finalized the physical data model a relational database implementation of the data structure can be made quickly and easily using SQL (Structured Query Language)[2]. SQL is the subject of an ANSI standard and the majority of database management systems (DBMS) provide an SQL interface. With SQL one may create database tables (data definition language), control access to the database (data control language) and update and query the data in the database (data manipulation language).

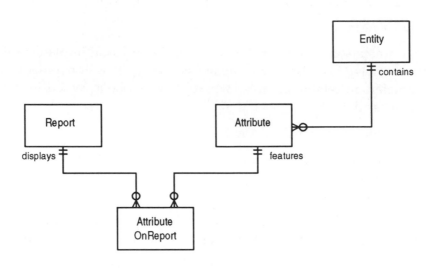

Figure 8.16

Although a detailed description of SQL is outside the scope of this book, we have provided an example set of SQL to show that the transition from an attribute list to an implemented database can be a very small step and one that can be fully automated with respect to table creation. Figure 8.17 is an entity diagram for a very simple order processing system.

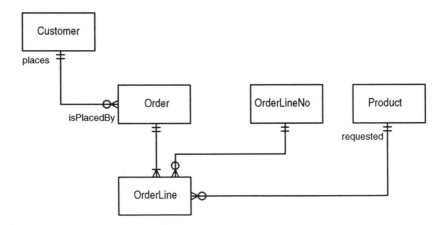

Figure 8.17: *Entity diagram for customer orders*

Assume that the entity diagram in figure 8.17 is represented by the following attribute lists.

    Customer
        customerNumber
        name
        address
    (o)   telNumber

    Order
        orderNumber
        dateOfOrder
        customerNumberPlaces
    Foreign: customerNumberPlaces → Customer

    OrderLine
        orderNumber
        orderLineNumber
        productNumber
        quantityRequested
    Foreign: orderNumber → Order
    Foreign: orderLineNumber → OrderLineNumber
    Foreign: productNumber → Product
    Unique: orderLineNumber, productNumber

    Product
        productNumber
        productDesc
        quantityCostPrice

    OrderLineNumber
        orderLineNumber

The customer table can be implemented in SQL by using the CREATE TABLE command. SQL reserved words are shown in capital letters.

    CREATE TABLE Customer
        (customerNumber   INTEGER   NOT NULL,
        name   CHAR (30)   NOT NULL,
        address   CHAR (40)   NOT NULL,
        telNumber   CHAR (15),
    PRIMARY KEY (customerNumber))

Attributes that are mandatory are flagged NOT NULL. The DBMS will require a value to be entered into this field when data is entered into the database. Optional attributes, such as telNumber, do not have the NOT

NULL clause and can be left empty. The PRIMARY KEY identifies the key of the table for use in referential integrity.

Each attribute's format and size is specified. Although this kind of information is not displayed in the attribute list representation of an entity, it is collected during the analysis phase of a project and and would be available from the repository. For the full repository structure see chapter 14 on meta-modelling.

Every table must also have a unique primary key index defined[3].

```
CREATE UNIQUE INDEX customerNumberIndex
    ON Customer (customerNumber)
```

The Order entity can be implemented as follows:

```
CREATE TABLE Order
    (orderNumber            INTEGER     NOT NULL,
    dateOfOrder             DATE        NOT NULL,
    customerNumberPlaces INTEGER        NOT NULL,
PRIMARY KEY (orderNumber),
FOREIGN KEY (customerNumberPlaces) REFERENCES Customer
    ON DELETE RESTRICT)
```

The Foreign clause in the attribute list specifying Customer as an owner of Order has generated a similar clause, FOREIGN KEY, in the SQL table definition statement. Relational integrity details are available in the repository though they are not shown on the attribute list. Here the RESTRICT option means that an occurrence of the Customer table may not be deleted while it references one or more orders. A relationship's referential integrity policy cannot be discerned from the attribute list notation but should be collected by the modeller (see chapter 3) and stored in the repository (see chapter 14).

The OrderLine entity is generated as shown.

```
CREATE TABLE OrderLine
    (orderNumber            INTEGER     NOT NULL,
    orderLineNumber         INTEGER     NOT NULL,
    productNumber           CHAR (6)    NOT NULL,
    quantityRequested       DECIMAL (9,3) NOT NULL,
PRIMARY KEY (orderNumber, orderLineNumber),
FOREIGN KEY (orderNumber) REFERENCES Order
    ON DELETE CASCADE,
FOREIGN KEY (productNumber) REFERENCES Product
    ON DELETE RESTRICT)
```

The FOREIGN KEY clause on the orderNumber attribute specifies CASCADE as the policy for maintenance of referential integrity: when an occurrence of Order is deleted the DBMS will cascade the deletion downwards killing all the lines associated with that order. To prevent a product being deleted while order lines referencing that product live on, the relevant foreign key clause specifies RESTRICT ON DELETE. Note that in each case the ON DELETE clause refers to policy on deletion of the owner.

Why are there only two foreign clauses in the SQL statement when the attribute list shows three? The missing foreign clause is orderLineNumber. We made this an entity in the logical data model as it is part of the primary key of OrderLine. The physical database designer has rationalized the table out of existence - another fact available from the repository as defined in chapter 14. It will probably have been replaced with a record of the last line number used on a parameter table.

Each table must have a unique index defined covering the items that constitute its primary key. Alternate keys, such as the combination of orderLineNumber and productNumber in the OrderLine table, are implemented by adding a second unique index.

```
CREATE UNIQUE INDEX orderProdIndex
    ON OrderLine (orderNumber, ProductNumber)
```

The product table can be implemented as follows.

```
CREATE TABLE Product
    (productNumber      CHAR (6)        NOT NULL,
    productDesc         CHAR (35)       NOT NULL,
    quantityCostPrice   DECIMAL (8,2) NOT NULL,
PRIMARY KEY (productNumber))
```

Each foreign key should be indexed in the interests of efficiency. The indexing of custNumberPlaces as a foreign key of Order as shown below.

```
CREATE INDEX custNumberPlacesIndex
    ON Order (customerNumberPlaces)
```

The creation of these indexes reflects the relationships in the entity diagram. Queries of the data in the database involve traversal of relationships and indexes should improve performance.

8.3.2   Querying the database using SQL

SQL was used to create the database; it is also used to populate and maintain the data in the database. Having established a database we will want to access the data in different ways. Consider a requirement to list all of a customer's orders. Using the SQL SELECT statement a query can be written that will join the Customer table to the Order table and produce a report in customerNumber, dateOfOrder sequence:

```
SELECT name, address, dateOfOrder, orderNumber
FROM Customer, Order
WHERE Customer.customerNumber = Order.customerNumber
ORDER BY name, dateOfOrder
```

In the above example we have performed an inner join of Customer and Order (only those customers with one or more orders will be output on the report), the join condition being specified in the WHERE clause. This query can be thought of as traversing the relationship from Customer to Order. Joins can involve many tables and can be written in different ways. The above example is intended as a simple illustration only.

Chapter summary

Logical data modelling needs to be done with blinkers on: it should assume that there are no performance targets, that code will be as complex as it needs to be to use data in fifth normal form and that all data will be held online indefinitely with no security implications. It should also assume that the hardware and RDBMS for the first implementation of the application have not been specified, even if in real life they have. The logical model should be completed under these assumptions and then frozen.

A copy of the logical model will become the starting point for physical design but denormalizations will almost certainly be introduced. Performance speed will be the main motive for denormalizing but other reasons will include code simplification, system distribution, archiving needs, security and interfaces with existing systems.

Denormalizations incur penalties. They almost always complicate insertions, deletions and updates of data (after all, that was why we normalized in the first place). They always take up more attribute storage space. Because denormalizations rob a data model of its intuitive semantics, they may confuse analysts and programmers trying to maintain the system in later years.

The physical database designer should quantify the expected performance benefits from any proposed denormalization. These can then be compared and offset against the drawbacks.

Once the data design is complete, a physical implementation of it can be generated automatically. Data definition code can be created from the information held in the repository.

NOTES

1. Refer to:
   Ullman, J. D., (1981). *Principles of Database Systems.* Computer Science Press.

2. There are many books available that cover SQL. One that contains numerous examples and some interesting case studies is:
   Carter, J., (1992). *Programming in SQL with Oracle , Ingres and dBASE IV.* Blackwell Scientific, Oxford.

3. For details of referential integrity in the context of IBM's DB2 database see:
   Date, C. J., & White, C.J., (1988). *A Guide to DB2.* Third edition. Addison-Wesley, Reading, Mass.

Questions

1. What information should a database designer gather before deciding on a specific denormalization?

2. Describe three denormalization techniques that assist with archiving.

3. The slimming club mentioned in section 4.9.1 wants to calculate and store the average weight of its members every week. Advise on the denormalization of its data model.

4. Explain the difference between a dense and a sparse index.

5. Explain the following terms.

   (a) primary key index
   (b) foreign key index
   (c) partial key index

6. Specify two denormalizations that can assist with data security.

7. Under what circumstances can horizontal partitioning improve performance?

8.   What are the costs and benefits of denormalization?

9.   Write the SQL data definition code to implement the data structures provided in your answer to question 3.

10.   Write an SQL SELECT statement to list all the addresses at which a particular member of the slimming club, whose membership number is 04412, has ever lived.

Part 2

Object modelling

9

Object modelling

Introduction

Data modelling is a powerful and rigorous way of modelling the data requirements of information systems, but it has a number of implementation-specific features. The logical data model is particularly suited to data-intensive management information applications, especially in situations where it is known that the implementation is going to use relational database technology.

Part 1 of this book was concerned with a form of logical data modelling that has its roots in the relational model requiring that certain tenets be adhered to, as described in chapter 7. These rules should be followed if the relational model is used as the basis for data modelling. However, we should bear in mind that the relational model is but one basis for data modelling, and also that the relational model gives priority to one particular implementation medium, namely the relational database. Applications that are not management information (MIS) orientated, e.g., CAD/CAM

(Computer Aided Design/Manufacturing), CASE (Computer Aided Software Engineering), or multi-media, can be difficult to implement using purely relational technology.

Although we may be able to model the required data structures using relational tables, the large number of tables needed to model more complicated data structures (particularly subtyping and composition structures) means the implementation may lead to poor performance and be rather difficult to administer and maintain. Even in situations where we know the implementation will involve a relational database there are still good reasons for modelling the requirements in a more implementation-independent manner. The system might be re-implemented at a later date using a database that is supported by a different type of data model, such as the Object-Oriented model. A model that gives more attention to the meaning of the data, rather than the structure of relational tables, will enable a more conceptual approach to be taken and aid better understanding and communication between users and developers.

Certainly one can use the data model as the basis of a requirements specification. SSADM (Structured Systems Analysis and Design Methodology) is a data-centred method that uses a relational style of data modelling. However, not everybody would agree that SSADM is necessarily the most appropriate method for the development of, for example, graphical interfaces or complex objects such as the engineering drawings maintained in a CAD/CAM application. Logical data modelling was introduced in part 1 because it gives a sound and rigorous basis for understanding entities and relationships, it can be implemented directly onto relational databases (currently the most widely-used implementation medium for MIS), and is consistent with SSADM.

With a simple model that contains only entities, relationships and attributes it has been possible to model complex situations, including subtyping, multiple inheritance, and the effects of time. However, there are some issues that we wish to address by the introduction of object modelling. By using an object model we can capture a situation in such a way that the model could be used to support many different implementation approaches (of which the relational model is but one). The object model is introduced to remove the implementation-specific features of the data model and to provide a basis for defining the behaviour of data through an Object-Oriented paradigm.

Many benefits have been claimed for an Object-Oriented approach to systems development, including reusability, reliability, scalability, faster development, easier maintenance, greater extensability, a closer correspondence with the real world, and a more effective way of handling complexity[1]. From a data modelling perspective we will focus on the management of complexity. In chapter 8 it was noted that the elegant logical data structures built by the data modeller are often savaged in physical design, albeit for the best of reasons, one of which being the simplification of application code. If it is possible to combine the way data behaves with the way that it is represented then perhaps rather than compromising the logical data structure it will be possible to hide it so that one does not need to know how the data is structured to make use of it - one will just need to know what the data can do. If the gap between logical design, physical design and implementation can be narrowed then the logical design should be recognizable in its implemented form.

Specific objectives of the introduction of the object model are:

data representation
- to avoid the use of foreign keys for the implementation of associations;
- to allow many-to-many associations;
- to reconsider the need for uniqueness;
- to use generalization/specialization structures rather than one-to-one relationships;
- to introduce an assembly/composition structure (chapter 10);
- to introduce ternary associations (chapter 10);
- to introduce time-stamping (chapter 10).

data behaviour and functional requirements
- to model data behaviour (chapter 11);
- to model functional requirements (chapter 12).

This chapter is concerned with how data is represented in an object model. Understanding the similarities and differences between data models and object models is essential for any data modeller who wants to understand the relationship between structured methods and Object-Oriented analysis.

9.1   The object model

To distinguish between the data model and the object model the following terminology will be used:

data model	object model
entity	class
occurrence	instance (or object)
relationship	association
attribute	attribute (or property)
entity subtype	subclass
entity supertype	superclass

The introduction of the terms class and object in the object model, as contrasted with entity and occurrence in the data model, signals our intention to create a basis for the introduction of behaviour into the object model. Classes and entities both address the representation of data, but classes describe also the behaviour of the data. Relationships are implemented by matching column values from one table with column values from another table while associations do not imply the use of foreign keys. Attribute has been retained in the object model as it seems to be an appropriate label in both models.

The graphical notations for the data and object models are also distinguishable - rectangles are used for entities in the data model and rounded rectangles are used for classes in the object model. Although the terms in the above table can be thought of as equivalents in a broad sense, it would be an over-simplification to see them as interchangeable since they represent different underlying assumptions about data modelling. One of the aims of this book is to identify a migration path for developers from the relational world to the Object-Oriented world and, going in the reverse direction, to show how an object model might be turned into a data model that could be implemented on a relational database. One way in which we hope to achieve this is by highlighting some of the similarities and differences between the two approaches.

9.2   Entities and classes

In the data model it has been assumed that an entity is equivalent to or, more accurately, can be implemented as a table. Relationships are said to exist between entities and are implemented using foreign keys. In the data model entities are seen as collections of attributes, where the grouping of those attributes should be consistent with the requirements of normalization. The data model in figure 9.1 will be used to contrast some aspects of the data and object models.

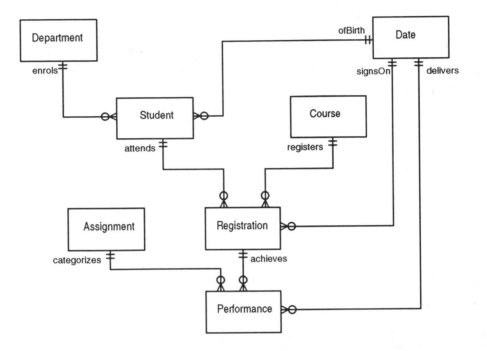

Figure 9.1: *Entity diagram*

The entity diagram in figure 9.1 is represented as an attribute list as follows:

Department
    <u>deptNumber</u>
    deptName
Unique: deptName

Student
    <u>studentNumber</u>
    nameFirst
    nameSecond
    dateOfBirth
    deptNumberEnrols
Foreign: deptNumberEnrols → Department
Foreign: dateOfBirth → Date

Course
    <u>courseCode</u>
    courseTitle
    credits

Registration
    studentNumber
    courseCode
    dateSignsOn
Foreign: studentNumber → Student
Foreign: courseCode → Course
Foreign: dateSignsOn → Date

Assignment
    assignment

Performance
    studentNumber
    courseCode
    assignment
    dateDelivers
(o)   grade
Foreign: studentNumber, courseCode → Registration
Foreign: assignment → Assignment
Foreign: dateDelivers → Date

The grade attribute in the Performance entity has been flagged as optional since there will be a delay between an assignment being handed in (dateDelivers) and the assignment being marked.

The student entity can be represented as a set of associations between a student class and the **primitive** classes that define how a student is represented, as shown in figure 9.2 (b). As will be seen later in this chapter, the concept of primary and foreign keys is not directly relevant in the object model and hence it does not matter where the association line enters the class box.

In figure 9.2 (b) a number of facts have been asserted for Student:

- a student must have one studentNumber;

- a student must be born on one date;

- a student must have one first name;

- a student must have one second name.

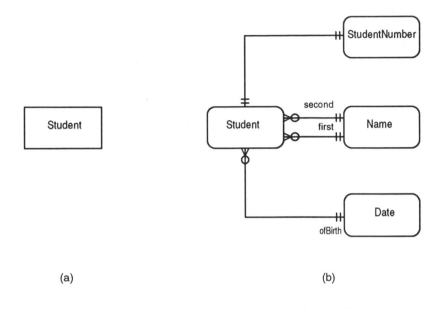

(a)   (b)

Figure 9.2: *Student entity (a) and Student class (b)*

The classes in figure 9.2 (b) are primitive - they cannot or need not be broken down into further components. Further classes can be constructed from primitive classes, a process we refer to as **clustering**. The classes StudentNumber, Name, and Date can be clustered into the Student class and then be represented diagrammatically as in figure 9.3. Attribute names (e.g., nameFirst) have been constructed from a combination of the class being clustered (e.g., Name) and the name of the association that is being absorbed (e.g., first). Where there is no association name then the class name can be used as the attribute name (e.g., studentNumber). As with attributes in a data model, attribute names in the object model begin with a lower case letter.

Figure 9.3: *Clustered Student class*

Three dots are used to indicate that a class has attributes (i.e., it is not a primitive class) but that they are not shown on the diagram. Attributes might be suppressed when there are too many of them to make the diagram readable (figure 9.4).

Figure 9.4: *Student class (attributes suppressed)*

The data model representation can be thought of as a collection of facts that have been clustered in such a way as to form entities. An equivalent object model for the data model in figure 9.1 is shown in figure 9.5, where each of the attributes has become a class in its own right.

Thus there is a class of object called StudentNumber, where an instance of that class might be 03020493. The distinction between entities and attributes that is at the heart of the data model is no longer as significant in the object model - everything is a class. Whether a class is primitive or not depends upon the requirements of the situation being modelled; the same issue is encountered in data modelling when deciding if an attribute needs to become an entity.

Assume that we have decided to cluster the primitive classes in figure 9.5 as shown by the dotted outlines, recognizing that the things of significance in this situation are Department, Student, Course, Registration, and Performance. These classes can then be represented at a higher level of abstraction as in figure 9.6.

In chapter 7 we considered how relational data analysis could be used in a bottom-up manner to complement the top-down approach of entity diagramming. Similarly, the clustering of primitive classes to create composite objects represents a bottom-up approach in which basic facts are asserted. A top-down approach is obtained by **levelling** in which high-level objects are identified and decomposed down through levels of abstraction to the point at which they have primitive classes as attributes.

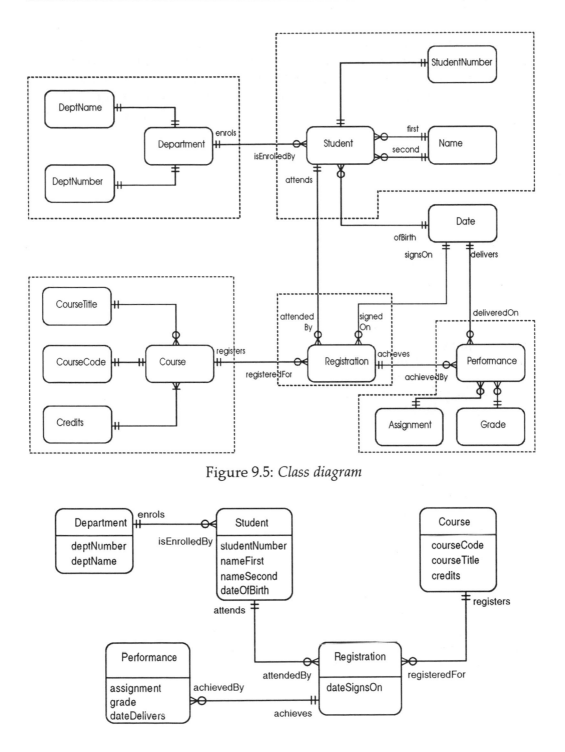

Figure 9.5: *Class diagram*

Figure 9.6: *Clustered class diagram*

The top-down approach should result in classes that are meaningful to users; the bottom-up approach should allow business facts, e.g., each student must be registered in one department, to be captured in a more rigorous way. As with data modelling it is not a question of either/or - the techniques should be used together to gain understanding of the problem domain in detail and in concept.

9.3   Representing class diagrams

Entity diagrams were represented as attribute lists in part 1. Similarly, class diagrams can be represented in text format. The class diagram in figure 9.6 can be shown as follows:

        Department
                deptNumber
                deptName

        Student
                studentNumber
                nameFirst
                nameSecond
                dateOfBirth

        Course
                courseCode
                courseTitle
                credits

        Registration
                dateSignsOn

        Performance
                assignment
                dateDelivers
        (o)   grade

The above textual representation is effectively a list of clustered classes and their attributes. All the attributes shown are primitive. There are no Foreign clauses in the above specification; none of the attributes reflects an association between classes at the level of the class diagram shown in figure 9.6. Dates are not foreign keys since the Date class is not shown in figure 9.6. If Date were modelled as an independent class then all of the date attributes would disappear, to be replaced by associations. Perhaps even more startling for the data modeller there are no attributes underlined to identify uniquely instances of the classes. This is also true of the class diagram in figure 9.6 since where an association line enters a class box has no significance.

Clearly associations are dealt with rather differently from relationships in the data model. This topic is the subject of the next section.

9.4   Relationships and associations

In the data model tables are joined by matching columns that share the same domain. The data model in figure 9.1 shows foreign key relationships (Department with Student, Date with Student, Date with Performance) and primary key relationships (Student and Course with Registration, Assignment with Performance, Registration with Performance). In the data model these relationships are implemented using foreign keys. In part 1 of the book in order to distinguish and clarify relationships we recommended that the relationship name is made part of the attribute name as necessary; the attribute dateOfBirth represents the relationship between Student and Date with the relationship name, of birth, being encoded in the attribute name.

It is not necessary to add the relationship name into the attribute name in the data model where there is a single relationship between entities (for example we would know that a foreign key deptNumber in Student would refer to the relationship isRegisteredBy if this is the only relationship between Student and Department). Where there are multiple relationships between entities then the role played by the attribute will need to be encoded into the attribute name in order to make the attributes distinguishable. In part 1 we recommended that relationship names be concatenated with attribute names as necessary to allow foreign key attributes to be generated automatically. By doing this it is possible to derive all the necessary foreign keys (foreign and primary foreign) from relationship and attribute names (see chapter 14).

Although this is the way in which relationships are implemented in the data model we should remember that it is but one way of implementing a relationship. In the object model we shall think of relationships in more conceptual terms. We shall refer to associations to remind us that we are thinking no longer of the data model. An association can be thought of as a mapping between two classes (figure 9.7).

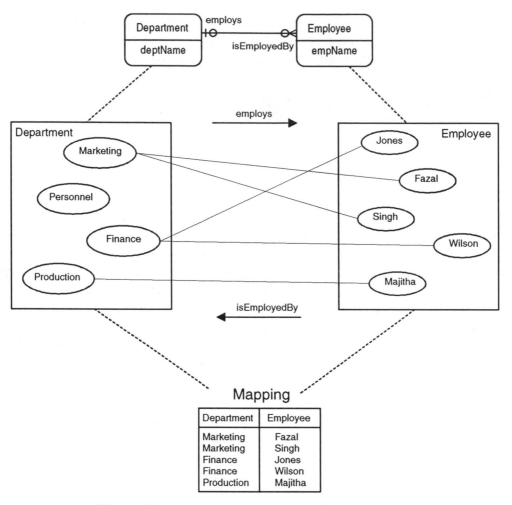

Figure 9.7: *Associations as mapping between classes*

In figure 9.7, the Department and Employee classes are associated by the function employs and its inverse isEmployedBy. These functions can be thought of as a mapping between the Department and Employee classes. In the object model in figure 9.6 there are a number of associations:

class	function	class	inverse function	class
Department	enrols	Student	isEnrolledBy	Department
Student	attends	Registration	isAttendedBy	Student
Course	registers	Registration	registeredFor	Course
Registration	achieves	Performance	achievedBy	Registration

In summary, there are some good reasons for not including attributes that represent foreign keys in class definitions:

- foreign keys are an implementation detail of the data model;

- foreign keys are a duplication of the meaning already contained in the relationship and therefore should be (and are) derivable[*];

- foreign keys can violate the requirement for encapsulation of classes (see chapter 11 for details of encapsulation).

9.4.1   One-to-one associations

A difference between the data and object models can be seen clearly in the treatment of 1:1 relationships.   In figure 9.8, both data and object models show that a department must have one manager.

(a) entity diagram - relational data model

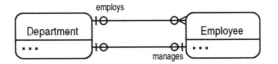

(b) class diagram - object model

Figure 9.8: *1:1 relationships/associations*

Because the manages relationship in the data model is represented as a constrained 1:n from Employee to Department it is evident that the Department entity contains a foreign key, perhaps empNumberManages (empNumber being the primary key of Employee). The choice of whether empNumber appeared in Department as a foreign key or whether the key of

---

[*] In fact all of the foreign keys shown in part 1 *are* derivable. The attribute list is a report from a repository and the foreign key attributes are derivable data (see chapter 14).

Department, deptNumber, appeared in Employee as deptNumberManagedBy was, to some extent, an arbitrary decision, although we might decide to put the foreign key in Department, as is the case in figure 9.8, if it is felt more likely that an employee will be allowed to manage many departments in the future than it is that a department will have many managers.

In the object model the notion of foreign keys is irrelevant and all one need say is that any department must have one manager and any employee may manage one department. How the association is implemented is not relevant in the object model. The Employee manages Department association should be visualized similarly to the Department employs Employee association in figure 9.7.

9.4.2   Many-to-many associations

The data model requires that many-to-many relationships be resolved. Where an association represents a two-way list and no further classes of interest are being hidden in the association, then in the object model the many-to-many association can be retained. In the early stages of requirements analysis there may be a number of these associations; as the requirements are better understood then most of the many-to-many associations will be resolved as the need for new classes is recognized.

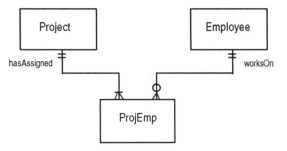

(a) entity diagram - relational data model

(b) class diagram - object model

Figure 9.9: *m:n relationships/associations*

In figure 9.9 (b) the many-to-many relationship between Project and Employee might be appropriate in an object model since it reflects the understanding that each employee may work on many projects and each project must have one or more employees assigned to it. In the object model we will try to avoid the introduction of artificial resolving classes that do not add any useful meaning to the model.

In the data model all m:n relationships must be resolved and the equivalent data model might be as shown in figure 9.9 (a). As with the one-to-many and one-to-one associations, in the object model we need only think of the many-to-many as a mapping supported by functions:

class	function	class	inverse function	class
Project	hasAssigned	Employee	worksOn	Project

However, if there are attributes associated with the Project/Employee association then it is likely that a new class will be introduced to the object model with the result that it resembles more closely the equivalent data model[2].

9.5   Uniqueness

In the object model there is no requirement to specify primary keys. However, every object is assumed to have a unique identity. In the example in figure 9.7 class instances have been shown. The instances of a class are also known as the **extension** of that class. The **intension** of a class specifies the characteristics that objects should have if they are to be considered members of that class. In an object model it is usually the intension that is being modelled; instances of a class (the extension) can be shown on a class diagram, but this is less common. Figure 9.7 illustrated both intension and extension. The mapping between objects is maintained regardless of whether or not the objects are identifiable from their representation (i.e., their attributes). Thus, if in the problem situation there are two employees named Wilson they are separate instances of the class Employee and, in the object model, can maintain their individual mapping to a department.

Obviously this is not implementable in a data model. It is a requirement of the relational model that each row of a relation be uniquely identifiable from the primary key, which is some combination of the relation's attributes (though this is not necessarily a requirement of relational databases, where tables can be established with duplicate rows). There is an additional constraint in the relational model that says that the primary key of a row may not be changed; the row must be deleted and then a new added. The identity of a row is visible in the attributes that make up the primary key, and identity cannot be changed.

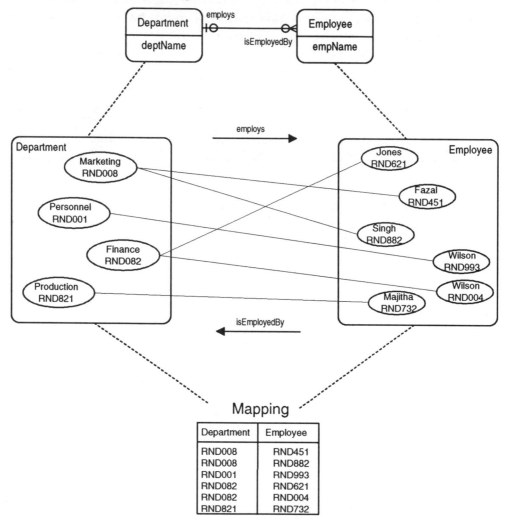

Figure 9.10: *Associations and identity*

In an O-O database identity is implemented through the object identifier, or OID, which ensures that every object is distinguishable[2]. However, the OID should not be made available to either developers or application users. It is therefore possible to have a number of distinct objects that look to be the same (i.e., their attributes are recursively equal). For example it would be possible to have two employees called Wilson, each of which is an object (and therefore unique) and capable of maintaining separate associations with other objects (e.g., one with Finance and the other with Personnel).

For illustrative purposes, random numbers have been used in figure 9.10 to simulate object identifiers, showing how a mapping might be achieved. In an object model the concern is not with how the mapping is achieved (the use of OIDs is one implementation technique); it is enough to know that each instance of a class will have its own identity and should be thought of as having a separate existence that persists regardless of its representation (attributes). Therefore it is not possible to guarantee that instances can be distinguished on the basis of their representation. Objects that are representationally equal are not necessarily the same object and although objects have unique identities this does not mean that they can be distinguished using visible attributes. Unique characteristics, if needed, must come from the representation of the object and not from an OID.

Uniqueness of representation can be derived in a number of ways:

- uniqueness not required;
- uniqueness from internal roles;
- uniqueness from external roles;
- uniqueness from the introduction of an artificial identifier.

Each of these approaches to representational uniqueness is now considered in turn.

9.5.1   Uniqueness not required

In the example in figure 9.10 employees were allowed to exist with the same name. Although all instances of employee must be distinct objects it might not be possible to distinguish between them on the basis of their representation. Using a Course class as an example (figure 9.11), if no uniqueness constraint is specified then it is possible that a number of course instances (representing different courses) could exist with the same data values.

Although each course is separate existentially, it will not necessarily be possible to tell which is which simply from an inspection of the data. In some cases this may not be an issue whilst in other situations considerable operational problems might arise if it is not possible to distinguish class instances on the basis of their representation.

Figure 9.11: *Course class*

Assume that the specification of the Course class is as follows:

Course
    courseTitle
    credits

No uniqueness constraint has been placed upon the class definition. If two courses, for example systems analysis, are added with the same attributes then it will not be possible to distinguish between them on the basis of representation.

This means that the class diagram in figure 9.6 will be valid even without any of the identifiers studentNumber, courseCode, deptNumber (figure 9.12).

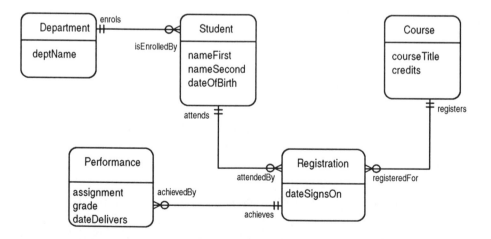

Figure 9.12: *Class diagram without identifiers*

9.5.2   Uniqueness from internal roles

As we have already seen, the clustered classes are made up of a number of roles, such as Student has nameFirst. A student is uniquely identifiable if a role instance (or a combination of role instances) may not appear more than once. For example, consider a Student class (figure 9.13) that does not have the attribute studentNumber.

Figure 9.13: *Student class*

Perhaps students are uniquely identifiable by a combination of the following roles:

Student has first name   and
Student has second name   and
Student was born on date

The specification of the Student class can now be amended:

```
Student
        nameFirst
        nameSecond
        dateOfBirth
Unique:         nameFirst,
                nameSecond,
                dateOfBirth
```

The Unique constraint will ensure that two or more students cannot have the same combination of first name, second name, and date of birth.

9.5.3   Uniqueness from external roles

Associations with other classes can also contribute to the uniqueness of instances. In figure 9.14, Registration has associations with Student and Course. It is now possible to use the fact that all registrations are made by a student for a course to assist in the unique representation of registration instances. The definition of the Registration class is now:

Registration
        dateSignsOn
Unique: attendedBy Student,
                registeredFor Course

Uniqueness has been achieved through the external associations attendedBy Student and registeredFor Course. For Registration to have representation uniqueness it is necessary that Student and Course have uniqueness clauses defined.

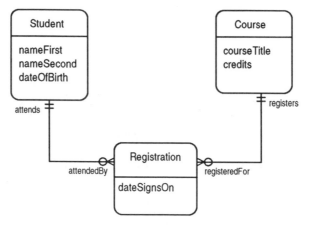

Figure 9.14: *Registration class*

The approach taken in the object model to associations and uniqueness of representation makes the entity diagramming convention, in which primary key relationships enter the top of the entity box and foreign key relationships enter the side of the box, inappropriate in a class diagram. But as we have seen, associations can contribute to the uniqueness of representation.

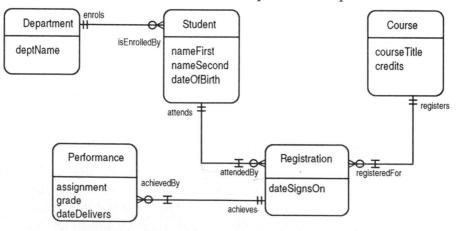

Figure 9.15: *Associations contributing to identity*

Where uniqueness is required and is derived from an association, then a bar with ends (an "I") should be placed on the association line (figure 9.15). The "I" symbol shows that Student and Course contribute to the uniqueness of Registration. For this to happen it is necessary for uniqueness constraints to be specified for the contributing classes (i.e., students and courses must have representational uniqueness).

9.5.4   Uniqueness from the introduction of an artificial identifier

To ensure representational uniqueness an artificial identifier can be introduced, such as studentNumber (figure 9.16).

The class diagram in figure 9.16 requires that a unique identifier be given to every instance of Student. This is not entirely dissimilar from the idea of an OID, but studentNumber is a **visible** part of the representation of the Student class, whereas the OID is not. Thus, even in O-O models and in O-O databases it may be necessary to introduce artificial identifiers.

```
Student

studentNumber
nameFirst
nameSecond
dateOfBirth
```

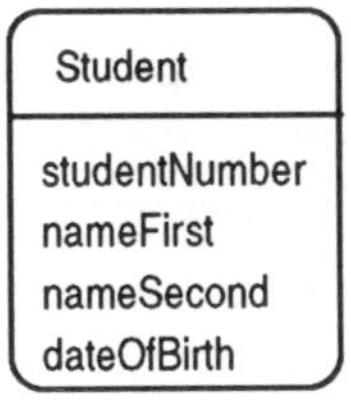

Figure 9.16: *Student class with artificial identifier*

The definition of the student class is now:

        Student
                studentNumber
                nameFirst
                nameSecond
                dateOfBirth
        Unique: studentNumber

But is the specification of representational uniqueness a requirement of the object model? One can argue that artificial identifiers are something introduced into the "real world" and that they are implementation considerations and therefore not relevant to the object model. Data modellers with a strong background in relational theory and relational databases often find it very difficult to let go of the idea that every entity/table must be uniquely identifiable from a combination of its attributes. It is not appropriate to give unthinkingly every class a unique identifier just because the relational model demands it. But it is also often rather difficult to distinguish between artificial and real-world identifiers. Once an identifier is introduced into a computer system and is used it then becomes part of the real world. Artificial identifiers, such as part number, were used in manual systems as a way of ensuring a unique identification well before the introduction of computer systems. Consequently, it is recommended that artificial identifiers are used judiciously, avoiding the extremes of giving everything an artificial identifier or avoiding them altogether.

9.6   Subclasses

Subtype entities are implemented in the data model using one-to-one relationships. The implementation of subtype entities in the data model used the basic concepts established in chapters 2 and 3. Using primary key relationships gave the basic construct of subtype and supertype entities, but became rather convoluted when it came to modelling multiple inheritance. The data model does not provide explicit support for subtypes. Most relational databases do not support subtype structures explicitly either, which means the physical implementation is usually compromised in the interests of performance.

In the object model subclasses are recognized explicitly and differentiated from associations by the presence of a solid triangle. Figure 9.17 (a) is the entity diagram shown in figure 4.11 in chapter 4 with its object model equivalent in figure 9.17 (b). The triangle replaces the arc used in the data model and has the additional benefit of making the subclasses immediately recognizable. The cardinality of the subclasses follows the same convention as that used for exclusivity arcs in the data model. A partial specification of the object model is as follows (note the use of the keyword isKindOf to indicate subclassification):

```
ITStaff
       employeeNumber
       name
       address
Unique:        employeeNumber

SupportStaff isKindOf ITStaff
       mobileTelNumber
```

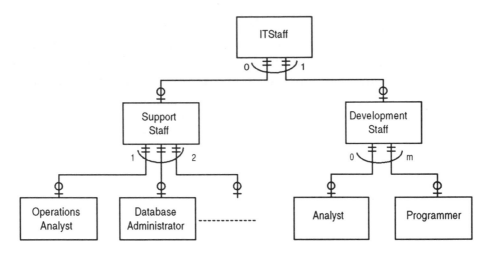

(a) entity diagram - relational data model

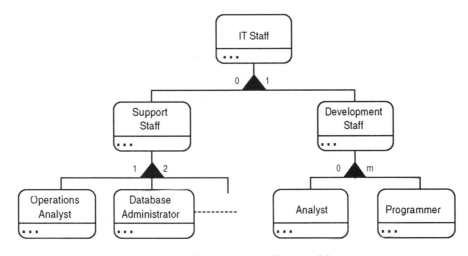

(b) class diagram - object model

Figure 9.17: *Subtypes and subclasses*

DevelopmentStaff isKindOf ITStaff

Analyst isKindOf DevelopmentStaff
    certNumberSSADM
    dateSSADMCertificated

Programmer isKindOf DevelopmentStaff
    dateAttendedJSP

With respect to multiple inheritance, there is no longer a concern with primary and foreign key relationships. It is acceptable to say that a jewelled sword is a kind of treasure and is a kind of weapon. Figure 9.18 (a) is the entity diagram shown in figure 4.18 in chapter 4 with its object model equivalent in figure 9.18 (b).

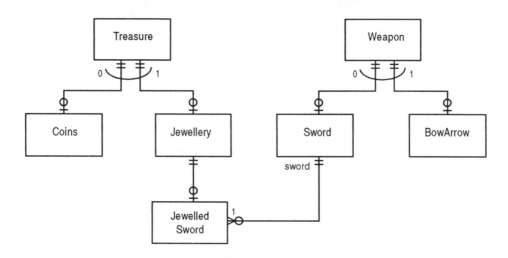

(a) entity diagram - relational data model

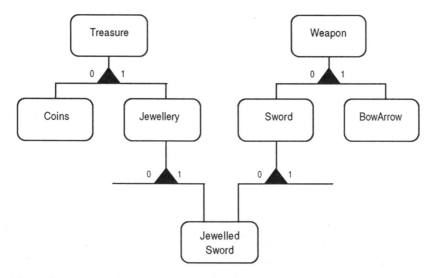

(b) class diagram - object model

Figure 9.18: *Multiple inheritance*

The object model specification for multiple inheritance would be as follows:

JewelledSword isKindOf Jewellery, isKindOf Sword

In the data model, an occurrence of a subtype requires that an occurrence of its supertype entity also exist. The number of tables grows with the number of levels of subtyping, requiring join operations to put the occurrence back together if the implementation is made on a relational database. In the object model subclassification is a distinct concept; the implementation of subtypes through 1:1 relationships is at best a simulation of the classification structures of the object model.

Before leaving multiple inheritance it is perhaps worth pointing out that some modellers would not allow multiple inheritance from different classes since it could be argued that all objects must be classified as one thing or another and that classes should not overlap. A jewelled sword is either a treasure or it is a weapon, but it should not be classified as both; if a jewelled sword is needed then there should be an independent class JewelledSword which duplicates the roles of Treasure and Weapon as necessary. This argument might conclude that multiple inheritance from different classes is a programming trick that should not be used in object modelling. However, taking a pragmatic approach one can argue that multiple inheritance from different classes is not widely used in analysis (hence the use here of the rather contrived example of Treasure and Weapon) and that it is best avoided unless there is a compelling reason to introduce it at the analysis stage.

Chapter summary

This chapter has addressed issues of representation - what the data looks like. Classes are constructed from primitive classes through a process of clustering, which is a bottom-up approach. A top-down approach to class modelling involves levelling where more abstract classes are decomposed until classes with primitive attributes are arrived at. As with data modelling, a combination of top-down and bottom-up approaches is used in practice. Some aspects of the data model are implementation-specific and can lead to artificial models, particularly with respect to identity (primary keys), relationships (foreign keys) and many-to-many relationships. The object model is less restrictive and should help modellers to create a richer and more meaningful model of a situation. Generalization/specialization is a fundamental concept in the object model and can only be approximated through the use of one-to-one relationships in the data model.

NOTES

1. For a description of the benefits and potential of Object-Oriented methods and technology see:

> Martin, J., & Odell, J., (1992). *Object-Oriented Analysis and Design.* Prentice-Hall. Englewood Cliffs.
>
> Graham, I., (1994). *Object-Oriented Methods.* Second edition. Addison Wesley.

2. In some modelling notations it is possible to hang attributes off associations. For example, in OMT (Rumbaugh et al, 1991) the attributes salary and job title would be attached to the employs association:

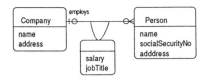

The argument is that salary and jobTitle do not belong to either Company or Person. We do not put attributes on associations and prefer to model this situation using a new class, such as Post:

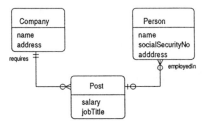

One reason for modelling the association's attributes as a class is that more detail of cardinality can be given. We might also model this situation using a subclass of Person, namely Employee. This means that the employs association, which originally had attributes salary and jobTitle, has been absorbed into a class that reflects the employs association, making a more comfortable home for salary and jobTitle than Person:

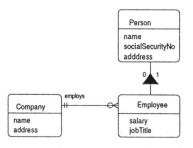

With m:n associations it is not appropriate to introduce a subtype and in such cases the resolving class, although it has attributes of its own, can seem rather artificial (hence the appeal of placing attributes on the association). However, on balance we have chosen to introduce new classes rather than place attributes on associations. For further details of OMT see:

Rumbaugh, J., Blaha, M., Premerlani, W., Eddy, F., Lorensen, W., (1991). *Object-Oriented Modeling and Design*. Prentice-Hall, Englewood Cliffs, New Jersey.

3. For further details of OODBMS see:

Bertino, E., & Martino, M., (1993). *Object-Oriented Database Systems: concepts and architectures*. Addison Wesley.

Hughes, J., (1991). *Object-Oriented Databases*. Prentice-Hall, Englewood Cliffs, New Jersey.

Questions

1. What implementation-specific constraints of the data model can be loosened by the introduction of the object model?

2. Model the following scenario using a class diagram and an equivalent entity diagram:

   a software package must run on one or more hardware platforms;
   a hardware platform may support many software packages.

3. Modify your solution to question 2 to include the memory requirement for each software package (assuming that the memory requirement for any particular software package varies from platform to platform).

4. The BookCopy class is used to represent the individual copies of books held by a library. Multiple copies of a single title, such as "Wuthering Heights", can be held. Model the class BookCopy using each of the following approaches to uniqueness:

   - uniqueness not required;
   - uniqueness from internal roles;
   - uniqueness from external roles;
   - uniqueness from the introduction of an artificial identifier.

   Provide sample attibutes of BookCopy and any other classes to illustrate the different approaches to uniqueness.

5. For each of the approaches to uniqueness adopted above describe how the software representation of a book copy corresponds to a physical copy of a book on the library shelves. Explain how you could take a book at random of the shelf and find its associated instance on a computer system.

6.   Separate classes exist for human resources (Consultant) and for machines (Robot). A new type of resource has been developed that is part human and part robot (Android). Develop an entity diagram and attribute list for Consultant, Robot, and Android. How does your class model differ from the entity diagram produced for question 9 in chapter 4?

7.   The following facts are available:

The Heritage Society maintains details of orchestras. An orchestra must have a name (e.g., Hallé Orchestra), may get an arts council grant (in which case the Society wishes to record the amount of the grant), and must have one principal conductor. Details of conductors required to be held include name, address, and home telephone number (if they are on the telephone). At any one time a conductor may be responsible for only one orchestra. Each orchestra has a repertoire of standard pieces of music (e.g., Beethoven's fifth symphony). Each piece of music is composed by one composer. The Society needs to know the playing time of each standard work. Details held of composers include name, nationality, date of birth, and the date they died (this is not completed for composers who are still alive). Each orchestra hires a number of musicians; each musician may work for only one orchestra at any one time. The Heritage Society wants to record the name and address of all musicians qualified for orchestral work. For those musicians currently hired by an Orchestra the Society needs to record the amount each musician is paid per performance - this is a fixed sum negotiated by each musician on an individual basis. A musician must play one or more instruments. The Society records details of instrument type (e.g., violin) and instrument family (e.g., woodwind, strings) and wishes to be able to report on which types of instrument are played by which musicians.

Represent these facts as an unclustered class diagram.

8.   Cluster the class diagram produced in question 7.

9.   Produce an attribute list for the clustered class diagram produced in question 8.

10.   Specify uniqueness constraints for all of the classes specified in your solution to question 8. Justify any artificial identifiers that you might need to introduce.

10

Further object modelling

Introduction

In this chapter we take the ideas of representation further and explore the
following topics:

- explicit composition structures
- association degree
- time-stamping
- constraints
- generation of a data model

10.1 Composition

In the object model it is useful to be able to show how objects can be made up
from other objects forming **complex** objects. The class diagram in figure 10.1
shows that a car is composed of an engine, body, transmission, and a number
of wheels.

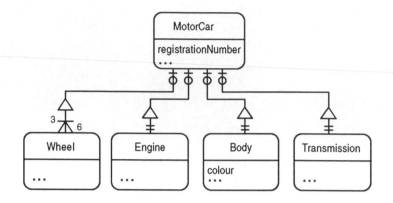

Figure 10.1: *Representation of MotorCar as a composite class*

Each motor car must have one engine, one body, one transmission, and a number of wheels (at least three and no more than 6). At any one time not all wheels, engines, bodies, and transmissions will be part of a motor car and therefore the minimum cardinality of Wheel, Engine, Body, and Transmission with respect to MotorCar is zero. This is an explicit representation of a composition structure, in which the diagramming convention adopted is to use a hollow triangle. Note that composition is different from generalization; engines and wheels are not types of motor car - they are the component parts of a motor car. The composition can also be shown implicitly (figure 10.2).

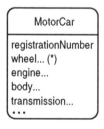

Figure 10.2: *Implicit composition*

The non-primitive attributes of MotorCar are indicated by an attribute name with a suffix of three dots. Repeating attributes are indicated by an asterisk (for example, wheel). Figures 10.1 and 10.2 refer to motor cars; they could be applied to one particular instance of MotorCar, such as the Vauxhall Astra with the registration A184 TGW. The model of the class VehicleModel, an instance of which is Vauxhall Astra, would be different from MotorCar (figure 10.3).

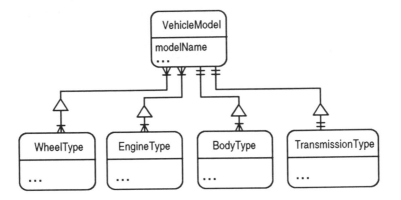

Figure 10.3: *Representation of VehicleModel as a composite class*

Different cardinalities apply to the types of component than to the actual components. A vehicle model can use a number of different types of engine and every type of engine must be used in one or more vehicle models. By contrast, a transmission type must be used on one vehicle model and each vehicle model must have one transmission type.[1] Returning to the Department and Student scenario introduced in chapter 9, we might decide to make Performance a part of Registration (figure 10.4).

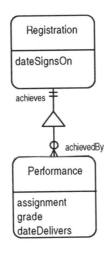

Figure 10.4: *Performance as part of Registration*

In data representation terms the composition structure is a strengthening of an association; from the diagram we can tell that classes linked by composition share a stronger affinity than those linked by associations that do not have a composition triangle. We can show Registration as an implicit structure:

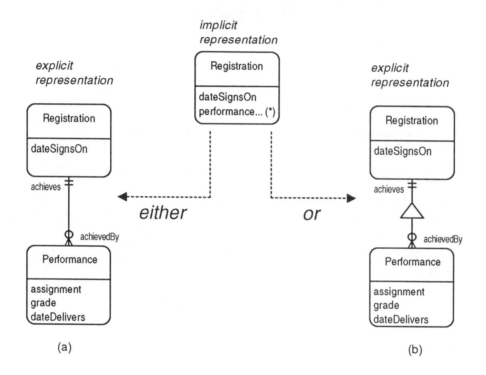

Figure 10.5

Is Registration a composite class? In Figure 10.5 (a) there is no composition symbol linking Performance to Registration. The implicit representation of Registration is in this case just a technique that can be used to simplify the diagram for presentation purposes. Figure 10.5 (b) shows that there is a stronger association between Performance and Registration and although it does not have great significance for the representational aspects of the class specifications, we will see in chapter 11 that there are implications for the behavioural aspects of the class specifications. In the data model the implicit structure is illegal since it has repeating items, which is a violation of first normal form. In the data model the implicit structure must be represented as in figure 10.5 (a).

We can use composition to good effect in the well-worn customer order scenario (figure 10.6).

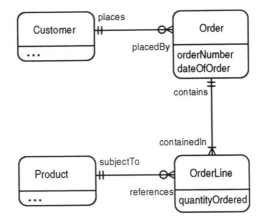

Figure 10.6: *Customer order*

In figure 10.7, OrderLine is modelled as a component part of Order.

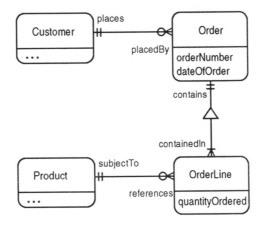

Figure 10.7: *Order shown as a composition*

An order comprises the attributes orderNumber and dateOfOrder together with one or more order lines. Suppressing the component parts of the order class results in the class diagram in figure 10.8.

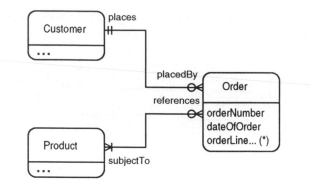

Figure 10.8: *Order with component parts suppressed*

It is necessary to show the association between Order and Product with cardinality of many-to-many as now each order must be associated with one or more products and each product may be associated with many orders. Showing implicit composition is a technique that can be used to simplify the class diagram, although by doing so we are hiding some of the details of the data representation.   However, when data behaviour is considered composition becomes a useful technique since it is possible to focus on how the instances of the composite class Order behave without being distracted by the internal representation of an order.

Representing figure 10.8 in textual format, using the clause isPartOf to indicate composition, gives:

        Order
                orderNumber
                dateOfOrder

        OrderLine isPartOf Order
                quantityOrdered

The relationships contained in figure 10.6 (Order without composition) and figure 10.7 (Order with composition) are the same:

class	function	class	inverse function	class
Customer	places	Order	isPlacedBy	Customer
Order	contains	OrderLine	containedIn	Order
Product	subjectTo	OrderLine	references	Product

The implicit structure in figure 10.8, once broken down into its component classes, is also represented by the above table.

In conclusion, composition structures are a useful means of incorporating more meaning in a data model by strengthening associations. With respect to data representation the implicit representation of composition structures is for diagramming purposes only. Composition structures have further implications when it comes to adding data behaviour to the model (chapter 11). Although the composition structure is not relevant to the data model since the data model does not address the behaviour of data, composition could be used as a presentation (diagramming) technique to show stronger relationships between entities.

10.2 Association degree

10.2.1 Binary associations

The associations and relationships considered so far have been of binary degree. Relationships in the data model presented in part 1 are always binary. Figure 10.9 shows a binary association between Department and Employee that represents two facts:

a department may employ many employees
and
an employee must be employed by one department

Figure 10.9: *Binary association*

The binary association is of degree two; there are two classes participating in an association.

10.2.2 Ternary associations

In the object model it is possible to have associations of degree higher than two. An association of degree three is known as a ternary association. For

example, consider the situation where a product may be represented by
many sales-persons in many cities (figure 10.10)[2].

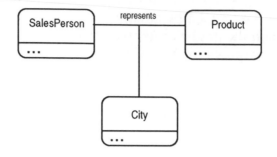

Figure 10.10: *Ternary association*

In figure 10.10 the represents association comprises a sales person, a city, and
a product, but without any specification of cardinality. Introducing a new
class is one way of modelling a ternary association - by decomposing it into
three binary associations (figure 10.11).

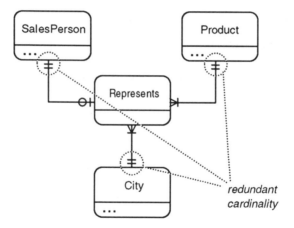

Figure 10.11: *Ternary association - resolving class*

From figure 10.11 we can tell that each product must be represented one or
more times, every city must be represented one or more times, and each
salesPerson may be a representative only once. We refer to these as
participative cardinalities. However, the Represents class is attempting to
fulfil the role of a ternary association with the result that much of the
potential richness has been lost in the graphical notation. As each instance of
Represents must be for one city, one product, and one salesPerson (this must

be true since the Represents class is modelling an association) the cardinalities of SalesPerson, City and Product are redundant. Perhaps we can put these slots to better use.

By introducing a new notation for associative classes the interpretation of the data model for ternary associations can be enhanced. This is indicated by the placing of a diamond within the Represents class box (figure 10.12).

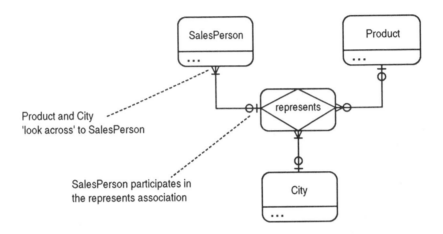

Figure 10.12: *Ternary association - resolving with an associative class*

In figure 10.12 the redundant slots are used to show "look across" cardinalities for the different pairs of classes. This means that we can infer from the diagram that:

- Each combination of salesPerson and city may represent at most one product;

- Each combination of salesPerson and product may be represented in at most one city;

- Each combination of city and product must be represented by one or more salesPersons.

The look across cardinality of city and product to salesPerson has a minimum value of one. This means that all combinations of city and product must exist in the represents associative class and be represented by at least one sales person. If there are p cities and q products than there will be (p * q) combinations that must be involved in ternary associations. Given two products and two cities the following combinations must be represented:

Product	City
Whizzo	Birmingham
Whizzo	Manchester
Zappo	Birmingham
Zappo	Manchester

The participation cardinalities remain unchanged and are interpreted as in figure 10.11. The data in figure 10.13 is consistent with the class diagram shown in figure 10.12.

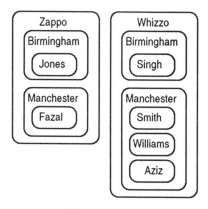

Figure 10.13

Ternary associations are always implemented using additional tables in the data model (figure 10.14). In this case the Represents entity becomes a subtype of SalesPerson and is renamed. If a sales person is allowed to represent more than one product or the same product in more than one city then the data model would become as in 10.14 (a), albeit with different cardinalities.

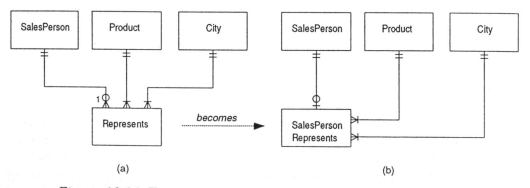

(a)   (b)

Figure 10.14: *Ternary association simulated by binary relationships*

Since the ternary association must be reduced to binary relationships it is not possible to represent the meaning of figure 10.13 in the data model; constraints would need to be specified separately to capture the business rules.

10.2.3   Associations of degree higher than three

In theory it is possible to have associations of degree four and higher. In practice associations of degree greater than three are uncommon. Most situations can be modelled using binary associations together with, to a much lesser extent, ternary associations.

10.3   Time-stamping

Chapter 5 showed how time could be modelled for attributes, entities, and relationships. Recording the history of attributes, classes, and associations over time is a common requirement and can be specified in the object model in shorthand.

10.3.1   Attribute time-stamping

Where the history of an attribute is required then in the clustered class the attribute is flagged with a "t" as in figure 10.15.

Figure 10.15: *Attribute time-stamp*

10.3.2   Association time-stamping

Associations may be time-stamped by the addition of a box to the association line (figure 10.16).

Figure 10.16: *Association time-stamp*

Time-stamping is a useful way of capturing a requirement to record the history of attributes, classes, and associations over time without complicating the diagram by modelling time using time classes. In chapter 5 data models that model time were shown and some further comparisons between object and data models are given in appendix A.

10.4   Object model constraints

Constraints have already been introduced in data modelling. There is no way of automatically enforcing constraints in the data model and as a result relational DBMSs tend to handle constraints in a variety of ways, from ignoring them altogether (in which case they have to be coded into application programs) to using triggers. The introduction of constraints sits rather better in the object model as it is possible to specify how the data behaves as well as how it is represented (this is discussed in chapter 11).

We will consider constraints that could apply to classes and to associations.

10.4.1   Class constraints

Examples of class constraints are: a car's mileage cannot decrease over time; the number of wheels must be more than two and less than seven (figure 10.17).

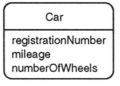

(mileage cannot decrease)
(2 < numberOfWheels < 7)

Figure 10.17: *Class constraints*

10.4.2   Association constraints

An example of an association constraint that is particularly useful (especially as it violates relational theory) is to make an association ordered. For example, although we have tended to model people's names as fixed in size (e.g., firstName, secondName) some people have many given names (perhaps they were named after a football team). If this is something of interest in the situation being modelled then we will want to show a m:n association between Person and GivenName; moreover we will want to preserve the order of the names. In a data model this would require that a sequence number is added to the primary key of the resolving entity, PersonGivenName. In the conceptual model we can represent this situation as in figure 10.18 (a), which can be read to mean each person must have one or more ordered given names. Clustering the class GivenName into Person gives figure 10.18 (b) (for diagramming purposes).

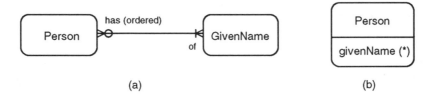

Figure 10.18: *Association constraint*

In chapter 5 we considered a constraint whereby the manager of a store must also be an employee of that store. In figure 10.19 this requirement is specified by the inclusion of a dotted line between the two associations.

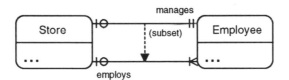

Figure 10.19: *Inter-association constraint*

10.5   From object model to data model

In this chapter some entity diagram equivalents for class diagrams have been shown (a fuller comparison is included in appendix A) in order to show firstly how the object and data models differ and to show secondly how a data model can be produced from an object model. To produce a data model it is necessary to specify uniqueness constraints for all the clustered classes in the object model. It is then possible to generate the data model automatically from the object model by the application of a set of rules - it *should* be possible to get your CASE tool to do this for you. Ternary associations will necessarily lose some of the richness of the diagramming convention introduced in this chapter.

Consider the unclustered object model represented in figure 10.20.

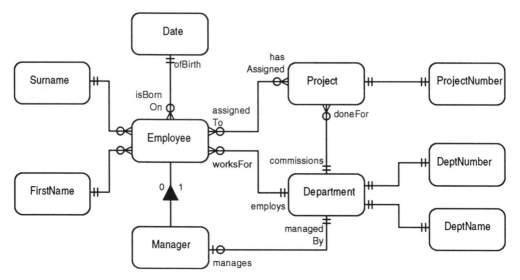

Figure 10.20: *Unclustered object model*

Clustering the object model in figure 10.20 results in figure 10.21.

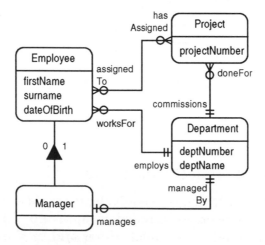

Figure 10.21: *Clustered object model*

If a data model is to be generated automatically from the clustered object data model it is essential that uniqueness constraints are specified for each clustered class.

The object model specification with uniqueness clauses is:

```
Employee
        firstName
        surname
        dateOfBirth
Unique:         firstName,
                surname

Manager isKindOf Employee

Department
        deptNumber
        deptName
Unique:         deptNumber
Unique:         deptName

Project
        projectNumber
Unique:         projectNumber
```

The associations in the object model are:

class	function	class	inverse function	class
Employee	worksFor	Department	employs	Employee
Employee	assignedTo	Project	hasAssigned	Employee
Manager	manages	Department	managedBy	Manager
Department	commissions	Project	doneFor	Department

A data model can now be generated from the object data model as in figure 10.22. The many-to-many association between Project and Employee has been resolved through the introduction of the entity EmployeeProject. This entity can be derived from the presence of a m:n cardinality and has a primary key that is generated from the unique identifiers of the two contributing classes. The one-to-one association between Department and Manager requires that a decision be made concerning which entity will hold the foreign key - in this example we have nominated Department. Where there is more than one unique clause then the modeller will need to specify which is to be used to identify class instances uniquely when generating a data model. Any unique clauses that include optional attributes can be discounted since the attributes making up a primary key are mandatory.

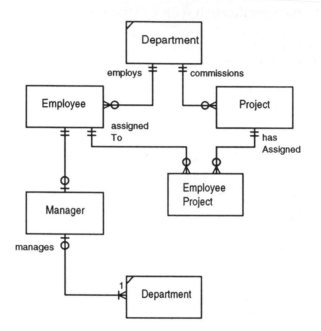

Figure 10.22: *Entity diagram*

Note that date has not emerged as an entity. This is because date is not used as part of a primary key in this simple example. In a data model an attribute that is part of a primary key becomes an entity in its own right and then appears in the Foreign clause of all the entities to which it is related, whether the relationship is a foreign key relationship or a primary key relationship. By making Date a root entity it would be possible to have it generated in the logical data model regardless of whether or not it formed part of a primary key.

The attribute list of the entity diagram is:

    Employee
            firstName
            surname
            dateOfBirth

    Manager
            firstName

surname
Foreign: firstName,
                        surname → Employee

Department
    deptNumber
    deptName
    firstNameManages
    surnameManages
Foreign: firstNameManages,
                        surnameManages → Manager

Project
    projectNumber
    deptNumberCommissions
Foreign: deptNumberCommissions → Department

EmployeeProject
    firstName
    surname
    projectNumber
Foreign: firstName, surname → Employee
Foreign: projectNumber → Project

10.5.1   Time-stamping

Now assume that the association between Employee and Department is to be time-stamped to provide a history of the departments that an employee has worked in. The section of the model affected by this requirement is shown in figure 10.23.

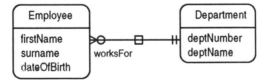

Figure 10.23: *Time-stamped association*

The association definition must be extended to show the maximum frequency of the time-stamping, which could be, for example, annually, monthly, daily, hourly. Assuming that the maximum frequency needed for this association is daily then the associations will be modified as follows:

class	function	class	inverse function	class	time stamp
Employee	worksFor	Department	employs	Employee	daily
Employee	assignedTo	Project	hasAssigned	Employee	
Manager	manages	Department	managedBy	Manager	
Department	commissions	Project	doneFor	Department	

The resultant data model for the Employee worksFor Department association is shown in figure 10.24.

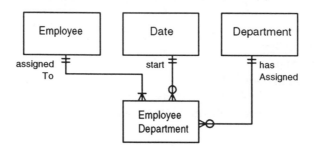

Figure 10.24: *Entity diagram for a time-stamped association*

10.5.2   Multiple levels of clustering on the class diagram

For the data model not to violate principles of normalization all the attributes of clustered classes (i.e., those classes that have been clustered into other classes) must be primitive. This means that classes may only be clustered to one level if repeating data items are to be avoided. In the Car class it will not be permissible to produce a data model with the attribute colourOfBodywork if this attribute is itself made up of further attributes. Figure 10.25 (a) shows the unclustered object model, (b) shows it clustered to one level, and (c) to two levels.

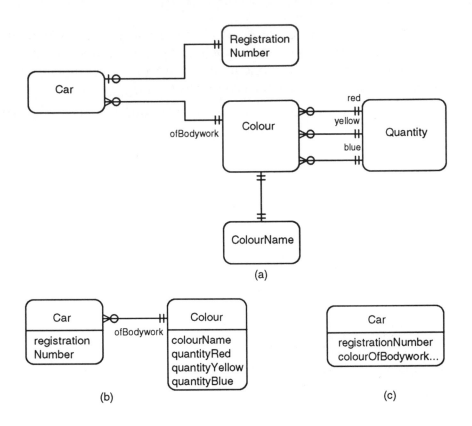

Figure 10.25: *Class diagram for Car*

The specification of the classes and associations will be as follows:

Car
      registrationNumber

Colour
      colourName
      quantityRed
      quantityYellow
      quantityBlue

class	function	class	inverse function	class
Car	hasBodywork	Colour	ofBodywork	Car

In the above example we have not made Colour a component of Car. If we did then the Colour class specification would include the clause isPartOf Car. Colour could well form a component of a number of composite classes, requiring one isPartOf clause for each composition.

In the data model we would settle for 10.25 (b) and model it as in figure 10.26.

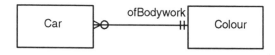

Figure 10.26: *Entity diagram for Car*

The attribute list that corresponds to figure 10.25 (b) is:

    Car
            registrationNumber
            colourOfBodywork
        Foreign: colourOfBodywork → Colour

    Colour
            colourName
            quantityRed
            quantityYellow
            quantityBlue

Chapter summary

In this chapter explicit composition structures were introduced to give a greater representational richness. Composition structures have further significance in the object model when it comes to adding data behaviour to data representation. Association cardinality of degree greater than two was introduced and enhanced using a combination of look across and participation. Shorthand notations for the time-stamping of attributes, class instances, and associations have been introduced in the object model; these structures can be expanded and implemented in a data model, the generic structures already having been described in chapter 5. Constraints can be used to specify rules that cannot be expressed using classes and associations. Finally, the mapping of an object model into a data model was illustrated.

NOTES

1. This situation can also be modelled using a bill of materials for the Vehicle Model class
    and a hierarchy for the MotorCar class. Vehicle models may use many types of engine,
    and an engine type may be used by many vehicle models. But a motor car must have one
    engine and an engine may be used in only one motor car. The bill of materials can be
    modelled recursively (see chapter 5) for component types (a component type can be
    anything from a type of bolt up to a vehicle model) and as a hierarchy for components (a
    component is an individual bolt up to a complete motor car):

    There is a constraint between these two recursive structures as we do not want to allow a
    car to be fitted with the wrong type of engine for its model. By introducing subclasses it is
    possible to show that some component types are engine types, wheel types, etc., and that
    some components are engines, wheels, motor cars, etc. For components the class diagram
    is:

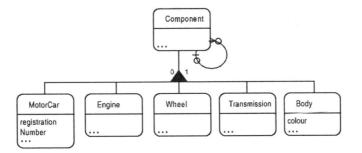

2. This example and technique have been taken from:
    Ferg, S., (1991). Cardinality Concepts in Entity-Relationship Modeling. In: T. J.
        Teorey (ed.), *Proceedings of the 10th International Conference on the Entity Relationship
        Approach*. San Mateo, Ca.

Questions

1. Prepare a class diagram using an assembly structure to show how the
    different components (monitor, base unit, disk drives, chips, etc.) build
    up into a personal computer.

2.   Printers can be of type laser or dot matrix and may supply printing services to many personal computers. Each computer may be attached to one printer. Extend the class diagram produced in question 1 to include printers and prepare a set of class definitions.

3.   Represent the personal computer assembly structure as a single class, PersonalComputer.

4.   Prepare a class diagram in which bicycles are represented as an assembly structure. Redesign the class diagram to show bicycles represented as a recursive structure with subclasses. What are the benefits of each of these different representations?

5.   Some of the properties offered for rent by an estate management company have gardens, some have central heating boilers, and some have both. The estate management company contracts service companies to maintain the gardens and boilers of those properties that have them. They need to maintain a history of the service companies contracted to maintain each property for insurance purposes. The company also offers properties for sale and wishes to capture each change to the selling price made by the vendor of the property. Produce a suitable class diagram for these aspects of the rental company without using time-stamping.

6.   Modify the class diagram produced in question 5 to include time-stamping and produce a class and association definitions.

7.   What are the rules for producing a data model from an object model?

8.   Develop a data model (entity diagram and attribute list) from the object model produced in question 6.

9.   Generate a data model for the following class

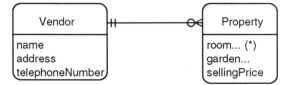

Assume that room and garden are described by primitive attributes such as width and breadth when developing the data model (devise appropriate attributes).

10.   How are compositions (assembly structures) in an object model represented in a data model?

11

Modelling behaviour

Introduction

So far, we have dealt exclusively with modelling data structures. The reasons for taking data as the starting point were discussed in the introduction to the book. Perhaps the most enduring myth of systems development is that a model of the data provides a more stable basis for the development of computer systems than does a model of the business processes. This idea has been enshrined in traditional structured development methods, although how effectively it has permeated through practice is more debatable. All of our dearly held beliefs come up for reappraisal at some time and data-centred development is no exception. Its primacy is being questioned as process-driven methods begin to be reasserted. It may be that this is fuelled in part by technological innovations such as group working software (e.g., Lotus Notes) and a general interest in all aspects of computer-supported cooperative work (CSCW). A process orientation can also be expected to be popular in response to Business Process Reengineering (BPR) initiatives. The primary emphasis in BPR is on defining purposeful activity and processes. However, Information Technology is not just for automation of old processes and neither is it merely technical support for new (reengineered) processes - it is also an enabler that can allow us to do things that would not have been possible previously, even if we could have imagined them.[1]

This book is concerned with data modelling. However, all data models have to make contact with the organization of work and the processes that are to be supported and data modellers cannot develop data structures without an understanding of the activity that the model in its implemented form will support. The object model described thus far addresses the *representation* of an organization's data. In this chapter the object model is extended to include the *behaviour* of the data. Behaviour is concerned with how instances change over time in response to business events.

The behavioural data model provides a step towards application functionality, but it still represents a viewpoint that is predominantly that of the system developer. The user is concerned with how a computer system might help them carry out their work in an organizational context, i.e., the functional requirements. This chapter is concerned with the behaviour of data rather than the functional requirements per se; the next chapter addresses the specification of functional requirements from a process perspective.

11.1   Adding behaviour to the data model

Having introduced some of the core elements of the O-O paradigm, namely classes, generalization/specialization and inheritance of representation, and composition, it is now time to look at the O-O paradigm in a little more depth before considering how behaviour can be added to an object model. The key concepts that will be covered here are: encapsulation, communication by messages, and inheritance.

11.1.1   Encapsulation

Encapsulation requires a service view of data (what does the object do?) to be adopted rather than an implementation view (how is the object constructed?). The representation of the object is hidden and therefore the only means of accessing and modifying an instance of a class is via the external interface operations defined for that instance's class.

The external interface operations supported by a class are known as **methods,** and the only way of changing the state of an object is by the invocation of an appropriate method. A method specifies the way in which the object will behave when it receives a message. For example, we would expect the Order class to support a method such as acceptOrder, which when invoked will cause a new instance of the class Order to be created. How the method is implemented is hidden from the sender of the message. The only way of communicating with an object is by invoking a method supported by the class of which the object receiving the message is a member. The packaging of the behaviour of the data with the representation is referred to as **encapsulation.**

11.1.2   Communication by messages

The concept of encapsulation (or information hiding) implies the need for instances of classes to communicate via narrowly defined interfaces using messages. There is no data sharing between instances of different classes. The methods supported by a class are invoked by the sending of a message.

Consider the unclustered data model of the class Car shown in figure 11.1 (a). By clustering the Car class the model in figure 11.1 (b) is arrived at.

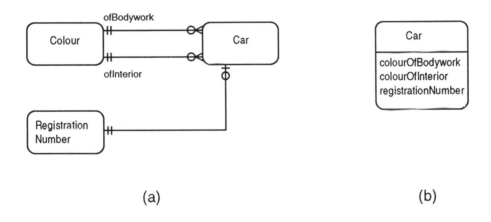

(a)   (b)

Figure 11.1: *Object model fragment for Car class*

Encapsulation requires the data structure of the Car class to be hidden. To change the bodywork colour of a car requires that a message be sent with a colour as an argument (the colour used as an argument is an object that is of the class Colour). The method invoked is responsible for changing the representation of the car object. To find out what colour interior a car has also requires a message to be sent because direct inspection of an attribute value would violate the requirement for encapsulation. In the case of finding out the interior colour, the method name is the same as the attribute name (although it need not be) - invoking the method will result in the return of an object that is of the class Colour. How the method is executed and how the representation of car objects is maintained is hidden from the sender of the message.

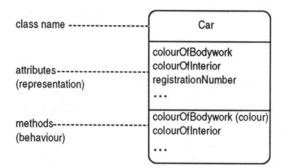

Figure 11.2: *Classes - attributes and methods*

The object model will now be extended to incorporate methods (how the data behaves) in addition to the representation (what it looks like) (figure 11.2). Representation and behaviour are encapsulated: the representation of an object is hidden and any requests to see or change the data must be made by passing messages that invoke methods.

To illustrate the idea of messages and methods figure 11.3 shows an instance of the class Car. Instances are depicted by rectangles, thus differentiating them from classes, which are shown as rounded rectangles. Sending the message colourOfBodywork (orange) to an instance of Car will invoke a method that will alter the representation of the car object receiving the message. Sending the message colourOfInterior without any arguments will result in "black" being returned (an object of the class Colour).

As methods are the only way of accessing the representation of an object, if there is no method specified for an attribute then that attribute is effectively invisible to the outside world. In figure 11.3 if the method colourOfBodywork is not specified then it is possible to change the colour of a car's bodywork by using the method colourOfBodywork (colour), but it is not possible to determine what the current colour of bodywork is.

car object (instance of class Car)

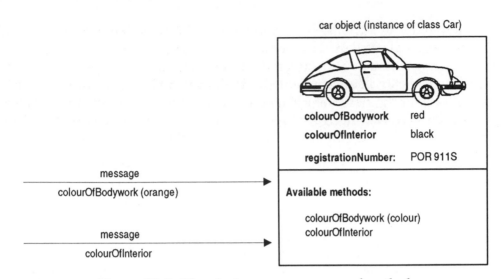

Figure 11.3: *Class instances - messages and methods*

11.1.3   Inheritance

Using the class structure, subclasses can inherit both representation and behaviour from superclasses. Representation (attributes and associations) are inherited by subclasses.

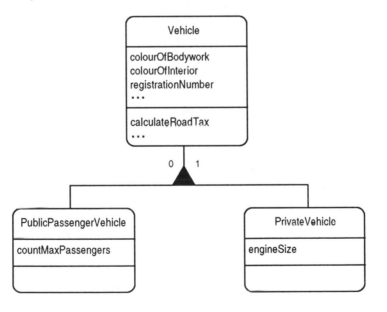

Figure 11.4: *Inheritance of behaviour*

For example, if the attribute colourOfPaintworkBody is defined for the class Vehicle, then that attribute is inherited by all subclasses of Vehicle, such as PublicPassengerVehicle and PrivateVehicle. The methods supported by the class structure can also be inherited. If the method calculateRoadTax has been defined for the class Vehicle then it can also be inherited by the different subclasses of Vehicle. In figure 11.4 the method calculateRoadTax is defined for the Vehicle class and then inherited by its subclasses.

Where the basis for calculation of road tax is different by class then the subclasses can re-implement the method calculateRoadTax. In figure 11.5 PublicPassengerVehicle calculates road tax based upon the number of passengers the vehicle is licenced to carry and PrivateVehicle on the basis of engine size. Any other vehicles that are occurrences of the superclass vehicle will use the original calculateRoadTax method. The methods inherited from a superclass can, as appropriate, either be re-used by the subclass or overridden (i.e., behaviour is redefined). Where it is not appropriate for a subclass to inherit a method from its superclass then this can be indicated by giving the method the suffix "(x)" in the subclass.

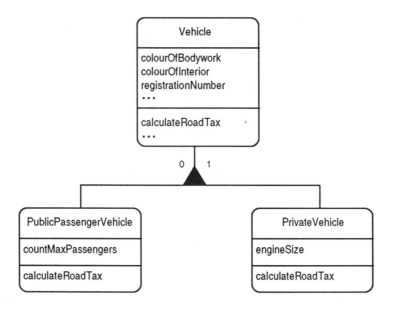

Figure 11.5: *Redefining behaviour*

There is now seen to be another good reason for introducing generalization/specialization: things may not only be representationally different - they may behave differently as well.

Multiple inheritance

Multiple inheritance has already been introduced with respect to the representation of an object. Behaviour can also be subject to multiple inheritance. Although multiple inheritance is a powerful technique, it can lead to conflicts when applied to object behaviour. Using the example of DevelopmentStaff, assume that both Analyst and Programmer implement the method calculateBonus in different ways (figure 11.6). AnalystProgrammer might inherit the method calculateBonus from Analyst, from Programmer, or redefine the method altogether.

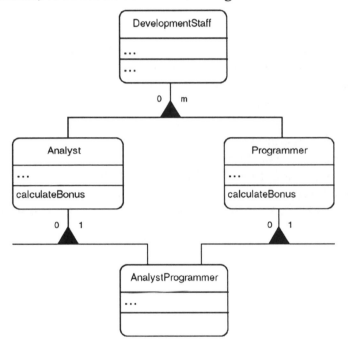

Figure 11.6: *Multiple inheritance and behaviour*

The introduction of multiple inheritance (whether it be multiple inheritance within a class or from different classes) to the data model can result in ambiguity where behaviour is concerned. Multiple inheritance should be used with some caution when specifying requirements and any ambiguities must be clarified.

11.1.4   Polymorphism

Because all objects know what class they belong to they know which methods they can respond to. The same method can apply to many classes and result in different behaviour depending upon the class of the object. Assume that the class Clock has the subclasses Analogue and Digital. Clocks of both types will respond to the message displayTime but will behave differently. The sender of the message need not be aware of the type of clock the recipient is when sending the message displayTime - the recipient will respond according to its class. New types of clock can be added, e.g., SunDial, and as long as the new subclasses support the generic method displayTime then no further changes will be needed to the clock system.

11.2   States and events

Now that the basics of the O-O paradigm have been introduced we will look at the relationship between representation and behaviour through the notion of states and events. The class diagrams introduced so far have been largely static. Over time, associations between instances change, reflecting the dynamic aspects of a situation. To illustrate the way in which data (representation) can change over time an example will be developed using a car rental company. The Rental Company accepts bookings from corporate account customers and then invoices them at the end of the month for all bookings that have been fulfilled (i.e., a vehicle has been made available) during that month. A booking may be in a number of different **states** during its life. For example, when a booking is first created it is in the state accepted; when the booking has been fulfilled and an invoice raised, the state of the booking will be invoiced. Assume that the possible states a booking may take are as shown in figure 11.7.

State
Accepted
Scheduled
Fulfilled
Invoiced
Paid
Cancelled
Archived

Figure 11.7: *Booking states*

How does a booking come into existence, change state (e.g., from accepted to scheduled) and finally die, that is, cease to be a fact that is of interest to the organization? States need to be considered jointly with events. An **event** is something that happens; for example, the fire alarm goes off, the telephone bill arrives, or, it starts to snow. Events are what cause the state of an object to change. Event-driven programming is used extensively in GUIs (graphical user interfaces), such as those that use Windows style interfaces. In event-driven programming, an object can be imagined as something waiting for an event to occur, such as, a user clicking the left hand button on the mouse, entering a string of text, or closing an application window. Events can be generated internally as well as externally; a clock function signals the end of a time interval, or another application requests a service.

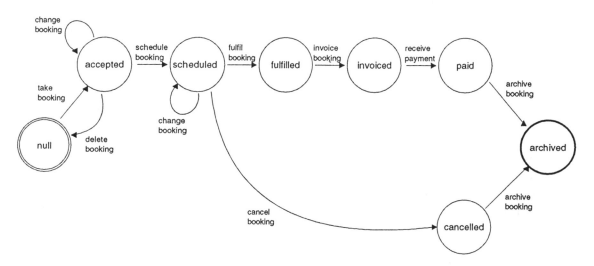

Figure 11.8: *State transition diagram for Booking*

An event may result in the state of an object changing. A change in state, for example where a fulfilled booking becomes an invoiced booking, is referred to as a **state transition**. Given a set of possible states that instances of the Booking class may be in, not all of the possible state transitions will be permissible - a booking should not be allowed, for example, to change from accepted to invoiced. Clearly, a means of defining which state transitions are valid is needed. In figure 11.8 a state transition diagram for the Booking class is shown. The circles represent the states that instances of the Booking class may hold. The vectors (arrows) represent the possible changes in state that a booking may be subjected to. The state changes are labelled with the event that causes the change in state.

11.2.1 Creation states

The null state is used to show the starting point and is shown within double circles. The null state represents a booking that does not yet exist. The creation state of a booking is accepted - this is the state of a booking when it becomes of interest to the system under consideration. This is not to say that the object necessarily does not exist in the problem situation, only that we are not currently interested in it. For example, when an employee is hired, the state of the employee might change from null to hired. Before the event hire employee took place the employee was in the null state because it was not of interest to the system under consideration. Obviously, the person to be hired had an existence prior to being hired as an employee, as reflected perhaps by that person's record on the social security system. But, until they take on the role isEmployedBy they are not a member of the class Employee.

By showing the null state it is possible to see the different creation states that an object may take as any transition from the null state represents alternative creation states. In the Booking example, there is only one creation state, accepted, but other classes might allow multiple creation states. Removing an instance from the Booking class is accomplished by making the state of the booking null. In figure 11.8 only accepted bookings can be removed: the event delete booking results in accepted bookings being put into the state null (i.e., removed from the Booking class). Once a booking has progressed beyond the accepted state it cannot be removed other than to become archived.

11.2.2   Cyclic transitions

Some events do not result in a change of state. For example, although the start date of an accepted booking can be changed, following this event the booking will still be in the state accepted. These events are shown as cyclic transitions (figure 11.9).

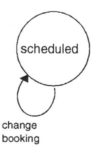

Figure 11.9: *Cyclical transition*

11.2.3   Closing states

The closing state is shown by a thicker circle. A class may allow multiple closing states, although in the case of Booking the only allowable closing state is archived. We will assume in this example that bookings in the state archived are outside the scope of the system, that is, they do not exist as far as the booking system is concerned. Archived bookings may still exist in manual files, on microfiche, or on computer bulk storage, they are just no longer relevant to the system under investigation.

11.2.4   Transitions - classes and instances

We must differentiate between the state transitions that are permissible for the class and the state transitions that apply to an instance of a class. Figure 11.8 showed the patterns of state transitions that are applicable to instances of the Booking class. Any individual booking (an instance of Booking) will find its own way through the generic Booking life cycle. For example, one particular booking might be created (i.e., accepted) only to be immediately deleted. Another booking might go through the more common cycle of accepted, scheduled, fulfilled, invoiced, paid, and archived.

11.2.5   Fence diagrams

In common with most areas of systems analysis, states and state transitions can be expressed using a variety of notations. The state transition diagram in figure 11.8 can be represented equivalently using a "fence" diagram (figure 11.10).

Not all classes will require state transition diagrams. Some classes may have instances that are either null or exists (i.e., have a single state as far as the system is concerned). Figure 11.11 shows a trivial life cycle for the class Customer.

Booking

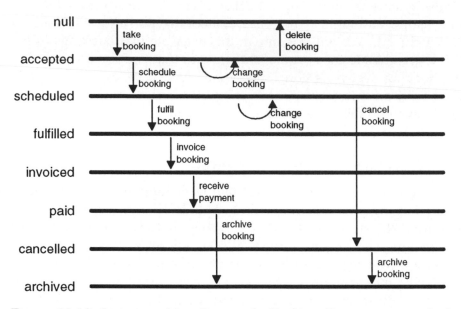

Figure 11.10: *State transition diagram for Booking (fence representation)*

Customer

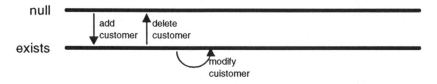

Figure 11.11: *State transition diagram for Customer*

Up until this point the representation of data structures has concentrated on the static aspects. What impact do dynamic aspects have upon a data model? In the next section the dynamic aspects of states and state transitions are represented in an object model.

11.3 Dynamic aspects of an object model

Given the states supported by the Booking class (figure 11.7), how might these states be represented in an object model? Each of the possible states of Booking instances must be capable of being reflected in an object model. The state of an object can be determined by an inspection of its representation, i.e., by the attributes and associations maintained by the object. When a booking is in the null state it is defined to be outside of the scope of the system under consideration and is consequently not shown in the object model. Similarly, bookings in the state archived are no longer of interest to the system and do not appear in the object model. Those bookings that are in the state accepted are shown in figure 11.12.

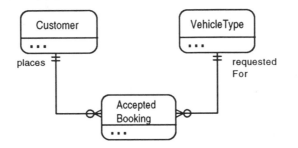

Figure 11.12: *Class diagram for bookings in the state accepted*

Bookings that have been accepted must be associated with one customer and with a vehicle type (e.g., economy, touring, executive, luxury, etc.). Once a booking has been scheduled then it must be associated with a specific vehicle. In some situations this vehicle might be of a different type from that requested when the booking was accepted, and it is a requirement to maintain a record of the vehicle type requested when the booking was accepted. Those bookings that have been scheduled are shown in figure 11.13.

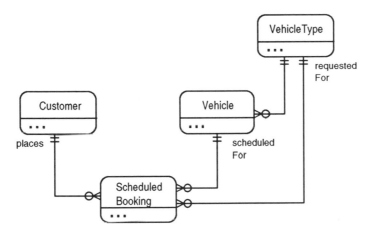

Figure 11.13: *Class diagram for bookings in the state scheduled*

When the booking is fulfilled it is possible that the vehicle supplied is different from that scheduled, perhaps because the vehicle failed a pre-booking inspection. The Rental Company needs to record which vehicle was actually supplied to fulfil the booking (figure 11.14).

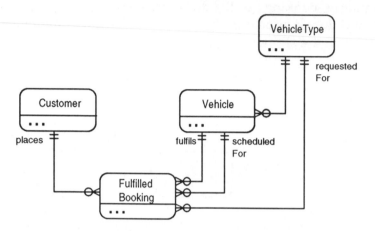

Figure 11.14: *Class diagram for bookings in the state fulfilled*

Invoices are raised at the end of each month for all those bookings that are in the state fulfilled. If we assume that the association between a booking and a customer is non-transferable then, once an invoice has been raised, the association between Customer and Booking becomes redundant - it can be derived through the association of Booking with Invoice and Invoice with Customer (figure 11.15).

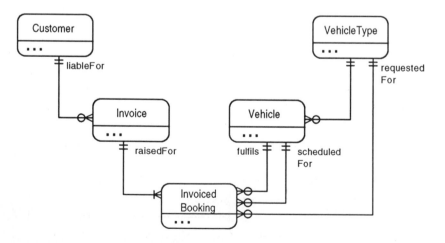

Figure 11.15: *Class diagram for bookings in the state invoiced*

Once the invoice associated with a booking has been paid, the state of the booking changes to paid. Rather more accurately, the association of the booking changes from an association with an invoice in the state unpaid to one with an invoice in the state paid. Thus, interactions take place between instances of Booking and instances of Invoice, where the state of the Invoice instances may contribute to the state of Booking instances. Bookings that are in the state paid are represented in figure 11.16. For illustration purposes, the simplifying assumption has been made that invoices are either unpaid or paid in full. Once an invoice is (fully) paid then all of the bookings associated with that invoice are classified as paid.

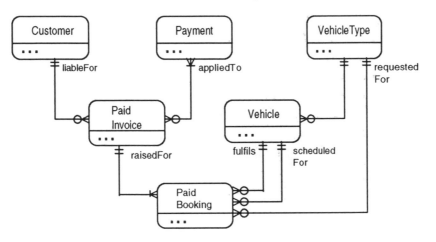

Figure 11.16: *Class diagram for bookings in the state paid*

The life of the booking has been characterized by the acquisition and relinquishment of associations as state changes take place in response to events. To show this situation in a single, static class diagram loses some of the richness. In figure 11.17, some of the associations have to be shown as optional. Bookings that have just been created do not have a vehicle scheduled and the vehicle that will fulfil the booking is not known. A booking will be associated with a customer in the early part of its life, but once an invoice is raised, the customer can be derived from the Invoice/Customer association. Thus in the static class diagram Booking is shown to have a mutually exclusive association with Customer and Invoice, requiring that both associations are shown to be optional (although the cardinality of the exclusivity arc means that, at any one time, a booking must maintain one (and only one) of the associations included in the exclusivity clause). And this is how we often end up modelling data, attempting to capture the dynamic aspects of data in an essentially static representation.

The class diagram in figure 11.17 allows the different Booking states to be represented. However, it is the series of data structures in figures 11.12 through 11.16 (together with a state transition diagram) that give a more meaningful representation of the way the data can change over time.

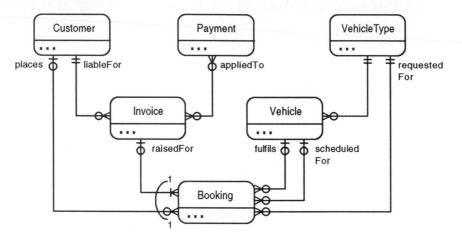

Figure 11.17: *Static class diagram for Booking*

11.3.1   States and subclasses

We have seen that the state of a booking is defined by its representation in data. In chapter 4 we saw that an exclusivity arc usually indicates that the introduction of subtypes should be considered. Similarly, in the object model an exclusivity arc can be replaced by a generalization/specialization structure: the subclasses InvoicedBooking and UninvoicedBooking could be added to remove the exclusivity arc. Taking this further, it is possible to see all of the booking states as subtypes (figure 11.18).

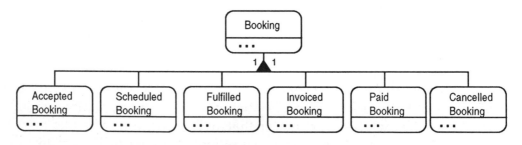

Figure 11.18: *Booking states represented as subclasses*

The subclass cardinality requires all bookings to be in one and only one state. The state subclassification of Booking is orthogonal to any other subclassification of Booking that might be made for the purposes of generalization/specialization of static representation.

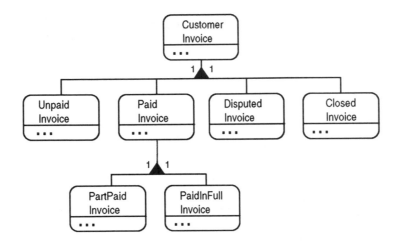

Figure 11.19: *States and substates*

States can also be subclassed to produce substates (figure 11.19). This might be appropriate where customer invoices that have been partly paid need to be identified.

We have shown that the state of an instance is defined by its representation, i.e., its attributes and its associations, and can therefore be captured in an object model. For example, it is possible that the only difference between the subclasses FulfilledBooking and InvoicedBooking is that FulfilledBooking has a direct association with Customer while InvoicedBooking has an association with Invoice and hence an indirect association with Customer.

11.3.2   Breaking associations

The data structures for cancelled bookings have not been shown. How might cancelled bookings be represented as a class diagram and how can cancelled bookings be distinguished from scheduled bookings? This depends upon what facts we wish to record about cancelled bookings. If all details of the booking are to be kept then the only difference between a scheduled booking and a cancelled booking is that cancelled bookings have an additional attribute, dateOfCancellation. If it is not necessary to retain all the details of the booking then some of the attributes and associations might be relinquished; for example, the association Vehicle scheduledFor Booking might be broken (figure 11.20).

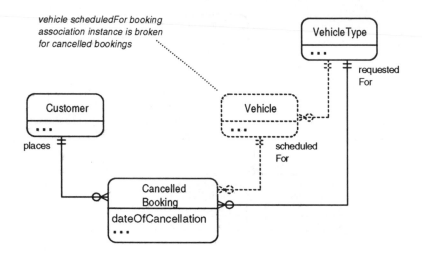

Figure 11.20: *Class diagram for bookings in the state cancelled*

11.4   Defining behaviour - methods

So, if the behaviour of the data is encapsulated with the representation of the data, then to communicate with an instance of Booking it will be necessary to pass a message. As noted above, even to find out the value of an attribute requires that a message be sent, for example to find out the mileage at the start of the booking:

booking mileageStart

In this case, booking is the object that will receive the message and mileageStart is the method that has been invoked. The method will return an object that is an instance of the Mileage class. Whether the Booking class has an attribute named mileageStart, or whether it is derived from other attributes or associations is not of consequence to the sender of the message - the data structure of Booking is hidden. Such a method might be specified as in figure 11.21, assuming that mileageStart is a primitive attribute of Booking.

Method	mileageStart
Type	Instance
Class	Booking
Precondition	none
Action	mileageStart = booking.mileageStart
Postcondition	none

Figure 11.21: *Method specification - attribute value*

In figure 11.21 mileageStart is a *method* supported by objects of the *class* Booking; it is also supported by subclasses of Booking through inheritance. The *precondition* and *postcondition* are not relevant since this is a method that does not change the representation of a booking and therefore cannot result in a change to its state (these will be demonstrated later). The *type* of the method is either Class, Instance, or Class & Instance. A class method is typically invoked to create a new instance of a class - if the instance does not currently exist then it cannot be sent a message and instead a message is sent to the class requesting that a new instance be added. An instance method is implemented by the instances of the class. Some methods can be implemented for both classes and instances. The *action* specifies what the method does: in this case it returns a mileageStart object that has the same value as the mileageStart attribute of the booking object (contained in booking.mileageStart). Within the method, the attribute mileageStart has been referred to directly by concatenating the class name (starting with a lower case letter as it is referring to a specific instance), booking, and the attribute name, mileageStart, separated by a period. This is the only time that an attribute should be referred to directly, i.e., where the method is attached to the same class as the attribute to which it makes reference.

For analysis purposes we will assume that a number of shorthand methods exist. The methods add, to create a new instance of a class, and delete, to destroy an instance of a class, are assumed to be available. For attributes, we assume that a method exists to find the current value of each attribute of a class, for example:

colourOfBodywork

and that a method also exists to set the value of an attribute, for example:

colourOfBodywork (colour)

A further convention is the use of the state method to find out what the state of an object is:

state

will return the state of an instance (for example, in Booking this could be scheduled, invoiced, etc.). A further shorthand notation is to use a colon to indicate a state, for example:

IF booking:invoiced THEN...

It must be borne in mind that the fundamental basis of the O-O paradigm is that implementation details are hidden and therefore that attributes are not visible. Although most O-O methods show attributes on class diagrams this is for guidance only. The only way to find an attribute value is by passing a message.

11.4.1   Methods for derived attributes

Methods are also used to specify derived attributes, such as mileageTotal which is derived from the attributes mileageStart and mileageEnd (figure 11.22). Derived attributes are not usually shown in the data model, but as it is possible to specify behaviour in the object model, derived attributes make a useful shorthand notation. Derived attributes do not add anything to the data model that is not already there, but they do make the specification of business requirements much simpler and can add substantially to the communicative power of the object model. Whether the derived attribute is held in a relational table or calculated as needed is an issue for implementation.

Method	mileageTotal
Type	Instance
Class	Booking
Precondition	none
Action	mileageTotal = booking.mileageEnd - booking.mileageStart
Postcondition	none

Figure 11.22: *Method specification - derived attribute*

On the class diagram derived attributes can be distinguished by the suffix (d). An explicit method must be specified for each derived attribute. Remember that the attribute list in a class box on a class diagram is an aide memoire - methods are the only way of accessing attribute values (figure 11.23).

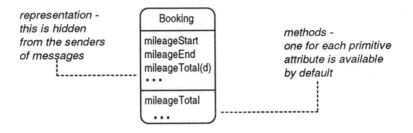

Figure 11.23: *Derived attributes in the class diagram*

11.4.2   Methods that change the state of an instance

When a method can result in a change of state, the precondition and postcondition should be used. Consider the method cancelBooking which is supported by the ScheduledBooking subclass of Booking. Any booking in the state scheduled will be reclassified (reflecting a change in state) as a cancelled booking. If the states are modelled explicitly as subclasses, the precondition is not adding anything since only bookings that are in the state scheduled will implement this method. The state of the booking is changed to cancelled and the attribute cancelledOnDate is set.

Method	cancelBooking (cancellationDate)
Type	Instance
Class	ScheduledBooking
Precondition	booking: ScheduledBooking
Action	booking = CancelledBooking booking.dateOfCancellation = cancellationDate
Postcondition	booking: CancelledBooking

Figure 11.24: *Method specification - cancelBooking*

The only way to cancel a booking is to use the method cancelBooking, which requires a cancellation date as an argument. The method cancelBooking results in a change in state of a booking object. As the state transition diagram shows, there is a number of state transitions allowed and a set of methods for the Booking class will be needed to manage those state transitions. Assuming that a method exists to return the contents of each of the attributes of the Booking class then the methods supported by Booking to manage state transitions are as shown in figure 11.25. The default methods add and delete have been redefined by takeBooking and archiveBooking.

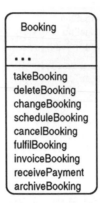

Figure 11.25: *Methods required for Booking state transitions*

The states of Booking can also be represented as subclasses of Booking and the methods distributed to the subclasses (figure 11.26).

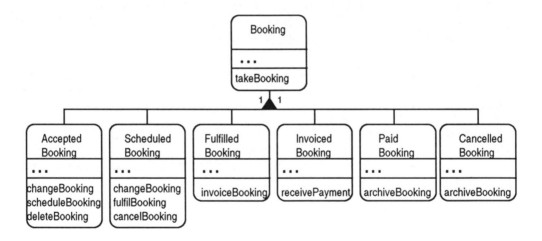

Figure 11.26: *Methods attached to Booking subclasses*

Note that a subclass for bookings in the state null has not been included since these by definition do not exist (or they already exist but are not of interest to the system under consideration). The method takeBooking is a class method that will create a booking in the state accepted and should not be inherited by the subclasses.

Not all states support all methods and some methods are implemented more than once. The archiveBooking method has been implemented separately by the InvoicedBooking and CancelledBooking classes (perhaps the archiving rules are different depending upon whether the booking was previously invoiced or cancelled). This does not result in confusion about which version of the method to use since the class of the object receiving the message will determine which method is invoked. If the message cancelBooking is sent to an invoiced booking then the method will fail as that method is not supported by the InvoicedBooking class. It can be seen that encapsulation can build a degree of safety into an application; objects can only respond using the methods that have been defined for their class or superclass. Objects respond differently to the same message depending upon how the method invoked has been implemented for their class. This is related to the O-O concept of polymorphism introduced above.

11.5   Associations and messages

A class diagram for Car and Colour is shown in figure 11.27, in which 11.27 (a) shows how Car and Colour are represented, while 11.27 (b) shows how they appear from a behavioural perspective.

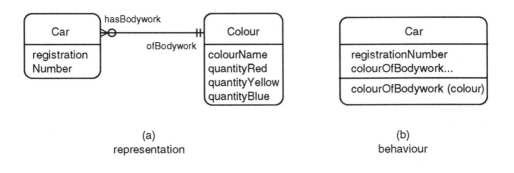

Figure 11.27: *Car and Colour classes - representation and behaviour*

When colour was an attribute of Car we assumed that a default method, colourOfBodywork (colour), existed that could be invoked to change the colour of a car's bodywork. Now that colour is not a primitive attribute of Car how will the method colourOfBodywork be implemented? Consider the sample instances for figure 11.27 (a) that are depicted in figure 11.28.

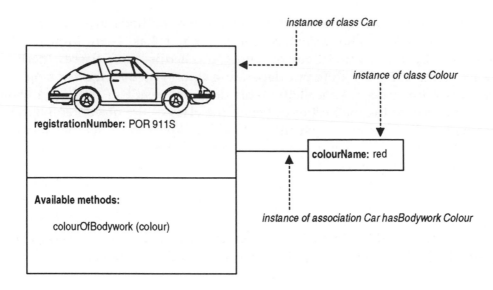

Figure 11.28: *Car and colour instances*

The method now sends a message to the association Car hasBodywork Colour and creates an instance of the association, such as POR911S has bodywork colour pink (figure 11.29). An instance of car has been connected to an instance of colour, but the only way to change the colour that a car is connected to is to invoke the message colourOfBodywork. So, if the implementation of Colour is changed (for example, the colour mixing scheme is changed to cyan, magenta, yellow, black) then the colourOfBodywork (colour) method does not need to change since the internals of the Colour class are hidden from the Car class.

Method	colourOfBodywork (colour)
Type	Instance
Class	Car
Precondition	none
Action	hasBodywork (colour)
Postcondition	none

Figure 11.29

11.6   Message paths

Business events trigger operations that may result in further events, those events triggering further operations....... A business event might be employee resigns, student is awarded degree, or customer places order. For example, assume that when a customer places an order the following process is initiated:

1. A check is made to see whether or not the customer is an existing or a new customer. If the customer does not currently exist then a new customer object must be added.

2. A new order is added, for which an order date, a date the goods are required, and a customer must be supplied.

3. For each product added to the order a product, the price quoted, and quantity required must be supplied.

4. For each order line the stock level of the product is checked to see whether there is a sufficient quantity on hand to meet the order. A shipment is created for each order line to record the quantity made available to the customer.

A logical message path maps the flow of messages needed to complete a business transaction that was triggered by a particular business event. A **business event processor** is an object that responds to business events and manages the completion of business transactions. The triggering of the business event processor might result from an operator using a computer keyboard, but could equally well be caused by another application, or from a sensor such as a thermostat. In figure 11.30 the business event customer places order and the resulting logical message path are shown.

The circled numbers in figure 11.30 relate to the steps in the customer places order process described above. Attributes have been suppressed to give a behavioural view of the message flow. Messages concerned with searching for instances have not been shown (for example, find whether the customer exists, or to find the product to be ordered) although messages required to find specifics, such as the current stock level, have been shown.

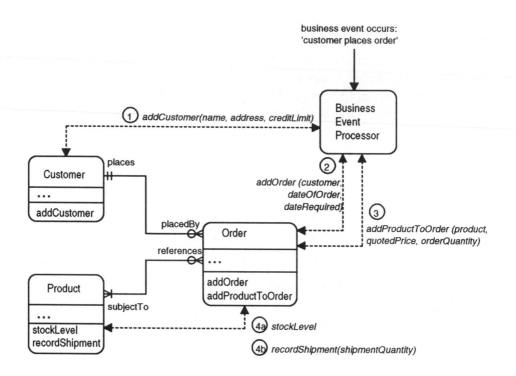

Figure 11.30: *Business event and logical message path*

11.6.1   Composition and messages

The Order class has OrderLine as a part. In figure 11.31 the composition has been shown implicitly. Because the association was strengthened into a composition, messages should be sent to the orders and not directly to order lines. If the composition structure is to encapsulate behaviour then the representation should be hidden. Therefore, to add an order the addOrder and addProductToOrder methods must be used. Looking inside the Order class it is possible to see how the addOrder and addProductToOrder methods are implemented. We cannot do this as users of the Order class, but we can in the role of designer of the Order class.

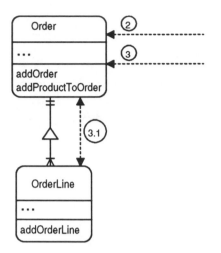

Figure 11.31: *Internal messages within Order*

Message 2 creates a new order through the addOrder method. Message 3 requests the service addProductToOrder. This method is implemented by the sending of message 3.1 to create a new order line, although this is not visible to the sender of message 3. Order does not need to know how OrderLine is implemented to be able to use its services - it is possible that OrderLine is also a composite class that would require further messages to be sent to implement addOrderLine. Even if addOrderLine is a primitive method today, who knows what it might become in the future? If the interfaces are maintained then change will be localized to the OrderLine class and Order will be unaffected.

Thus it can be seen that composition structures can be treated as any other association: messages must be used to communicate between the different levels of composition if encapsulation is to be maintained. In many cases the decision about how to combine classes into composition structures, together with the resulting implications for the definition of methods, is perhaps more pertinent to design (how shall we build the system) rather than analysis (what shall we build).

Message paths are useful insofar as they show that an object model can support the business events the application must support. However, the message path gives little idea of the dependencies between events and does not lend itself easily to a functional decomposition of business processes. It is for this reason that we turn in the next chapter to the modelling of events to provide a means of specifying how a business event processor should behave.

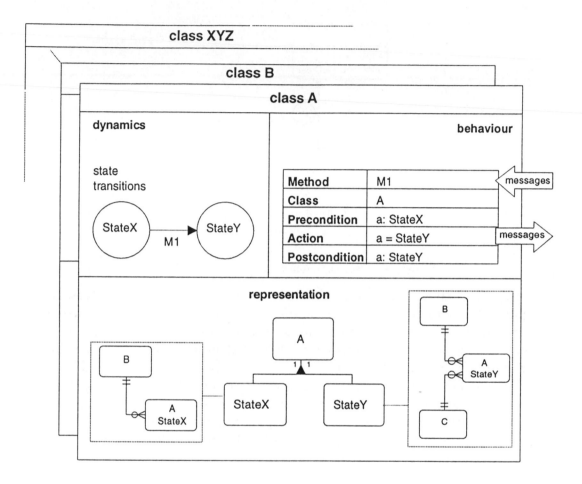

Figure 11.32: *Data - representation, behaviour and dynamics*

Chapter summary

The notion of states was introduced to object modelling to represent the dynamic aspects: how class instances change over time. Events cause changes in states. These states can be modelled using data representation (attributes and associations) together with state transition diagrams.

Encapsulation ties the behaviour of the data together with its representation, resulting in the definition of methods and the need for communication by messages. The approach to data modelling introduced in this chapter draws heavily on the O-O paradigm and has the potential for more understandable analysis and, if carried down into design and implementation, should lead to systems that are more flexible and maintainable.

A business event processor responds to events and manages business transactions. Logical message paths are used to determine whether or not an object model has sufficient behavioural capabilities to support the business event processing requirements. Figure 11.32 summarizes the object model: representation describes the data structure of a class; methods define the behaviour of the data; and state transitions describe the dynamic aspects of the data.

NOTES

1. Business Process Reengineering (BPR) is concerned with radical change and innovation. A major popular text is:

> Hammer, M., & Champy, J., (1993). *Reengineering the Corporation, A Manifesto for Business Revolution*. Nicholas Brealey, London.

Interested readers are recommended to look at Davenport's work, which takes a less populist view of BPR:

> Davenport, T.H., (1993). *Process Innovation: reengineering work through Information Technology*. Harvard Business School Press, Boston.

Questions

1. What is encapsulation? Why does it lead to the need to communicate using messages?

2. What might be some of the benefits of polymorphism for personal computer applications that need to drive different types of printer?

3. Prepare a state transition diagram for a traffic light.

4. Represent the traffic light state transition diagram using a fence diagram.

5. An estate management company offers properties for sale. Properties can be in the state available, under offer, sold, or withdrawn. Assuming that sold and withdrawn are closing states, prepare a state transition diagram.

6.   Represent the states that properties can be in as subclasses of Property.

7.   What methods should be defined for Property?

8.   Prepare a specification for the method acceptOffer.

9.   When an offer for a property is received the following actions take place:
  1 A check is made to see if the purchaser is registered with the estate management company - if not then a new purchaser must be added.
  2 The offer is added for which the property, offer date, offer time, and amount must be supplied.
  3 If the property is available the offer is accepted tentatively; if the property is currently under offer then the offer is recorded as a reserve offer.
  4 The vendor is contacted and the offer is either accepted or rejected.

  Create a class diagram and a logical message path to show the flow of messages triggered by the business event offer received for property.

10. Expand the implicit Property class shown into an explicit assembly structure that contains Property, Room and Garden classes.

```
┌─────────────────┐
│    Property     │
├─────────────────┤
│ room... (*)     │
│ garden...       │
│ sellingPrice    │
└─────────────────┘
```

Show the message path for adding a new room to a property:

  (a)   for the implicit Property class
  (b)   for the explicit Property class

12

Modelling processes

Introduction

In chapter 11 the data model was extended so that a class, in addition to defining the representation of data, also defined how the data would behave. In modelling behaviour an event-driven approach was adopted with an emphasis on modelling the different states that instances of a class may take. This view of an information system reinforces the view of the developer insofar as it is concerned with data structures and behaviour rather than the processes that the information system is to support. Although the idea of a business event processor was introduced in chapter 11, no indication was given concerning how to model the processes supported by a business event processor. The **event schema** is now introduced as a form of process modelling that is sympathetic to an O-O approach. However, given that the primary topic of this book is data modelling it is possible here to give but a brief introduction to process modelling.

Before looking at the event schema the structured systems analysis approach to process modelling is described in overview.

12.1   Structured Systems Analysis

Many structured systems analysis methodologies, such as SSADM (Structured Systems Analysis and Design Methodology) and IEM (Information Engineering Method) consider the business requirement from three viewpoints: data (entities), process (algorithms) and dynamics (state). The nature of the target application can lead the analyst and designer to put greater emphasis on one viewpoint or another.   For example, mathematical/scientific applications tend to have the algorithmic component emphasized, real-time control systems the dynamics (state transitions) and information systems the data.

Our concern here is primarily with the development of information systems, an activity in which historically developers have espoused a data-driven approach.   The data-driven approach to development may provide a degree of stability whilst maintaining flexibility, but, because of the separation of data representation and behaviour, it has supplied only a partial solution.   More and more, computer systems will be expected to address the three viewpoints.   For example, manufacturing processes controlled real-time might provide data to a central database where complex algorithms are applied to predict the requirements for raw materials; management information is then disseminated, perhaps using multi-media, to involved parties such as the finance department.

Structured analysis methods address the need to model data, process and dynamics. SSADM is a widely used methodology that is intended to be data driven, emphasizing the centrality of the logical data structure (data model), with processes being defined using data flow diagrams (DFDs) and behaviour over time being modelled using entity life histories (ELHs).   Much effort can be expended keeping the three viewpoints* of the system

---

* The use of different viewpoints and the resulting differences and conflicts that they can throw up is not a bad thing.   We recommended that top-down and bottom-up approaches be used in data modelling and consider that different viewpoints on the development process will each give a potentially valuable insight.   All methods and techniques involve blindness. By viewing an application in data terms we will to some extent de-emphasize the functional aspects; conversely a functional view will de-emphasize the data structures.   If we see these different approaches as metaphorical then we can recognize that they are a way of seeing and also a way of not seeing.

synchronised and in resolving differences that arise from the analysis viewpoints. Figure 12.1 shows the relationship of the three views of a system espoused by structured methods.

Each application being developed is, to a greater or lesser extent, independent of other applications already developed or simultaneously under development. Attempts are made at the enterprise level to share data models and to reduce duplicate development of functionality. Unfortunately, these efforts often end up as fruitless exercises in bureaucracy that are ineffective in influencing the way in which project teams actually build applications. Also, sharing data does not necessarily lead to the sharing of the processes that act upon that data. The data might be said to be normalized, but the same cannot be said of the processes.

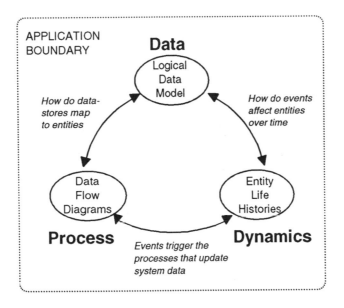

Figure 12.1: *Structured systems analysis*

One of the difficulties in applying structured methods is that they are themselves complex, this complexity giving rise to issues of management. If we believe that Information System (IS) development is an inherently complex task then we should look for techniques that help us in managing this complexity. Structured methods are one approach to managing complexity, where the three views of the required system are kept in synchronisation by constant cross-referencing and consistency checking. Automation of the structured approach can be achieved by introducing

CASE tools, which at least remove much of the gruelling task of checking the specification for internal consistency and make it possible to maintain specifications as requirements change over time. The use of CASE tools makes the structured methods approach to systems development practicable.

Even so, it can be difficult to recognise commonality once process definitions are separated from data definitions. Processing is defined using the stratagem of functional decomposition, the breaking down of a problem into ever smaller components. Data modelling is applying the principle of abstraction, concentrating attention on areas relevant to the problem to be solved. Both functional decomposition and abstraction are important techniques for managing complexity. However, by separating process from data at the analysis stage of the development cycle, the technical quality of the final system becomes very much dependent upon the quality of the system design. The design team must find the commonality of processing that a top-down, functional decomposition approach is in danger of missing.

Structured methods have been used for many years and although they are unchanged in essence, it is possible to see shifts of emphasis. The DeMarco[1] approach placed the data flow diagram (process specification) at the heart of the analysis process, with the logical data structure being developed in support of the processing specification. Over the last twenty years of structured methods the logical data structure has moved to a central position, as evidenced in the brief foregoing discussion of SSADM. This represents a move away from individual system development efforts that emphasize application functionality via a functional decomposition approach towards the search for more stable mappings of the problem situation that can be shared. In version 4 of SSADM, by attaching operations to entity life histories there is an opportunity to use SSADM in a pseudo-O-O manner. However this would be more dependent upon the developer than the method[2].

At the current time it is possible to discern a trend towards a greater concern with process as well as data in the evolution of structured methods. However, this should not necessarily be seen as a failure of data-driven development or a full-circle return to where structured methods started out. The development of structured methods has gone from process centred to data centred and now is moving toward object centred, i.e., the integration of process and data.

12.1.1   Data Flow Diagrams (DFDs)

Having observed that process modelling is experiencing a resurgence, we note that currently the principal way of modelling processes in a structured methods environment is the data flow diagram (DFD)[3]. The DFD[*] (in a very basic form) consists of:

data stores, which hold temporary or permanent data:

```
D4  Suppliers
```

processes (e.g., Accept Order):

data flows:

————————————▶

external sources/recipients:

(Supplier)

The DFD shows how data enters and leaves the system, the processes that act upon the data, and what data must be stored (figure 12.2). DFDs show the flows of data necessary to support the processes - they do not typically show the timing and sequencing of processes. DFDs are decomposed hierarchically; each process box at one level can be decomposed into a separate DFD at a lower level. Three or four levels of DFDs would not be unusual. This hierarchical ordering is a functional decomposition and can be a very powerful way of describing processes.

---

[*] One should be aware that in SSADM, DFDs are used to support the identification of functions and events and that it is these, rather than the required system DFD, that are used in the logical design stage.

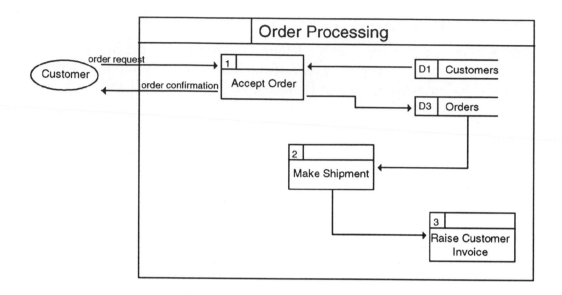

Figure 12.2: *Data flow diagram (DFD)*

12.1.2   Some difficulties with DFDs

DFDs are founded upon the idea of data flows, the idea that data flows from process to process, process to datastore, and datastore to process. It is easy to forget that this is a metaphor and to begin to imagine data literally flowing around the organization. By contrast, a metaphor for the data model might be the "bucket" - there is a bucket of data available that can be dipped into, the data changed, and then the data put back for somebody else to use. By using the data flow metaphor there is a danger that the analyst will be trapped in thinking about how things are done at the moment and will find it difficult to be creative in re-visioning the existing processes. Although the analyst will undoubtedly need to look at the existing systems at some point in the development life-cycle, there are good arguments for not starting with the existing system, particularly if the aim is "obliteration" rather than automation[4] and a Business Process Reengineering approach is being adopted.

12.1.3   A change of metaphor

Some of the difficulties with DFDs relate to the separation of data, process, and dynamics (figure 12.1). It is also possible to see an information system as in figure 12.3, in which the metaphor of **tools** and **materials** has been adopted[5]. The data structures (representation and encapsulated behaviour) represent the materials available to those who are undertaking organizational activity. Materials are in the Universe of Discourse (UoD). The way in which we organize our work is the subject of the Organization of Work (OoW) to which the tools metaphor can be applied. Tools are what we use to help us accomplish purposeful activity. Although the developer tends to focus on the materials, the user is more concerned with the tools. The tools are called business event processors (in contrast to "applications") as the approach taken to modelling processes will be event-driven rather than procedural. Once a process has been defined that deals with a particular business event then the aim should be to re-use that process rather than to recreate it. Much of the potential for re-use will come from the application of generalization/specialization to processes (tools) as well as to data classes (materials).

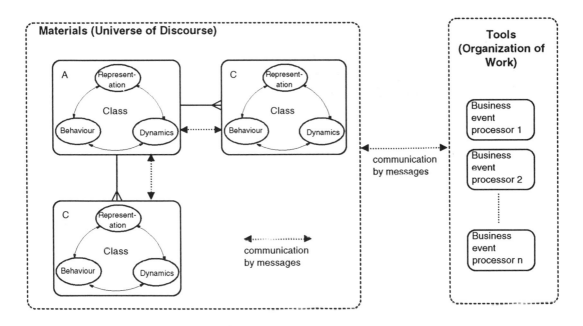

Figure 12.3: *Tools and Materials*

Communication is by messages. Tools should make use of materials on the basis of a material's behaviour and how that material has been implemented should be hidden from the tool. The user of a tool may invoke processes and similarly should not be aware of how that process has been implemented. We have considered in the previous chapters how to model the representation and behaviour of data (the materials) and will now look at one way of modelling processes (the tools that use the data materials).

12.2   Event schemas

Event schemas can be used to specify processes but rather than using data-flows and data-stores as the data flow diagram does, operations and events are modelled[6].

Operations give rise to the occurrence of events that can trigger other operations (figure 12.4). External operations result in external events that can trigger internal operations resulting in further events. Control conditions specify how the preceding events result in a subsequent operation being triggered.

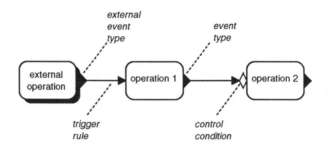

Figure 12.4: *Event schema notation*

Consider again the customer order process described in chapter 11:

1. A check is made to see whether or not the customer is an existing or a new customer. If the customer does not currently exist then a new customer object must be added.

2. A new order is added, for which an order date, a date the goods are required, and a customer must be supplied.

3. For each product added to the order a product, the price quoted, and quantity required must be supplied.

4. For each order line the stock level of the product is checked to see whether there is a sufficient quantity on hand to meet the order. A shipment is created for each order line to record the quantity made available to the customer.

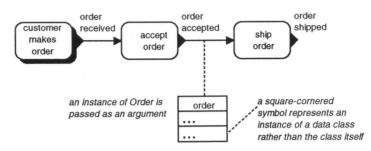

Figure 12.5: *Event schema for customer orders*

This process can be shown as an event schema (figure 12.5). An occurrence of the external event customer makes order triggers the operation accept order, which results in the creation of an order object (a material). The accept order operation results in the event order accepted occurring - this event triggers the operation ship order. An order object (indicated by the square-cornered symbol) is passed to the ship order process as an argument.

The operation accept order is implemented by a method. That method is itself composed of operations that are in turn implemented by methods. Operations that are primitive interact with the object model via the passing of messages. Thus the data abstraction of the object model is complemented by a hierarchical decomposition of processes. In figure 12.6 the accept order operation has been decomposed into further operations.

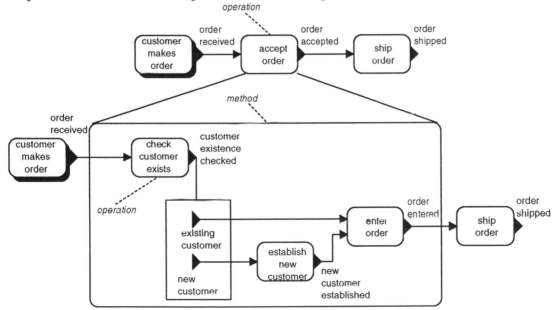

Figure 12.6: *Event schema for accept order operation*

An operation is an object and therefore it will exhibit behaviour when passed a message. This also means that the implementation detail of an operation must be hidden; operations are black boxes that carry out some task, turning an input into an output. How the operation accomplishes its task is hidden and this means that the internal workings of an operation can be changed without affecting other operations, provided that the operation's interface to the outside world is maintained. So, if the accept order process needs to be changed, perhaps to introduce a check against a credit limit, then the change can be localized to the accept order operation. Because operations are objects they can be specialized. For example, the accept order operation might be specialized to cater for corporate customers, who are treated differently from off the street customers (see section 12.4).

12.2.1   Event schema and object model interaction

The Vehicle Rental Company is used to illustrate how an event schema interacts with an object model. The event schema in figure 12.7 shows at a high level of abstraction the events and operations associated with mobility requests.

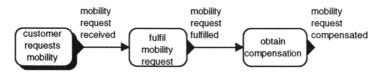

Figure 12.7: *Event schema for bookings*

It is worth pointing out at this stage that the analyst should be wary of adopting the terminology of the current system without some thought. It would be tempting to use concepts such as vehicle booking and invoice, but in figure 12.7 the concepts mobility request and compensation are used. Mobility requests are more general than vehicle bookings - in satisfying mobility requests an organization might consider the recommendation of bicycles, public transport, car-sharing schemes, and even virtual mobility (e.g., video-conferencing or virtual reality). At this level one is concerned with *what* is to be done. The method for an operation describes *how* an operation is to be accomplished, and in the case of mobility requests it may well involve taking bookings for rental vehicles. However, by working at a higher level of abstraction new opportunities can be surfaced that are not visible when one is stuck with ideas such as vehicle booking[7].

Similarly, obtain compensation provides rather more scope than an operation that is concerned with raising invoices and matching payments. Compensation need not be cash (it could be a cash equivalent such as shares in a company) and it need not be financial (it could be a barter of services). Even if compensation must be financial and in cash, it need not necessarily involve the raising of an invoice - customers could be given online access to the booking system and the responsibility for making a payment at the end of the month for the bookings fulfilled in that month (a physical invoice need not be raised, although appropriate accounting entries must still be made).

Assuming that the fulfil mobility request operation involves the materials introduced in the data model in chapter 11, then the event schema might be as in figure 12.8.

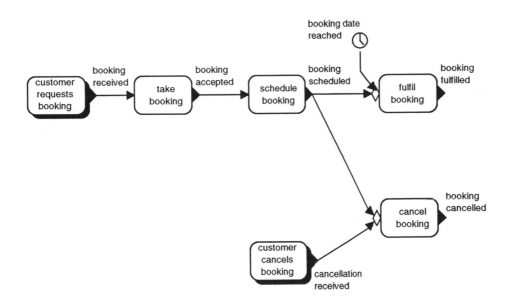

Figure 12.8: *Event schema for the fulfil mobility request operation*

Control conditions, represented by a diamond, can be specified as Boolean operators. For example, the control condition for the operation fulfil booking requires that an external clock event (booking date reached) *and* the event booking scheduled occur before it is invoked. Figure 12.9 shows the event schema for the operation obtain compensation. Invoices have been introduced for illustrative purposes to show one way of obtaining compensation - they are not the only means.

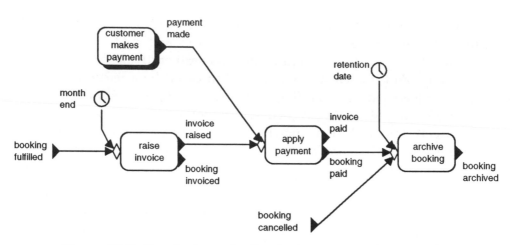

Figure 12.9: *Event schema for the obtain compensation operation*

At the lowest level an operation's method will invoke methods supported by the object model. Assuming that the operation cancel booking, shown in figure 12.8 is at a primitive level (i.e., where no further event schema decomposition is specified), then it will invoke an object model method to carry out its operation. Method specifications were introduced in chapter 11 for material classes; method specifications can be prepared also for operations (figure 12.10). This method is of the class Operation and like any other method must be invoked by the passing of a message. A date object specifying when the cancellation was made must be passed to the operation as well as the booking to be cancelled.

Operation	cancel booking (booking, canDate)
Precondition	cancellation received AND booking scheduled
Action	booking cancelBooking (canDate)
Postcondition	booking cancelled

Figure 12.10: *Method specification - cancel booking operation*

The specification in figure 12.10 is similar to a material class method, the main difference being that this method is attached to an operation. The operation "cancel booking" is an instance of the class Operation (tools) and is analogous to Booking being an instance of the class DataClass (materials).

12.2.2   Event schemas and substates

Consider a change in business policy whereby bookings cancelled with insufficient notice are subject to a cancellation charge. This requires a change in the state transition model as cancelled bookings may now result in the raising of an invoice (figure 12.11).

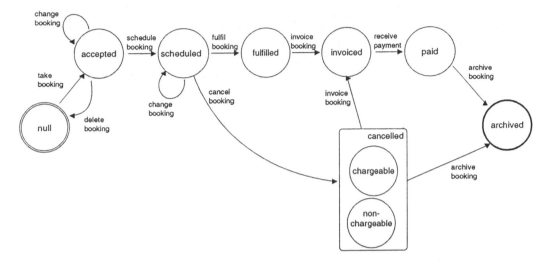

Figure 12.11: *Cancelled bookings - modified state transition diagram*

There are now substates of cancelled bookings, those that attract a cancellation charge and those that do not. A modified event schema is shown in figure 12.12.

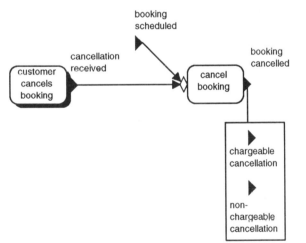

Figure 12.12: *Cancelled bookings - modified event schema*

Following completion of the cancel booking operation the event "booking cancelled" occurs. This event has been subclassified into the events chargeable cancellation, which triggers the "raise invoice" operation, and non-chargeable cancellation, which triggers the "archive booking" operation. The method for the revised cancel booking operation is shown in figure 12.13.

Operation	cancel booking (booking, canDate)
Precondition	cancellation received AND booking scheduled

Action	booking cancelBooking (canDate)
	IF booking: ChargeableCancelledBooking THEN
	    chargeable cancellation
	ELSE
	    non-chargeable cancellation
	END

Postcondition	booking cancelled

Figure 12.13: *Method specification - cancel booking*

The method of the operation cancel booking results in a message being sent to the booking. Following successful execution of this method the booking will be either in the state chargeable or in the state non-chargeable. The cancel booking operation then needs to determine the state of the booking in order to set the appropriate postcondition. The cancelBooking method might now be as in figure 12.14.

Method	cancelBooking (cancellationDate)
Type	Instance
Class	ScheduledBooking
Precondition	booking: ScheduledBooking

Action	daysNotice = booking.dateStart - booking.dateOfCancellation
	IF daysNotice < 2 THEN
	    cancellationCharge EQ booking.bookingCost * 1.0
	ELSE IF daysNotice < 5 THEN
	    cancellationCharge EQ booking.bookingCost * 0.5
	ELSE IF daysNotice < 10 THEN
	    cancellationCharge EQ booking.bookingCost * 0.1
	END
	IF cancellationCharge EQ 0 THEN
	    booking = NonChargeableCancelledBooking
	    booking.dateOfCancellation = cancellationDate
	ELSE IF
	    booking = ChargeableCancelledBooking
	    booking.dateOfCancellation = cancellationDate
	    booking.cancellationCharge = cancellationCharge
	END

Postcondition	booking: cancelledBooking

Figure 12.14: *Method specification - cancellationCharge*

The business rule for cancellations has been encapsulated with the material to which it relates (in this case bookings). If the policy on cancellations changes then it only need be changed in one place.

12.2.3   Generalization/specialization of operations

Generalization is used in recognition of common features and specialization in recognition of differentiating features. In data structures it is possible to recognize that employee and customer share common features by generalizing them into person; by making staff and manager specializations of employee it was possible to differentiate between them whilst retaining the knowledge that both managers and staff are employees. To get re-use of process specifications it is important to be able to use generalization and specialization for operations. In figure 12.15 the operation create payment has been specialized into create cheque payment and create EDI payment (EDI stands for electronic data interchange). These operation specializations share the common features of create payment. The operation create EDI payment has been further specialized to recognize different forms of electronic payment.

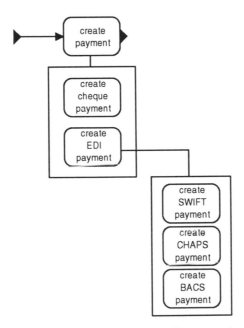

Figure 12.15: *Generalization/specialization of operations*

In a banking environment a generic model of the create payment operation would allow the commonality of all payments to be identified but at the same time allow payment media to be differentiated. In practical terms this might lead to the realization that there need not be separate payment processes defined for accounts payable (non-banking suppliers), employee costs (salaries and expenses), interest charges, loan repayments, etc. Once the general need for a payment process has been identified it can be specialized to address the different payment forms required.

Chapter summary

Process modelling has been based upon the metaphor of tools that make use of materials. The diagramming notation for processes (tools) used event schemas, providing a closer tie to the dynamic aspects of the object model than traditional techniques such as data flow diagrams (DFDs).

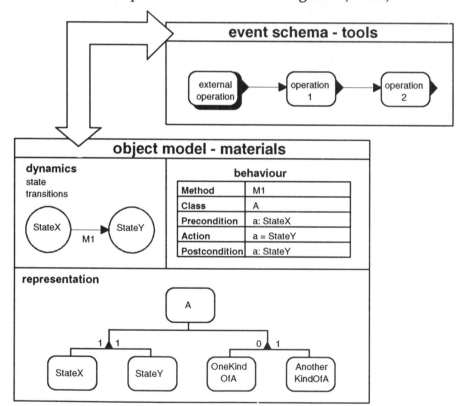

Figure 12.16: *Process modelling and object (data) modelling*

The generalization/specialization of operations could lead to further re-use and is complementary to the re-use of materials (data classes). Figure 12.16 summarizes the tools and materials metaphor.

NOTES

1. See:
   > DeMarco, T., (1979). *Structured Analysis and System Specification.* Yourdon Press, Englewood Cliffs, NJ.

2. As one might expect structured methods are attempting to adopt the O-O paradigm within existing frameworks. For example, see:
   > Montgomery, S. L., (1994). *Object-Oriented Information Engineering.* Academic Press, Cambridge, MA.
   > Robinson, K., & Berrisford G., (1994). *Object-Oriented SSADM.* Prentice-Hall International.

3. For a clear and thorough description of process modelling for structured methods (function hierarchies, functional dependencies, DFDs, state transition diagrams) see:
   > Barker, R., & Longman, C., (1992). *CASE*Method, Function and Process Modelling.* Addison-Wesley.

4. See:
   > Hammer, M., (1990). Reengineering Work: Don't Automate, Obliterate. *Harvard Business Review*, 68(4), July-August: 104-112.

5. The tools and materials metaphor has been used in O-O analysis and design in a banking environment, and is described in:
   > Budde, R., Christ-Neumann, M., & Sylla, K., (1992). Tools and Materials: an analysis and design metaphor. In: Bjerknes, G., Bratteteig, T., & Kautz, K., editors. *Proceedings of the 15th International Systems Research seminar in Scandinavia - IRIS).* University of Oslo.

6. The event schema is described in:
   > Martin, J., & Odell, J., (1992). *Object-Oriented Analysis and Design.* Prentice-Hall. Englewood Cliffs.

   There are a number of alternative texts available that address O-O analysis. The Coad & Yourdon text is fine for representation and behaviour, i.e., the materials, but has little to say about the organization of work, i.e., the tools.
   > Coad P., & Yourdon, E., (1991). *Object-Oriented Analysis* (2nd edition). Yourdon Press, Prentice-Hall.

   The OMT method has more to say about analysis but advocates a form of DFD for process modelling:
   > Rumbaugh, J., Blaha, M., Premerlani, W., Eddy, F., Lorensen, W., (1991). *Object-Oriented Modeling and Design.* Prentice-Hall, Englewood Cliffs, New Jersey.

7. For further details of conceptual modelling for Business Process Reengineering see:
       Vidgen, R., Rose, J., Wood, J.R.G., & Wood-Harper, A.T, (1994). Business process
       reengineering: the need for a methodology to re-vision the organization. In:
       *Proceedings of IFIP TC8, Business Process Re-Engineering: Information System
       Opportunities & Challenges, May 8 - 11.*

Questions

1.   What are some of the benefits and disadvantages of data flow diagrams
      (DFDs) in the context of an O-O approach?

2.   Create a DFD for the estate management company to reflect the
      following description of business events:

      When a purchaser makes an offer for a property the estate management
      company first checks to see if the purchaser is on their records, and if not adds
      them. If the property is currently under offer then the offer is rejected. If the
      property is available then the offer is recorded and the vendor contacted. The
      vendor can either accept or reject the offer. If the offer is accepted then it
      remains so until either the offer is cancelled or an exchange of contracts is
      made. Contracts having been exchanged, the sale is completed once the
      completion date is reached.

3.   Create an event schema for the scenario outlined in question 2 above.

4.   The operation hire staff requires that different procedures be followed
      for permanent and temporary staff. For permanent staff different
      procedures are followed depending upon whether the position is a
      management   grade   or   a   clerical   grade.   Create   a
      generalization/specialization structure for the "hire staff" operation.

5.   In the interests of good customer relations the Vehicle Rental Company
      wishes to give office managers the discretion to make chargeable
      cancelled bookings non-chargeable. Modify the state transition
      diagram in figure 11.11 to reflect this and prepare a specification for the
      operation "make chargeable cancellation non-chargeable" with the
      business rule that only chargeable cancellations with a notice period of
      2 days or more and a value of less than £100 can be made non-
      chargeable.

Part 3

Theory and practice

13

Large-scale data models

Introduction

Most data models are compiled during the development of a particular computer system. Occasionally an organization will commission a corporate data modelling exercise to map the data used in all its activities. Corporate data models, whose purpose is to allow the development of a set of coherent applications sharing data resources, can grow to a strength of two or three hundred entities. But even the data model for a typical application system will have thirty to sixty entities. Managing the development of a data model of significant size calls for a number of techniques and disciplines.

13.1 Approaches to data modelling

13.1.1 Business understanding

Data modelling is a way of representing our understanding of a business. It doesn't matter how competent an analyst is in the use of data modelling techniques, she will get nowhere without understanding the business first. In a relatively short space of time the data modeller must attempt to understand the business as well as the users do. It is not enough to understand what happens when everything runs smoothly: the analyst must also find out what action is taken in exceptional circumstances or when something goes wrong. Nor is it enough for the data modeller to understand data in the same way that a competent user does: she must consider it in a wider context and in a more abstract way.

Business understanding comes from several different sources.

The public domain

A lot of business knowledge is available in textbooks, journals, training courses and screen-based information systems. We would encourage data modellers to insist on access to whatever is necessary.

Current systems

Organization-specific data can be traced from the existing systems, whether manual or computerized, which are destined to be replaced. All inputs to and outputs from the existing computer systems should be determined from examination of existing database tables, input screens, forms, registers, reports, ledgers, card indices and such sources. It is not uncommon to find significant data attributes buried in the program code of some older legacy systems. While analysing current systems it is important to separate the logical data which they use from the way those data are implemented: although at present it may be very important to the users to know which page of a journal a warehouse delivery is recorded on, it is not going to matter in the new implementation.

Having advised the data analyst to trace data from current systems, we should stress that we do not recommend extended and formal documentation of current processes. Such exercises tend to dissipate enthusiasm and inhibit creative thinking. The team should begin to document the required system as soon as the starting gun is fired and keep that in mind as its objective at all times.

Policy statements

Computer systems fossilize existing ways of doing things. They are usually replaced not because they have stopped working but because they don't allow enough flexibility for new types and methods of business. The invitation to design a new system is a rare opportunity to change the course of a business and one which should be grasped with both hands. Check out senior management mission statements and find out how the business is moving. Where would the organization like to be in three or four years' time?

Experienced users

Go to the top - but don't forget to go to the bottom as well. A great deal of data is not recorded anywhere except in the brains of those who operate the business at the moment. These may be the people who feel their lifestyles and even livelihoods threatened by the new system. Among the skills of the good data modeller will be the polite persistence required to elicit what needs to be known. This doesn't come naturally to everyone and it is worth remembering that training in social skills, such as assertiveness training, is available.

13.1.2   Top-down versus bottom-up

There are two techniques of entity spotting: top-down and bottom-up. Roughly speaking, top-down modelling techniques are those described in chapters 2 to 6. The bottom-up technique of relational data analysis was the subject of chapter 7.

The top-down approach requires the modeller first to take a bird's eye view of the information requirements of the project as a whole and then to focus in gradually to perceive more detail. The fundamental entities will be spotted before anything else: the employee in a payroll application; the account in an accounting system; the room in a hotel booking package. These can be recognized before any of their attributes are known.

Top-down analysis was traditionally recommended by structured methodologies for modelling process rather than data. To be able to describe the overall functionality of a system in broad brush terms and then to break it down into more detailed component functions was seen as a way of keeping each component to a manageable size, so that it could be comprehended as a whole by an intelligent human's brain. Up to a certain point, process can be analysed in more and more detail. As the magnifying glass gets stronger new detail emerges. But what of data? Data seem to be flat like a carpet. Until an entity's attributes are known there is little to be said; once they are known there is very little more to add. Data do not seem to be as susceptible to the magnifying glass as processes are.

The bottom-up approach means mounting a systematic search for each piece of information, an activity that can be given rigour by relational data analysis. For each atomic item of data, a key is determined. The key can be found by asking, "What would I have to tell the system in order to get a single value for this attribute returned to me as an answer?" For example, it would be no good asking what an employee's basic salary used to be. You would have to say how long ago you want to go back. So the key of salary involves both employee and date.

Many of the attributes unearthed in this way turn out to have the same key. Items of data individually discovered by bottom-up analysis seem to cluster together and suggest the existence of an entity at their heart. By occasionally revealing itself in this way, an entity earns its subsidiary definition as "the focal point of a number of attributes". It is as though we are looking up at the night sky and picking out constellations when all we can really see are the pinpoints of light from thousands of stars and planets. However, it is by no means uncommon to find a single attribute with a complicated concatenated key which it doesn't share with anything else.

Both top-down and bottom-up approaches must be taken. Without a top-down approach generalizations will be missed; a bottom-up approach is required to ensure sufficient detail is captured. The data modeller's job is to make the two meet in the middle.

13.1.3   Creativity

Although it may sometimes seem to be limited by a small subset of permissible structures, data modelling actually allows great scope for creativity. To determine an appropriate way to reduce a complex business activity to a model, the data modeller often needs to dream up several different possibilities and analyse the implications of each one before selecting the most useful. Usually this requires some mental juggling with a business' less well defined concepts. Learning to be imaginative is probably much harder for the average adult than learning data modelling techniques, since creativity is so systematically drummed out of most of us by the conventional education system. Try one of Edward de Bono's books for methods of freeing up thinking processes.

The tools of the trade should be used to capture creative thoughts and not to suppress them. Although most data modellers will have access to a CASE tool to help in the production of presentable data model diagrams, at the beginning of the analysis phase diagrams will be drafted with pencil and paper. At this stage the practitioner might feel more comfortable drawing entities as ellipses and relationships as arcs: the smooth curves can be drawn quickly and tend not to inhibit creative thought as boxes and pipes do. Try drawing data model diagrams during interviews instead of taking notes. The ability to think directly in terms of data structures is a useful instinct.

13.2   Populating the meta-model

The results of the analysis work are stored in a data dictionary or repository. If the team is fortunate the repository will be automated (as a CASE tool or IPSE - integrated product support environment) with an underlying meta-model similar to the one described in chapter 14. If not, then standard word processing, database and graphics software must be used to simulate a CASE environment. The help that a dedicated application tool gives in checking, maintaining and presenting the data model will also have to be simulated.

13.2.1   Version control

Data modelling is an iterative process. The first-cut data model will usually provide a broad structure of generalizations and specializations which seem to support and streamline the business functions required. Once these have been approved, further versions will flesh out the structure. The second cut might contain all the data needed for normal processing and the third could add default and exception data. At every stage the model will be tested and further requirements identified. Eventually the data model should be tested at attribute level against the logical processing specification to ensure that all the functionality envisaged can be supported.

The final version becomes the foundation for the physical model. Note that developing the physical data model is itself an iterative procedure, although the questions which will be asked at each stage will be of a fundamentally different nature than those asked of the logical model.

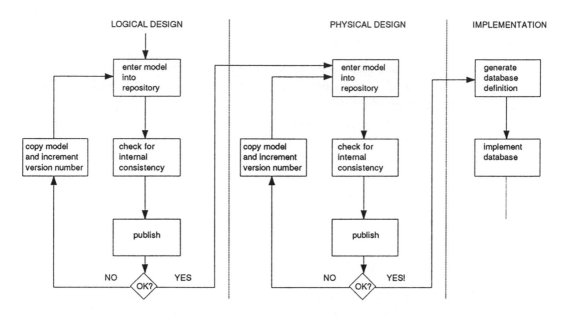

Figure 13.1: *Flow chart showing data modelling iterations*

Some CASE tools give better support to version control than others. At its simplest, creating a new version of the data model means taking a copy of the previous one and using that to continue development. At each stage new and experimental ideas may be incorporated: these might survive to become integral parts of the model or they may be discarded. The ability to regress unsuccessful changes is a useful feature of good version control mechanisms.

13.2.2   Integrity checks

Every time the data model is presented for approval it must be internally consistent. An internally consistent data model has been checked to ensure that, for example,

- every entity has a primary key;

- entities do not contain non-existent attributes;

- every attribute features in at least one entity;

- every relationship joins two entities which exist.

During the course of populating the meta-model, inconsistencies will inevitably arise but they should all be resolved before a version of the model is pronounced complete. Most CASE tools have integrity checking routines which will search for internal inconsistencies and report them to the modeller.

13.3   Presenting the data model

Care must be taken to present the large-scale data model to users and to other developers in digestible chunks. It is also important that reports from the meta-model can be replicated if further copies are requested or if comparable reports are required after each iteration of the model.

13.3.1   The definitive diagram set

Of all the possible reports from the repository, entity diagrams are most widely used to propagate an understanding of the data model. Diagrams which follow the techniques recommended in chapters 2-6 convey all the semantics of the model and nearly all the implementation detail required for the relational platform.

Any piece of paper larger than A4 size probably has too much information on it to be comprehended at a glance. But that is the least of its crimes. It is difficult to read on the bus on the way home. It does not fit into the standard filing system. It needs to be printed on a special printer. It needs to be photocopied on special paper. It is difficult to bind into a report in a standard way. The worst possible data model diagram stretches across several sheets of paper which need to be glued together by the data modeller every time a copy is required and is colour coded in highlighter pen.

We would recommend that the data modeller create a definitive set of data model diagrams which describe the entire model in black and white on sheets of A4 paper. The entities in the data model need to be distributed among these diagrams so that each entity is at home on one diagram. Each diagram should have a maximum of around fifteen resident entities.

Looking at an entity on its home diagram, the reader is guaranteed to see all of its primary key and foreign key owners. To achieve this, some of the owner entities, which might live on other diagrams, are replicated. To make it clear which entities are resident and which are just visiting, a dotted line is drawn around the residents.

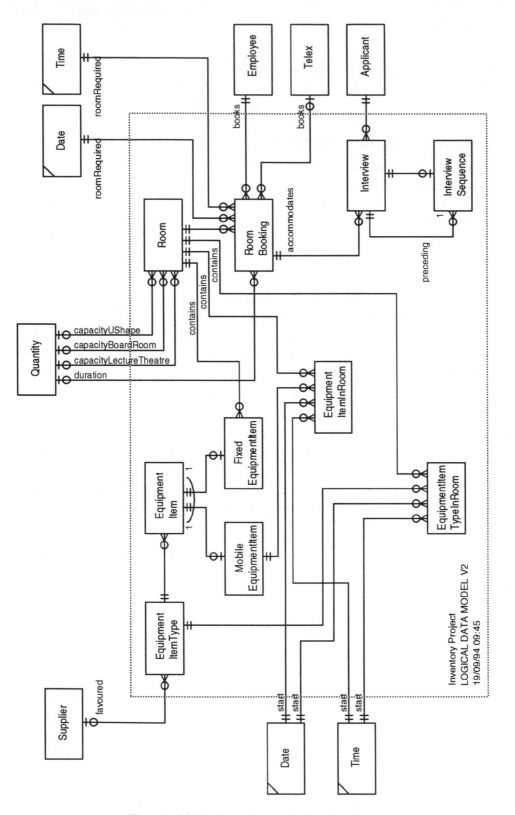

Figure 13.2: *Page from a definitive diagram set*

The reader is not guaranteed to see all of the details of a resident entity, although if a detail entity happens to reside on the same diagram the relationship will be shown. By implication, each relationship is represented on one and only one diagram: the home diagram of its detail entity.

How are the entities divided among the diagrams in a definitive document set? The authors are not proposing any rules. Entities tend to cluster together into broad subject areas. The more relationships which are internal to a data model diagram - that is, they do not require a visit from a non-resident entity - the better. The requirement to minimise the number of visitor entities in the document set as a whole could be expressed as an algorithm which would cluster entities automatically. A CASE tool which offered to automate the production of the definitive diagram set from the contents of the repository would need to incorporate such an algorithm.

13.3.2   The summary diagram

The definitive diagram set guarantees a complete picture of the data model. It may be supplemented by other diagram types if required. In particular, various techniques for suppressing parts of the data model are used to provide summary diagrams.

- Key-only entities have no owners and can therefore be dropped from the summary diagram without consequences;

- Certain other entities which have no owners, and therefore no foreign key attributes, can be dropped even though they do have non-key attributes;

- Many-to-many resolvers can be dropped if they have no relationships other than those with the entities they resolve. On the diagram, the m:n relationship between those two entities can be shown, just as it can be on class diagrams;

- Subtypes can be rolled up into their supertypes. Any foreign key relationships of the subtype must be imputed to the supertype;

- History details can be dropped.

A summary diagram can be extremely useful as a means of giving an overview of the project data. It should be clearly labelled to show that it is not part of the definitive diagram set and to state which of the sparsing techniques above have been used in its construction.

Chapter summary

Creating a corporate or large-scale project data model requires a disciplined approach. The model must be stored in a formal repository or on a pseudo repository. Version control should be used to ensure that the model is only presented when it is internally consistent.

Entity diagrams are reports from the repository and could, in theory, be generated automatically from it. In a definitive set of project diagrams each entity is at home on only one diagram. On that diagram all its primary and foreign key owners must be shown. The definitive diagram set can be used to help verify the entities and their attributes in the repository.

Summary diagrams may be produced in addition to the definitive document set. A summary diagram should state what compression techniques have been used in its production.

Questions

1.   Name four sources of business data.

2.   Describe the differences between top-down and bottom-up data analysis.

3.   Specify four characteristics of an internally consistent data model.

4.   Must a data model be internally consistent at all times?

5.   On how many diagrams in the definitive document set is an entity at home?

6.   How is a visiting entity shown on a diagram in the definitive document set?

7.   On how many diagrams is a relationship shown in the definitive document set?

8.   Looking at an entity on its home diagram, the reader can see on the same page

      (a)   all of its primary key owners - true or false?
      (b)   all of its foreign key owners - true or false?
      (c)   all of its detail entities - true or false?
      (d)   all of its subtypes - true or false?

9.   Devise an algorithm for minimising the number of visiting entities in a definitive diagram set.

10.   Describe four techniques used in creating summary data diagrams.

14

Meta-modelling

Introduction

The computer systems development process is a business like any other. It too has data that need to be recorded. Its processes have to be understood and documented as information system development methods. They are often computerized: CASE (Computer Aided Systems Engineering) tools are application packages for those whose business is developing systems.

Just like any other business, that of systems development is susceptible to the technique of data modelling. Every CASE tool and indeed every development methodology has at its heart a data model called a meta-model. Because the meta-model contains data about data it is not appropriate to set it on the same plane as ordinary business data models: it sits above them and controls how they work. "Meta" is a Greek prefix meaning above.

CASE tools were originally designed to automate computer code production. Early meta-models therefore described not logical data but physical process components such as modules and programs. Subsequently, efforts were made to automate earlier phases of the systems development life cycle. Data dictionaries were built to capture the data structures and process logic discovered during the analysis phase. The mathematical premise of relational data theory meant that the logical data components of the meta-model, such as the entity and the attribute, were well defined and relatively straightforward to model. When structured systems analysis methodologies set about formalising behaviour in the same way, the meta-model acquired new components such as functions and processes.

ICL's Data Dictionary System (DDS), a cumbersome mainframe CASE tool built round a pioneering meta-model, divided its view of the world of systems development into four quadrants Figure 14.1).

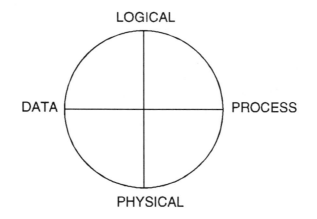

Figure 14.1: *The four quadrants of the DDS meta-model*

Part 1 of this book concerned itself with logical data structures, the top left hand quadrant, touching on physical data structures (the lower left hand quadrant) in chapter 8. Part 2 investigated the development of the data model to incorporate process logic. In doing so it rejected the structured systems developers' view of process - and therefore the whole of the top right hand quadrant of the DDS meta-model - in favour of an Object-Oriented approach based upon a metaphor of tools (business event processors and the organization of work) and materials (data representation and behaviour).

In this chapter we explore how the relational meta-model for logical data can be described using the relational techniques described in part 1.

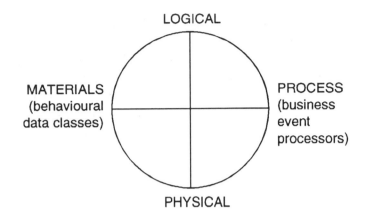

Figure 14.2: *An Object-Oriented meta-model*

14.1   Entities

Just as the business data model might have an entity called Vehicle, the meta-model has a meta-entity called Entity. As J 166 CHM was an occurrence of Vehicle, so Vehicle is an occurrence of Entity[*].

The meta-entity Entity must have a unique identifier which will distinguish its occurrences from one another. A name such as "Vehicle" is sufficient. Entity has an important non-key attribute, its description, which defines the scope of permitted occurrences. It has also been given an attribute called example, which allows the data modeller to enter a sample occurrence of each business entity for illustrative purposes. Another attribute holds the name of the diagram where the entity is at home. For cxample, all of the entities associated with customers might be grouped together for printing as an entity diagram segment (for an illustration of this see the case study in appendix B). The physical implementation flag is used to indicate whether a table should be generated for this entity when the data model is converted into a data definition language. Although there is usually a one-for-one correspondence between logical cntities and physical database tables we saw in chapter 8 that there are situations where an entity

---

[*] Those readers with an understanding of calculus might like to think of the meta-model as the derivative of the business model. The business model is a function such as $1 + e^x$ whose derivative is another function, in this case e^x. If e^x is itself differentiated the result is again e^x. Thus the meta-model of the meta-model is still the meta-model.

might not be implemented as a table. Typically this would be a key-only owner, such as OrderLineNumber.

With the exception of the flag ifPhysicalImplementation, which must take one of the values yes or no, the non-key attributes are optional. This is almost universally true in the meta-model, in recognition of the fact that the practitioner will develop a data model gradually and may wish to record the existence of a meta-entity before its full details are to hand.

Entity
    entityName
(o)   description
(o)   example
(o)   diagramNameHome
    ifPhysicalImplementation

We saw in chapter 4 that entities may have many subtypes. An entity can only have one supertype entity since multiple inheritance is accomplished either by the introduction of a constraint(s) (multiple inheritance within a subtype structure), or by the use of a 1:1 relationship(s) (multiple inheritance from different subtype structures). Therefore the situation where one entity is a subtype of another entity may be modelled using a 1:n recursive relationship (figure 14.3). This structure will be expanded and presented as an attribute list in section 14.5.

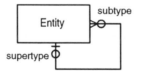

Figure 14.3: *Meta-model for entity subtype structures*

14.2   Attributes

Attribute is another meta-entity. An occurrence of Attribute might be colour. Again this name is enough to identify it uniquely among all the other attributes in the business model. The non-key attributes of Attribute include its description, its data type, its size and its range. They are all allowed to be null because they may not be known at the early stages of the project, though they would all be expected to be completed by the end of it.

Attribute
      <u>attributeName</u>
      entityName
      ifOptional
      ifDerived
(o)   description
(o)   dataType
(o)   sizeOutput
(o)   precisionOutput
(o)   valueMaximum
(o)   valueMinimum
(o)   example
Foreign: entityName → Entity
Foreign: dataType → DataType
Foreign: valueMinimum → Value
Foreign: valueMaximum → Value

14.2.1   Values and value ranges

DataType and Value are both key-only meta-entities related to attribute. The attribute entity has two relationships with Value, both optional even when the business model is published, showing the start and finish of the range of values that an attribute can take on. The attribute can take on any value between the minimum and the maximum. The minimum and maximum values which are physically possible for an attribute are fixed at implementation time by the amount of storage space which will be allocated to the attribute when it is implemented. For example, if an integer is allocated two eight-bit bytes of storage then it can take on values ranging from -32767 to +32767[*]. The logical data modeller should not be concerned with details of physical implementation but should specify a wide enough range to ensure that sufficient space is allocated in the physical design.

Where an attribute must be restricted to a particular set of values the entity AttributeValue, a many-to-many resolver between Attribute and Value, is used. For example, "male" and "female" are the only two permissible values of the attribute gender. The "value" female might also be a permitted value of the attribute reasonOppressed, hence the need for the resolver meta-entity AttributeValue.

Value
      <u>value</u>

---

[*] $32767 = 2^{15} - 1$ or $\sum 2^n$ for all n between 0 & 15 inclusive.

AttributeValue
    <u>value</u>
    <u>attributeName</u>
Foreign: value → Value
Foreign: attributeName → Attribute

14.2.2   Data types

There are several basic data types, such as character, integer, real number and true/false flag. A database which had developed into multi-media would require types such as graphic or sound sample. Because this list of possible values is effectively a domain it can be implemented in a key-only meta-entity called DataType.

DataType
    <u>dataType</u>

Suppose an attribute occurrence, such as colour, has its dataType attribute set to "character". This means that all occurrences of colour will be interpreted as character strings. Even if someone put a value of "27" into the field it would still be interpreted as a character string and the database would refuse any instruction to determine its cubed root.

The dataType date is recognized in most databases because so many business attributes are roles of the root attribute date. However, as noted in chapter 2, date attributes are in fact structured codes which are made up of parts which identify year, month and day. The key of Year might be a four-digit integer such as 1997; the key of Month a two-digit integer such as 11 and the key of DayOfMonth another two-digit integer. If each of these were an attribute in its own right, the integer data type would suffice to classify them all.

14.2.3   Output size and precision

Each Attribute has an output size which qualifies its data type. For example the character string holding colour may be twenty characters long. If the Attribute is to appear on any reports or screens then this is the width of the box or column needed to display it[*]. Screens and reports are usually painted by an automated tool which can read the attribute's output length directly

---

[*] If the output is in proportionally spaced type the screen design must allow for all the characters to be capital Ws, since they take up more space than any other letter!

from the meta-model, but exactly the same considerations apply if a programmer is painting the screen using a more primitive tool.

An integer's output size is the number of spaces required for its digits but not the minus sign or brackets which might be required to indicate when it is negative. Depending on the indicator chosen, the screen design can allow for them separately.

Integers and character strings are normally output in their entirety on screens and reports: they are expressed with full precision. Because a real number includes decimal places its output precision attribute must specify how much precision is required after the decimal point.

Some relational databases combine the dataType and outputSize meta-attributes and offer a domain of data types which is effectively an array of combinations of the two characteristics. For example, Sybase offers three different integer types called int, smallint and tinyint.

14.3   Attributes in entities

When an entity's attributes are listed in the attribute list format used throughout part 1 of this book it can be seen that some might be foreign key attributes inherited from owner entities. Because these attributes can be derived from relationships in the meta-model, only those that are not inherited are held. This implies that each attribute belongs ultimately to just one entity. Entity is the owner of Attribute and therefore entityName appears as a foreign key in Attribute.

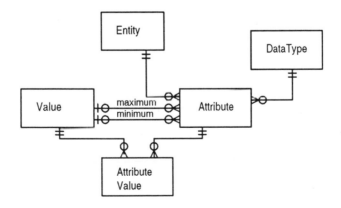

Figure 14.4

Here too optional and derived attributes can be marked. The marker meta-attributes are not allowed to be null: they will all be set to N automatically unless changed.

14.4   Relationships

All the relationships examined in part 1 were binary: that is to say, they linked two entities. Often there is only one relationship between any two entities but there can be several. Therefore the relationship must be identified by an arbitrary serial number as well as the names of both entities.

```
Relationship
        entityNameOwner
        entityNameDetail
        serialNumberRelationship
        relationshipDescription
        ifTransferable
Foreign:        entityNameOwner → Entity
Foreign:        entityNameDetail → Entity
Foreign:        serialNumberRelationship → SerialNumber
```

The meta-entity Relationship has a non-key attribute, indicating whether or not this relationship is transferable. It has a value of N unless actively changed.

14.4.1   Cardinality

A one-to-many relationship has a symmetry: it has an entity at each end and for each end we want to store details of minimum and maximum cardinality and referential integrity. The owner end should be allowed to take on a cardinality between 0 and 1, the detail an unfettered cardinality: otherwise both ends should be structured similarly. Owner and Detail are implemented as two meta-subtypes of Relationship which are in an exclusivity group to ensure that one owner and one detail exists for any relationship (figure 14.5).

14.4.2   Labels

The relationshipLabelOwner in the Owner entity is mandatory and, depending upon the value ifLabelPropagated, may be used to rolename foreign key attributes in a relational implementation. The meta-model would therefore enforce the naming conventions for a business model's attributes, as described in chapter 3. Because of its importance in generating foreign key attribute names the relationshipLabelOwner is required to be unique among all the relationships linking the same owner and detail. The attribute relationshipLabelDetail in the Detail entity is optional - it is never propagated and is often just an artificial inverse of the owner label. It is stored so that it can be output on diagrams and other reports as required.

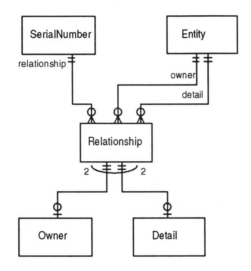

Figure 14.5: *Relationships*

Owner

        <u>entityNameOwner</u>
        <u>entityNameDetail</u>
        <u>serialNumberRelationship</u>
        relationshipLabelOwner
        ifLabelPropagated
(o)   minimumCardinality
(o)   maximumCardinality
(o)   policyOnInsertion
(o)   policyOnDeletion
Foreign: entityNameOwner,
            entityNameDetail,
            serialNumberRelationship → Relationship
Unique: entityNameOwner,
            entityNameDetail,
            relationshipLabelOwner

Detail
     <u>entityNameOwner</u>
     <u>entityNameDetail</u>
     <u>serialNumberRelationship</u>
(o)   relationshipLabelDetail
(o)   minimumCardinality
(o)   maximumCardinality
(o)   policyOnInsertion
(o)   policyOnDeletion
Foreign: entityNameOwner,
           entityNameDetail,
           serialNumberRelationship → Relationship

14.5   Primary and alternate keys

14.5.1   Alternate keys

An entity can have many keys, of which one is designated as the primary key and the others as alternate keys. Each key has to be uniquely identified in the meta-model and entityName plus serial number is used to create a compound meta-key. Since the alternate keys of an entity take no particular precedence over one another this serial number is necessarily arbitrary.

Key
     <u>entityName</u>
     <u>serialNumberKey</u>
Foreign: entityName → Entity
Foreign: serialNumberKey → SerialNumber

Key items are selected from the entity's attributes and its relationships with its owner entities. The latter will become foreign keys in a relational implementation of the business model, but are derivable in the meta-model. Since either an attribute or a relationship can play a part in more than one key, another many-to-many resolver is required.

KeyItem
     <u>entityName</u>
     <u>serialNumberKey</u>
     <u>serialNumberKeyItem</u>
Foreign: entityName,
           serialNumberKey → Key
Foreign: serialNumberKeyItem → SerialNumber

A key can be composed of attributes of an entity, from relationships, or a combination of both. Two meta-subtypes of KeyItem are needed:

AttributeInKey and RelationshipInKey. AttributeInKey has attributeName as a foreign key, constrained by the need to ensure that the chosen attribute is one of the entity's own attributes.

> AttributeInKey
> <u>entityName</u>
> <u>serialNumberKey</u>
> <u>serialNumberKeyItem</u>
> attributeName
> Foreign: entityName,
>   serialNumberKey,
>   serialNumberKeyItem → KeyItem
> Foreign: attributeName → Attribute
> Constraint: entityName,
>   attributeName in
>   Attribute.entityName,
>   Attribute.attributeName

If RelationshipInKey were modelled as a detail of Relationship and a subtype of KeyItem it would inherit the meta-attribute entityNameDetail twice. To avoid this problem SerialNumber and Entity both become foreign key owners of the subtype, representing the owner entity and the sequence number identifying the particular relationship between the owner and the detail. A constraint ensures that the Relationship meta-entity holds an occurrence of a relationship between the entities in question with the requisite serial number.

> RelationshipInKey
> <u>entityName</u>
> <u>serialNumberKey</u>
> <u>serialNumberKeyItem</u>
> entityNameOwner
> serialNumberRelationship
> Foreign: entityName,
>   serialNumberKey,
>   serialNumberKeyItem → KeyItem
> Foreign: entityNameOwner → Entity
> Foreign: serialNumberRelationship → SerialNumber
> Constraint: entityNameOwner,
>   entityName,
>   serialNumberRelationship in
>   Relationship.entityNameOwner,
>   Relationship.entityNameDetail,
>   Relationship.serialNumberRelationship

14.5.2   Primary keys

Not all entities will be treated the same when it comes to defining primary keys. In the logical data model the primary key of a subtype entity must be the same as the key of its (single) supertype. It is possible to distinguish between those business entities that are at the bottom of, or in an intermediate position in the subtype hierarchy, and those business entities that are at the top. Although it is desirable to be able to specify more than one key for any business entity, in the case of subtype entities the primary key must be inherited from its supertype entity. Therefore, primary keys should always be inherited from those business entities that are at the top of the subtype structure. The recursive relationship in figure 14.3 can now be recast to give figure 14.6.

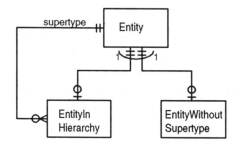

Figure 14.6: *Meta-model for entity subtype structures (resolved)*

One of the keys of an entity without supertype must be chosen as its primary key. This is achieved for business entities that have no supertype by use of the device described in chapter 5, section 5, which allows one of a number of detail occurrences to be nominated as the chief or as the owner's representative. The device would normally work by the addition of a reverse relationship between the original detail and the original owner. In this case, a reverse relationship between Key and EntityWithoutSupertype would result in a foreign key attribute, entityName, appearing in Entity. Since this foreign key attribute will always be the same as the entityName already specified, it would lead to needless duplication. To avoid the problem we make SerialNumber the new owner of EntityWithoutSupertype and use it to specify which of an entity's keys is primary. A constraint ensures that a suitably numbered key does exist for that entity.

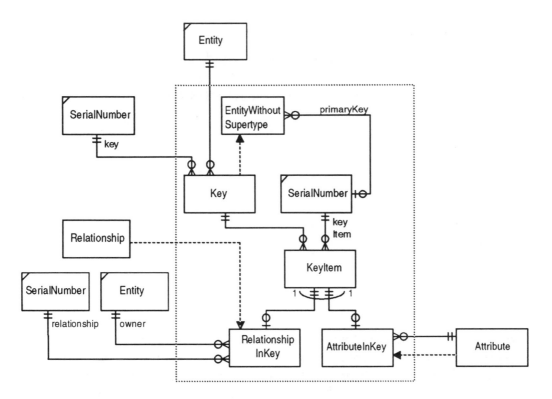

Figure 14.7: *Keys*

Each entity without supertype must have a primary key in the final version of the business model, but the meta-model does not insist on this during development. Thus SerialNumber is an optional owner in the reverse relationship. An alternative would have been to set the value of EntityWithoutSupertype.serialNumberPrimaryKey to 1 as a default. The meta-entity EntityWithoutSupertype is now expanded to show its primary key:

Entity
      entityName
(o)   description
(o)   example
(o)   diagramNameHome
      ifPhysicalImplementation

EntityWithoutSupertype
    <u>entityName</u>
(o)   serialNumberPrimaryKey
Foreign: entityName → Entity
Foreign: serialNumberPrimaryKey → SerialNumber
Constraint: entityName,
        serialNumberPrimaryKey in
        Key.entityName,
        Key.serialNumberKey

EntityInHierarchy
    <u>entityName</u>
    entityNameSupertype
Foreign: entityName → Entity
Foreign: entityNameSupertype → Entity

14.6 Exclusivity groups

Two types of exclusivity group are needed in the meta-model. The first is concerned with the grouping of subtype entities and the second with the grouping of 1:n relationships. As we saw in chapter 4, exclusivity groups on 1:n relationships often imply the need for subtype structures to be introduced.

14.6.1 Subtype groups

A group of entities which are members of a subtype group must all be subtypes of the same supertype. The subtype group has its own characteristics which determine whether one or more of the subtypes must exist. There must be at least two subtypes in a group.

SubtypeGroup
    <u>entityNameSubtypeGroupOwner</u>
    <u>serialNumberSubtypeGroup</u>
(o)   minimumCardinality
(o)   maximumCardinality
    ifCompleteEnumeration
Foreign: entityNameSubtypeGroupOwner → Entity
Foreign: serialNumberSubtypeGroup → SerialNumber

Again, the serial number used to identify the subtype group is arbitrarily chosen. None of the subtype groups in the data model has any precedence over any other. Non-key attributes showing minimum and maximum cardinality are allowed to be null for flexibility in the early stages of a project; the group is assumed to be a complete enumeration of the available subtypes unless the attribute is actively given a value of N.

If a subtype were guaranteed to be in no more than one subtype group then the EntityInHierarchy meta-entity could include an optional foreign key attribute holding the subtype group number. However, it is conceivable that a subtype could belong to more than one group simultaneously[1] so there must be a many-to-many resolver between EntityInHierarchy and SubtypeGroup. A constraint is needed to ensure that all of the entities that comprise the group do actually share the same supertype.

EntityInSubtypeGroup
      <u>entityNameSubtypeGroupOwner</u>
      <u>serialNumberSubtypeGroup</u>
      <u>entityName</u>

Foreign: entityNameSubtypeGroupOwner,
             serialNumberSubtypeGroup → SubtypeGroup

Foreign: entityName → EntityInHierarchy
Constraint: entityName,
             entityNameSubtypeGroupOwner in
             EntityInHierarchy.entityName,
             EntityInHierarchy.entityNameSupertype

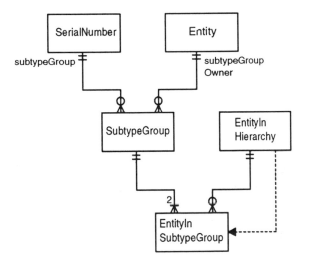

Figure 14.8: *Subtype groups*

14.6.2   Relationship groups

A group of entities which are members of an exclusivity group must all be potential details of the same owner, or must all be potential owners of the same detail - in fact it is the relationships, rather than the entities themselves, which form the group.

> RelationshipGroup
>   <u>entityNameRelationshipGroupOwner</u>
>   <u>serialNumberRelationshipGroup</u>
> (o)   minimumCardinality
> (o)   maximumCardinality
> Foreign: serialNumberRelationshipGroup → SerialNumber
> Foreign: entityNameRelationshipGroupOwner → Entity

Again, the serial number used to identify the group is arbitrarily chosen and none of the relationship groups in the data model has any precedence over any other. As with subtype groups, it is very rare for a relationship to be part of more than one group; if a relationship were guaranteed to be in no more than one group then the Relationship meta-entity could include an optional foreign key attribute holding the relationship group number. However, it is conceivable that a relationship could belong to more than one group simultaneously so there must be a many-to-many resolver between RelationshipGroup and Relationship.

However, if we were to make RelationshipInRelationshipGroup a detail of Relationship then this would lead to entityNameRelationshipGroupOwner being duplicated. Therefore the entity contributing to the relationship group and the serial number of the relationship with the relationship group owner become primary key owners of the resolver and a constraint has been introduced. The constraint has an OR clause to allow the owner of the relationship group to be either a detail of the contributing entities or to be an owner of the contributing entities. See appendix B for illustrations of the different types of relationship groups.

> RelationshipInRelationshipGroup
>   <u>entityNameRelationshipGroupOwner</u>
>   <u>serialNumberRelationshipGroup</u>
>   <u>entityName</u>
>   <u>serialNumberRelationship</u>
> Foreign: entityNameRelationshipGroupOwner,
>   serialNumberRelationshipGroup → RelationshipGroup
> Foreign: entityName → Entity
> Foreign: serialNumberRelationship → SerialNumber

Constraint: entityNameRelationshipGroupOwner,
entityName,
serialNumberRelationship in
Relationship.entityNameOwner
Relationship.entityNameDetail
Relationship.serialNumberRelationship
or in
Relationship.entityNameDetail
Relationship.entityNameOwner
Relationship.serialNumberRelationship

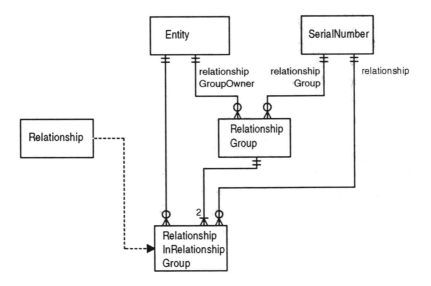

Figure 14.9: *Relationship groups*

14.7   The core meta-model

The meta-model sections of a relational data model presented above are combined in a single diagram (figure 14.10). The consolidated attribute list for the meta-model is shown in appendix C, together with a populated set of sample meta-entities.

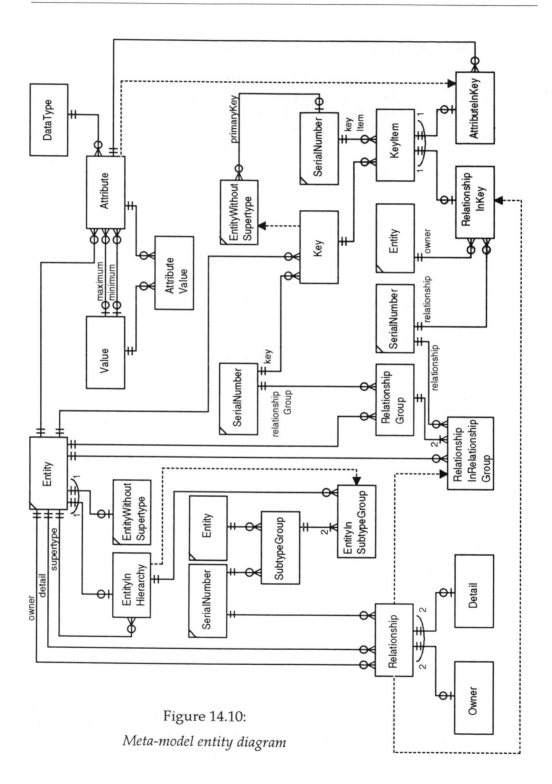

Figure 14.10:

Meta-model entity diagram

14.8   Further considerations

14.8.1   Volumetrics

Meta-models underlying CASE tools often allow volumetric data to be held against meta-entities: thus for example the meta-entity Entity would hold statistics on how many occurrences of each business entity might be expected on average and at peak and off-peak times. This data is unimportant to a logical data model though it is often discovered by the analyst at the same time as the logical data structure.

14.8.2   Projects and versions

This chapter has taken no account so far of the fact that a CASE tool will probably be required to hold business models for several different projects alongside each other. If we wanted to represent this fact in the meta-model we should have to invent another meta-entity called Project, keyed by projectName. The projectName identifier would be inherited by the keys of other meta-entities such as Relationship and thus by all its details. If Entities and Attributes were seen as the property of specific projects, their keys too would inherit projectName.

Used as a basis for a CASE tool the meta-model would acquire extra entities and attributes on physical implementation. It would need to record members of the project team as users. There would also need to be audit attributes on every meta-entity to record when and by which user it had last been updated.

14.8.3   Constraints and business rules

The meta-model in figure 14.10 utilizes constraints but does not provide a mechanism for modelling them. Some constraints are relatively simple and could be attached to entities; more complex constraints can involve a number of entities and fall into the more general category of business rules. The combining of rule-based systems with data-modelling (particularly if an Object-Oriented approach is adopted) is highly relevant and of great interest but outside the scope of this chapter.

Some simple business rules can be implemented using the value clause and can thus be implemented directly in a data model. See chapter 3 for an example of the use of a value clause.

14.9   Reporting from the meta-model

In the same way that users get reports from their business models, data modellers find reports from the meta-model invaluable throughout the course of the development of a system. The reports help the data modeller to enforce meta-relationships which were optional at the beginning of the development project but which are expected to be completed eventually.

One important report from the meta-model is the business model diagram. It will be apparent that all the symbols and annotations on a data model diagram are derivable from the meta-entities described. For example, whether relationship labels are shown in both directions, one direction or neither is a reporting option. In theory, once the full details have been entered into a CASE tool's project dictionary the tool could draw perfect data model diagrams for a project team's use. This facility could be built into every CASE tool immediately if it wasn't for the difficulty of creating algorithms to place symbols in two-dimensional space in such a way that they can be linked accurately and with a minimum of crossing lines. But it is the aesthetics of the diagram which are contributed by the artist, not its logic: that should all be backed up by meta-model table entries.

Chapter summary

Like any other area of business activity, systems development can be described by data modelling. The entity diagram, attribute list and relational schema can be pictured as reports that are produced from a repository (usually a CASE tool) that is itself the subject of a data model. Such a data model is called a meta-model. Although it might appear that an attribute list contains redundant data, it should be remembered that this is a report from a non-redundant meta-model.

The meta-model described here supports all aspects of data modelling as described in chapters 2 to 6, with the exception of constraints. However, other methodologies and CASE tools have come up with slightly different designs - rather as two analysts modelling an order processing system would debate some aspects of the model. The point is that in defining the structure of the meta-model a CASE tool designer effectively decides how the CASE tool will work. And of course the data modeller on the order processing system determines its major design principles too.

NOTES

1. Note that this isn't the same as multiple inheritance, which allows an entity to have two supertype owners simultaneously. Here we're talking about one supertype and one subtype, where the subtype may-or-must exist in one group and may-or-must exist in another group as well. The relationship between entity A and entity D in the following diagram illustrates this case:

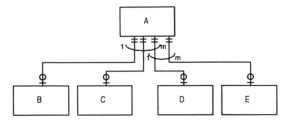

Questions

1.   Create a meta-model of a data flow diagram (DFD). Use any popular text on SSADM as your requirements specification.

2.   Use the object model conventions to create a meta-model for the logical data model (an object model equivalent for figure 14.10).

3.   How might composition structures and encapsulation of behaviour be introduced to the new meta-model produced in question 2?

4.   Produce an event schema for the data modelling process. If you were to implement the event schema, what might some of the screens look like?

5.   Create state transition diagrams for the meta-entities Entity and Attribute.

6.   Use the object model notation to create a meta-model for the object model itself.

7.   In this chapter we used the logical data model to meta-model itself. In question 6 the object model is used to meta-model itself. Is it appropriate to model the object model using its own conventions? What might a meta-meta-model look like?

15

Data modelling in context

Introduction

The first two parts of this book focussed on technique - data modelling and object modelling. Proficiency in the techniques of data modelling might well contribute towards successful computer systems development, but we are not under the illusion that technical proficiency will be sufficient. Your data modelling technique might well improve as a result of reading this book (indeed we hope that it will), but technique alone cannot guarantee success in computer systems development. Rather than finish with a conclusion that pretends to supply final answers we prefer to raise questions that point toward some of the issues that arise once a technical competence in data modelling has been achieved. Data modelling is based on some remarkably simple notions, namely entities and relationships (or classes and associations). Why then does it take so long to become practised in data modelling and why do so many development exercises fail, even when experienced and capable technical personnel are involved?

Despite attempts to make computer system development more rigorous, whether it be through a more formal process of requirements analysis or automation of the development process involving the use of Computer Aided Software Engineering (CASE), a considerable proportion of systems development results in products that cannot be said to provide user satisfaction. It has been reported that 75% of all system development efforts were cancelled, or the completed systems never used[1].

Common sense might lead us to believe that poor quality data models result from the modeller failing to reach a proper understanding of the facts of the situation or, having understood the situation correctly, not representing the facts faithfully in a data model. Common sense then leads us to an obvious solution: we must be more rigorous in eliciting requirements so that our models better mirror reality and we must develop better modelling techniques for representing that reality. But it is just not that easy. William Kent has discussed some of the difficulties encountered when identifying entities and relationships[2]. Using a wealth of examples, Kent demonstrates the practical difficulties associated with creating universal definitions for entities, particularly for entities that at first sight seem straightforward, such as street, building, and book, showing that the selection of entities and the definition of those entities cannot be separated from the context in which they will be used.

In talking about the common-sense approach to data modelling and the need to mirror reality more closely we have created a straw man that is supported by some major and questionable assumptions. In the next section we consider the assumption that a good data model is one that mirrors reality.

15.1   Four paradigms of data modelling

A paradigm provides an overall way for organizing our thoughts about the world. In science a paradigm determines what methods and explanations will be considered as acceptable. A framework for classifying paradigms is described by Burrell & Morgan[3], involving the categorization of assumptions on objectivist/subjectivist and order/conflict dimensions (figure 15.1). This framework has been applied widely in Information System research.[4]

The *objectivist* position is characterized by a realist ontology and a positivist epistemology. Ontology is concerned with the nature of reality. Epistemology is concerned with how we gain legitimate knowledge about the world, i.e., with truth. Loosely speaking, the objectivist assumes that objects and structures exist as empirical entities independent of human observers and that the appropriate way of acquiring knowledge of the world is by observation and the identification of causal relationships (correspondence to reality is the measure of a good theory). The *subjectivist* position holds that scientific method is not appropriate for explaining the social world as different people interpret the world in different ways and any agreement is inter-subjective. The appropriate way to investigate the social world is to recognize multiple realities and to adopt an interpretivist stance. The *order* view of the world sees order, stability, and integration; the *conflict* view sees coercion, disintegration, and places an emphasis on change. These two classifications yield four distinctive combinations: functionalism (objectivism/order); radical structuralism (objectivism/conflict); social relativism (subjectivism/order); and neohumanism (subjectivism/conflict). In figure 15.1, these positions have been represented by the metaphors of doctor, warrior, liberal teacher, and emancipator respectively.

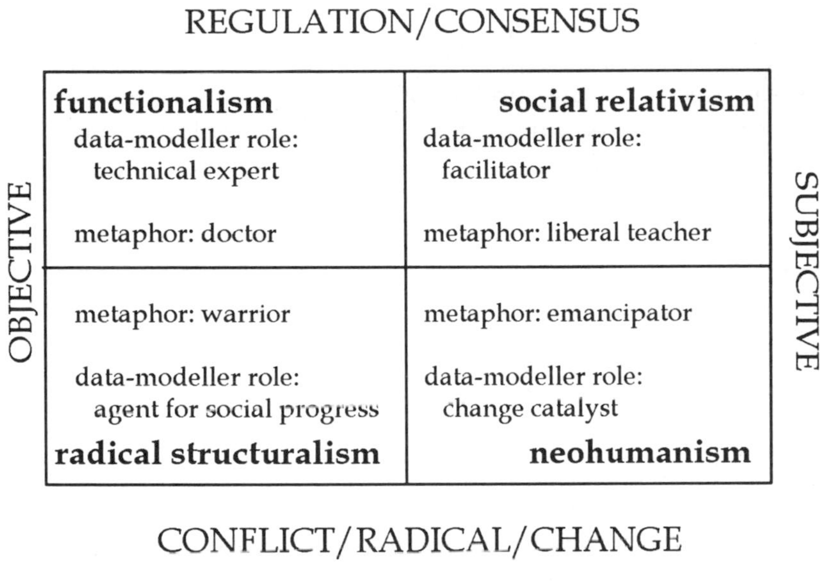

REGULATION/CONSENSUS

functionalism	**social relativism**
data-modeller role: technical expert	data-modeller role: facilitator
metaphor: doctor	metaphor: liberal teacher
metaphor: warrior	metaphor: emancipator
data-modeller role: agent for social progress	data-modeller role: change catalyst
radical structuralism	**neohumanism**

(left side: OBJECTIVE; right side: SUBJECTIVE)

CONFLICT/RADICAL/CHANGE

Figure 15.1: *Four paradigms of data modelling*

With respect to data modelling two questions are raised by this framework. Firstly, what is the ontological status of the data model, and secondly what is an appropriate way to go about the construction of a data model? How might an analyst approach the task of data modelling working within each of the different paradigms? Would we expect their assumptions about reality and truth, and order and conflict to have an influence on the form that the data model takes?

The technical expert, "doctor", sees data modelling as an objective exercise where entities and relationships can be said to exist independently of people (entities and relationships exist without a person being present to perceive them). Problems with data models are associated with a failure to capture and specify the real requirements. The solution is to improve the engineering process such that the requirements specification is accurate, complete, consistent, and unambiguous. The assumption that there is agreement on means and ends leads to a single data model that is suitable for and acceptable to all stakeholders. The data model is a value-free reflection of a singular reality and scientific method is the appropriate way of building a data model (data models are theories which can be empirically tested in the real world).

The "warrior" also perceives data modelling as an objective exercise, but assumes that there are conflicting interests and is therefore concerned with whose requirements are being addressed. For example, do the entities captured in the data model satisfy the needs of management at the expense of employees' needs? Data modelling is seen to be conflictual as it is not possible to satisfy the requirements of all the stakeholders. Socio-economic structures exist in the real world (hence the objectivist classification) and one of the responsibilities of the data modeller is to protect the interests of those disadvantaged by such structures. The data model is a reflection of real-world structures but because of socio-economic factors the data model is not value-free; the data modeller should support labour activities in the struggle against the owners.

The facilitator, "liberal teacher", considers reality to be socially constructed and that there are as many realities as there are people involved in the development exercise. Entities and relationships are therefore inter-subjectively agreed, requiring the participation of many of the parties affected by a proposed IS to be involved in agreeing what entities and relationships should be incorporated in the data model. The situation is perceived to be one of consensus, which means that the parties involved will be able to reach agreement concerning a suitable data model. Differences in perception of what constitutes an appropriate data model can be reconciled in the interests of the common good. In this case there is no single correct data model - an acceptable model will emerge through the *process* of constructing a data model. The more people whose interests are reflected in the model then the more likely it is that a shared understanding will be reached and a successful implementation achieved. A good data model is one which creates a shared understanding; the appropriate way to go about creating such a model is through participation and facilitation.

The "emancipator" would also consider that reality is socially-constructed, but recognizes the presence of conflict and hence the exercise of power. The emancipator is thus concerned with constructing a data model that takes into account the needs of the less powerful (less privileged) and the recognition of cultural repression. The emancipator adopts a critical stance and seeks to initiate change that will improve the situation, recognizing that there is unlikely to be a consensus and that any data model will be mediated through the exercise of power. A good data model is one which helps create a social reality that alleviates cultural repression; the appropriate way to go about creating such a data model is via a rational discourse that is emancipatory.

In assuming that a good data model is one that mirrors reality we are working within a positivist tradition in which the measure of a good theory (data model) is its correspondence with reality. The Burrell and Morgan framework shows that this is but one way of approaching the world. Do data modellers work within a functionalist paradigm?

15.1.1   Data modelling and functionalism

Many of the working definitions of an entity have been derived from Chen's seminal paper in which the entity-relationship model is considered to be a reflection of the real world[5]:

> The entity-relationship model adopts the more natural view that the real world consists of entities and relationships. It incorporates some of the important semantic information about the real world.....An entity is a "thing" which can be distinctly identified.

Paul Lewis gives a number of quotes from the data modelling and Object-Oriented (O-O) literature showing that many methods assume an objective ontology.[6] Lewis shows that there is a potential danger with O-O in the insistence that objects are a more natural representation of the real world. Such a stance sidelines the question of whether entities and classes are useful epistemological devices or whether they have ontological significance. Perhaps data modellers espouse a functionalist approach, but what do they do in practice? Martin & Odell refer to O-O as a model of reality:[7]

> The models we build in OO analysis reflect reality more naturally than the models in traditional systems analysis. Reality, after all, consists of objects

and events that change the state of those objects. Using OO techniques, we build software that more closely models the real world. When the real world changes, our software is easier to change - a real advantage. (page 67)

The authors of this work appear to have adopted an objectivist stance. However, in practice it is not so easy to stick to our functionalist principles and in the same text we find:

Analyzing organizational systems means creating an effective, shared set of concepts. Concepts underlie each and every organizational process. Concepts define a shared organizational reality and form the basis of an organizational language with which to communicate. (page 237)

This creation of shared meaning through the definition of concepts does not seem to sit easily with the objectivist flavour of the previous quote (although this could be due to there being dual authorship). Is it possible to accept both the above quotes without being inconsistent? We argue that the issue is not whether to be objective or subjective but that one implies the other and that any method that is based upon one of these ontological positions must accept and cater for the other. Substantiating this argument is the aim of the next section.

15.2   Dualities and dualisms

The original work by Burrell and Morgan proposes that the four paradigms are mutually exclusive and that methods should be developed independently within the individual philosophies - this is known as paradigmatic closure. The implication of paradigmatic closure is that data modelling methods should be based either upon the notion of an objective reality or upon the notion of a reality that is socially constructed (in which case data models can be said to create reality rather than to mirror it). Taking a strong objectivist position is difficult - we cannot demonstrate the existence of an objective reality (science cannot legitimate itself)[8]. But a strong subjectivist stance is not a lot more comfortable and runs the danger of an extreme relativism where anything goes. The problem we have created is in assuming that data modelling must be either objective or subjective. We have created a binary opposition between objectivism and subjectivism and cast them as a dualism.

Berger and Luckman proposed a framework where subjective meanings (externalization) become objective facticities (objectivation) which then "act back" as they socialize present and future generations (internalization).[9] Reality construction is the dialectical relationship of these three moments.

Giddens seems to have moved even further from the paradigmatic closure of the Burrell and Morgan framework by conceiving the objective and subjective to be present simultaneously, as represented in structuration theory.[10]   An important implication of structuration theory is that the objective/subjective distinction should be seen as a duality and that it is not possible to separate out objective and subjective components.

15.2.1   Structuration theory

Structuration theory allows us to see the subjective and the objective as a duality[11] rather than a dualism and is a framework that is being used more widely in IS research.[12] Giddens resolves the objective/subjective debate by seeing structure (objectivity) and agency/process (subjectivity) as a duality in which social action both reproduces and changes the social structure. Human action and social structure are considered in three dimensions: signification, legitimation, and domination. The dimensions are linked by three modalities: *interpretative scheme* - stocks of knowledge drawn upon by human actors to make sense of their own and others' actions; *facility* - the ability to allocate resources (human and material); *norm* - actions sanctioned by drawing upon standards concerning good and bad. Structuration theory allows for unintended consequences of intentional human activity and recognizes practical consciousness - that people are more knowledgeable than they can articulate.

15.2.2   Structuration theory and IS development

With respect to IS development and data modelling the notion of duality is shown in figure 15.2. The structures of signification represent organizational reality (the current organizational context). The activity of IS development is constrained by the structures of signification, but at the same time has the potential to change those structures of signification, i.e., to (re)create organizational reality by the introduction of the unfamiliar.

We define a method to be a set of procedures for getting things done. A methodology is a higher level construct that provides a rationale for choosing between different methods. Data modelling is a technique that can be employed by different development methods.[13]   According to these definitions Information Engineering and SSADM are both methods, despite one, IEM, being called a methodology. In figure 15.2 IS methods form part of the stock of knowledge used to make sense of the participants' actions. It is not appropriate to consider the process as objective (IS development mirrors organizational reality) or as subjective (organizational reality is created through IS development). Both objective and subjective aspects are present at the same time; without the notion of objectivity the notion of subjectivity is meaningless (and vice versa) - objective methods can be said to be objective because they are not subjective. The developer who adopts a predominantly objective approach to development will tend to reinforce the current structures of signification; the developer who can recognize that reality is also socially constructed is more likely to be involved in the re-creation of structures of signification. The situation can be seen to be further complicated by the aspects of domination and legitimation, tacit knowledge, and unintended consequences.

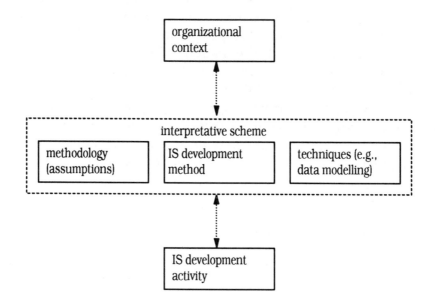

Figure 15.2: *IS development as a duality*

15.3   Information and data

Throughout this book we have tried to avoid the term information modelling and have concentrated on the modelling of data. We are also aware that we have made no attempt to define either.[14] We take information to be data plus the meaning attributed to it. Consider the item of data year to date sales. The sales person might interpret this datum in the context of annual bonus;

the sales manager in terms of sales team performance; the marketing manager might use it as input to the development of a marketing strategy.[15] As has been observed by Kent, data take on meaning (become information) in a context. By thinking of computer systems as stores of "information" we remove the very thing that distinguishes data from information - the process of meaning attribution, which is carried out in a context by people.   By assuming that the concept information has a real world existence we first reify it; by seeing it as embodied in computer systems we objectify it - information becomes a real world entity that we can go up to and touch. Boland argues that we have deferred the difficult issue of how meaning is negotiated. Following from Giddens, Boland argues that information is not a commodity - it is a skilled human accomplishment.[16]

But where is the meaning? The meaning is not entirely in the data model and it is not entirely in the situation being modelled - it lies somewhere between the two and cannot be located precisely. You might argue that once a situation has been described in a data model then others could use this "objective" description as the basis for computer system development. Unfortunately the act of reading a data model is itself interpretive and subject to the same difficulties experienced when the modeller interpreted the situation to produce a data model.   And it does not stop there: the implementation of a computer system is in part an interpretation of a data model and the use of that computer system is yet a further act of interpretation, this time by a user of that computer system.   It is not surprising that the meaning becomes hard to track down when it is subject to continual re-negotiation in a boundless context.

One of the problems in seeing information as something in the real world is that we lose sight of its metaphoric power. Information becomes a taken for granted literal truth. In the next section we consider how literal thinking can constrain the data modeller.

15.4   Metaphors, literal truths and data modelling

The notion of information adopted for the purposes of this book is of information as a metaphor. From Aristotle onwards, metaphor has often been defined as transference. Morgan defines metaphor:[17]

We use metaphor whenever we attempt to understand one element of experience in terms of another. Thus, metaphor proceeds through implicit or explicit assertions that A is (or is like) B. When we say "the man is a lion", we use the image of a lion to draw attention to the lion-like aspects of the man.

The metaphor frames our understanding of the man in a distinctive yet partial way (page 13).

The application of a metaphor is at the same time a way of not seeing, as it highlights one view while pushing others into the background. Richard Rorty argues that truth is a metaphor couched in language and is not a given that is 'out there'. Without sentences we do not have truth. Sentences are part of language and language is a human creation. Thus, only descriptions of the world can be true or false since we cannot say anything about the world other than through language. The world without humans cannot be true or false and truth must be made rather than found. Rather than seeing language as a medium between ourselves and the real world it is more pertinent to consider language as a metaphorical device, where the major distinction is between the familiar and the unfamiliar. Attention is then focussed on how we create the unfamiliar and the process by which it becomes familiar and thus literally true. Rorty distinguishes between irony and common sense.[18]

The common-sense approach accepts the current vocabulary as sufficient and sees reality as determining our vocabulary. The ironist distrusts the vocabulary that is inherited and approaches it critically. A common-sense data modeller will accept that customers are a real world phenomenon - all organizations have customers don't they? But many retail banking systems were built without a customer entity; these systems were product processing systems, reflecting the banks' account orientation in the 1960s and 1970s. Subsequently they have found it very difficult to change their computer systems (and their business) to a customer basis. The notion customer at one time was unfamiliar noise; as it became accepted and used widely it became a literal truth. To be creative, data modellers need to think metaphorically and to be willing to introduce unfamiliar noise. If the unfamiliar noise gets accepted and implemented successfully in a computer system then the metaphor dies and literal truths emerge.

The ironist data modeller will question the inherited vocabulary of the entities and relationships currently recognized by an organization; the common-sense data modeller will accept the existing categories that the organization uses and implement them as literal truths in a data model. Which approach would you rather take when attempting Business Process Reengineering?

15.5   Multiple perspectives

In chapter 8 we discussed the physical implementation of a data model. This is important and it is possible that a computer system might fail if, for example, the response times were too long. But there are many other causes of failure and many of them have little to do with the technical competence of the system developers. Data modellers who think in one perspective only are in danger of over-simplifying a complex situation. One way in which data modellers can be more sensitive to the situation in which they are working is to apply a multiple perspective approach.

The application of multiple perspectives to data modelling is not merely an exercise in looking at the same object from different angles or different peoples' perspectives (e.g., the user's view of the data model compared with the database administrator's). Unbounded Systems Thinking (UST) by Mitroff and Linstone proposes three perspectives: technical (T), organization (O), and personal (P)[19]. Paraphrasing from Mitroff and Linstone: the T perspective is concerned with a scientific world-view, logic, rationality, modelling and analysis, and a claim of objectivity; the O perspective is concerned with social entities, politics, and processes; and the P perspective world-view is of the individual and is concerned with power, influence, prestige, learning, and beliefs. Mitroff and Linstone recognize that the O and P perspectives overlap and that it can be difficult to separate them. Different forms of knowledge are appropriate to the different perspectives - the scientific approach might be relevant when taking a T perspective, but it is not appropriate for addressing O and P issues.

However, by recognizing different forms of knowledge the multiple perspective approach is associated with practical difficulties, some of which are now considered. As a result of their background and tradition, people tend to privilege one particular perspective over other perspectives. For example, data modellers are often happier when taking a technical perspective of a situation. However, attempting to 'right' the situation by privileging the organizational view while at the same time marginalizing technical issues is not necessarily a solution. The perspectives represent different knowledge interests and thus need to be considered jointly. Because they cannot be reduced in any meaningful sense to a single perspective, there are no simple rules for balancing the requirements of different perspectives. Indeed, the perspectives should be expected to produce conflicting requirements and this dissensus used as a basis for discussion and action. Thus, in using multiple perspectives we need to be able to use methods that reflect the different knowledge interests, to be aware of the limitations of the different methods, and to use judgement to reach a balance.

In this book we have focussed on how to describe data structures and have given little attention to the problems of interpreting the context in which data modelling takes place (an O perspective). One approach to modelling the context in which data will be used is SSM (Soft Systems Methodology). A description of the method is outside the scope of this book but readers are directed towards the work of Checkland.[20] Aspects of the P perspective can be addressed using the ETHICS method.[21] A development method that incorporates all three elements of the TOP model is the Multiview methodology.

Chapter summary

Diverse ideas have been brought together in this chapter partly to provide a contrast from the technique emphasis of the preceding chapters but also to attempt to explain why data modelling is so difficult, especially given the simplicity of the technique. One aim of this chapter has been to raise questions rather than provide answers; we make progress through asking new questions rather than finding new answers to old questions.

It might seem that this chapter is rather abstract and conceptual and of little relevance to practising data modellers. We believe that many of the ideas presented here lead to a practical agenda for data modelling.

Some of the ideas put forward for data modellers are:

- question continually the assumptions that you work with (these are usually implicit) and try to reflect upon experience[22];

- think in terms of dualities rather than dualisms and be comfortable with current structures while recognizing that you may be creating new structures;

- recognize that data is not value-free and that you can never wholly be an objective outsider;

- retain the notion that data models are metaphorical and that successful computer systems embody dead metaphors as literal truths;

- use multiple perspectives to gain a deeper understanding of the contradictions inherent in most situations. It is better to surface and be aware of contradictions than to ignore them.

Above all, data modellers should be prepared to take responsibility for the consequences of their actions. Professional modellers are involved - they are not bystanders.

1. As reported in:

> Lyytinen, K., & Hirschheim, R.A., (1987). Information Systems Failures - a survey and classification of the empirical literature. *Oxford Surveys in Information Technology*, volume 4, 258-309. Oxford University Press.

Jayaratna reported on a breakdown of US federal software projects (a total software budget of $6.2m) that showed: less than 2% of software products were used as delivered; 3% were used after change; 19% were abandoned or reworked; 29% were paid for but not delivered; and 47% were delivered but never used. Although these results may or may not be representative of software development in general they do lead one to question whether improving the technical abilities of system developers is sufficient to ensure that quality applications (i.e., applications which when used result in customer satisfaction) are delivered.

> Jayaratna, N., (1990). Systems Analysis: The Need for a Better Understanding. *International Journal of Management*, 10: 228-234.

2. Kent describes the challenges of data modelling in a lucid and entertaining way; all system developers should read this book:

> Kent, W., (1978). *Data and Reality: basic assumptions in data processing reconsidered.* Elsevier, Amsterdam.

3. The four paradigm framework presented here is described in detail in:

> Burrell, G., & Morgan, G., (1979). *Sociological Paradigms and Organizational Analysis.* Heinemann Educational Books, London

This book was difficult to get hold of; it has been reprinted by Arena, Ashgate Publishing Limited (1993).

4. Klein and Hirschheim have applied the four paradigms framework to IS development:

> Hirschheim, R.A., & Klein, H.K., (1989). Four Paradigms of Information Systems Development. *Communications of the ACM*, 32(10): 1199-1216.

In an earlier paper they applied the objective/subjective dimension to data modelling:

> Klein, H.K., & Hirschheim, R.A., (1987). A Comparative Framework of Data Modelling Paradigms and Approaches. *The Computer Journal*, 30(1): 8-15.

Avison and Wood-Harper have also drawn upon the four paradigm framework:

> Avison, D.E., & Wood-Harper, A.T., (1990). *Multiview: An Exploration in Information Systems Development.* Blackwell Scientific Publications, Oxford.

The representation of the framework presented in figure 15.1 draws upon all of the above sources. In this chapter we are more concerned with the assumptions of the data *modeller* rather than the paradigm that data *modelling* might be said to be typified by.

5. See:

> Chen, P., (1976). The entity-relationship model: towards a unified view of data. *ACM Transactions on Database Systems*, 1(1): 9-37.

6. Lewis gives a fascinating insight into the issues of data modelling in particular and computer system development in general:
    Lewis, P., (1994). *Information Systems Development*. Pitman.

7. See:
    Martin, J., & Odell, J., (1992). *Object-Oriented Analysis and Design*. Prentice-Hall. Englewood Cliffs.

8. For a discussion of some of the difficulties in science legitimating itself refer to:
    Lyotard, J.-F., (1984). *The Postmodern Condition: A Report on Knowledge*. Manchester University Press.

9. See:
    Berger, P. L., & Luckman, T., (1966). *The Social Construction of Reality*. Doubleday. GardenCity, New York.

10. See:
    Giddens, A., (1984). *The Constitution of Society*. Polity Press, Cambridge.

11. This argument has been presented by:
    Wilmott, H., (1990). Beyond paradigmatic closure in organizational enquiry. In: Hassard, J., & Pym, D., editors. *The theory and philosophy of organizations: Critical issues and new perspectives*. Routledge, London.
    From a different background Latour has argued a case for accepting the paradox that society is socially constructed (subjectivity) yet at the same time has a "real" existence (objectivity), as we soon find out when embarking on any attempt to create a new social reality.
    Latour, B., (1993). *We Have Never Been Modern*. Harvester Wheatsheaf.

12. For an application of structuration theory to IS research see:
    Walsham, G., & Han, C.-K., (1991). Structuration Theory and Information Systems Research. *Journal of Applied Systems Analysis*, 17: 77-85
    Walsham, G., (1993). *Interpreting Information Systems in Organizations*. Wiley, UK.

13. The notion of duality can be carried down into the data model itself. Fuzzy logic accepts dualities and recognizes dualisms as the ends of a spectrum. Some people are old. some people are young, but there is a grey area where people are "youngish". A very accessible introduction to fuzzy logic is:
    Kosko, B., (1993). *Fuzzy thinking: the new science of fuzzy logic*. Harper Collins. London.
    Graham has introduced fuzzy logic to create fuzzy objects:
    Graham, I., (1994). *Object-Oriented Methods*. Second edition. Addison Wesley.
    This is potentially a very powerful way of modelling data and it goes some way to tackling the problems raised by Kent. Although fuzzy logic might appear to be sympathetic with a structuration approach, it is important not to lose sight of the philosophical issues - there is a danger that fuzzy logic will be seen as a way of getting an even closer representation of a real world (Kosko does not really tackle this issue).

14. We have also made no attempt to define "system". That is another thorny issue and one which we do not tackle here, except to say that we adopt a structurational view of hard and soft approaches to systems thinking.

15. This example is taken from:
>   Wilson, B., (1991). Information Management. In: Jackson M., Mansell, G., Flood, R., Blackham, R., & Probert, S. *Systems Thinking in Europe*. Plenum Press, New York. Pages 89-97.

16. The foregoing argument has been taken from:
>   Boland, R.J., (1987). The In-formation of Information Systems. In: Boland, R.J., & Hirschheim, R., editors. *Critical Issues in Information Systems Research*. Wiley.

17 The work of Gareth Morgan on metaphor is:
>   Morgan, G., (1986). *Images of Organization*. Sage. Newbury Park, CA.
>   Morgan, G., (1993). *Imaginization*. Sage. Newbury Park, CA.

> A work that argues the importance of metaphor is:
>   Lakoff, G., & Johnson, M., (1980). *Metaphors we Live By*. The University of Chicago Press.

18. Chapter 4, "Private irony and liberal hope" contains a very readable account of irony and common sense, in:
>   Rorty, R., (1989). *Contingency, irony, and solidarity*. Cambridge University Press.

19. The multiple perspective approach is described in:
>   Mitroff, I., & Linstone, H., (1993). *The Unbounded Mind, breaking the chains of traditional business thinking*. Oxford University Press, New York.

20. SSM is described in:
>   Checkland, P., (1981). *Systems Thinking, Systems Practice*. Wiley, Chichester.
>   Checkland, P., & Scholes, J., (1990). *Soft Systems Methodology in Action*. Wiley, Chichester.

> For an IS emphasis see Lewis and also:
>   Wilson, B., (1990). *Systems: Concepts, Methdologies and Applications*. Wiley, Chichester.

21. ETHICS is described in:
>   Mumford, E., & Weair, M., (1979). *Computer systems in work design - the ETHICS method*. Associated Business Press. London.

22. Practice and theory can be thought of as being linked in a learning cycle (they can also be thought of as co-present). Reflection on practice can help data modellers to understand how and why some techniques and approaches worked in one situation but not in another. One of the most important characteristics of IS professionals is the ability to reflect upon their practice:
>   Schon, D., (1983). *The Reflective Practitioner: how professionals think in action*. Basic Books, NY.

> For further thoughts about computer systems see:
>   Dahlbom, B., & Mathiassen, L., (1993). *Computers in Context*. NCC Blackwell, Oxford.

Appendix A

Diagramming conventions

Class diagram
Association cardinality
A Mandatory / B Optional

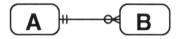

Instances of class A are associated with 0, 1 or more instances of class B

Instances of class B are associated with 1 instance of class A

A Optional / B Optional

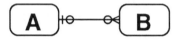

Instances of class A are associated with 0, 1 or more instances of class B

Instances of class B are associated with 0 or 1 instances of class A

A Mandatory / B Mandatory

Instances of class A are associated with 1 or more instances of class B

Instances of class B are associated with 1 instance of class A

A Optional / B Mandatory

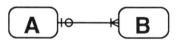

Instances of class A are associated with 1 or more instances of class B

Instances of class B are associated with 0 or 1 instances of class A

Entity diagram
Relationship cardinality
A Mandatory / B Optional

Occurrences of entity A are related
to 0, 1 or more occurrences of entity B

Occurrences of entity B are related
to 1 occurrence of entity A

A Optional / B Optional

Occurrences of entity A are related
to 0, 1 or more occurrences of entity B

Occurrences of entity B are related
to 0 or 1 occurrences of entity A

A Mandatory / B Mandatory

Occurrences of entity A are related
to 1 or more occurrences of entity B

Occurrences of entity B are related
to 1 occurrence of entity A

A Optional / B Mandatory

Occurrences of entity A are related
to 1 or more occurrences of entity B

Occurrences of entity B are related
to 0 or 1 occurrences of entity A

Class diagram
Association cardinality

A Mandatory / B Optional

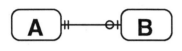

Instances of class A are associated with 0 or 1 instances of class B

Instances of class B are associated with 1 instance of class A

A Optional / B Optional

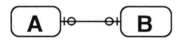

Instances of class A are associated with 0 or 1 instances of class B

Instances of class B are associated with 0 or 1 instances of class A

A Mandatory / B Mandatory

Instances of class A are associated with 1 instance of class B

Instances of class B are associated with 1 instance of class A

Entity diagram
Relationship cardinality

A Mandatory / B Optional

Occurrences of entity A are related to 0 or 1 occurrences of entity B

Occurrences of entity B are related to 1 occurrence of entity A

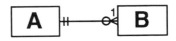

A Optional / B Optional

Occurrences of entity A are related to 0 or 1 occurrences of entity B

Occurrences of entity B are related to 0 or 1 occurrences of entity A

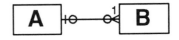

A Mandatory / B Mandatory

Occurrences of entity A are related to 1 occurrence of entity B

Occurrences of entity B are related to 1 occurrence of entity A

Class diagram
Association cardinality

A Optional / B Optional

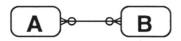

Instances of class A are associated
with 0, 1 or many instances of class B

Instances of class B are associated
with 0, 1 or many instances of class A

A Mandatory / B Optional

Instances of class A are associated
with 0, 1 or many instances of class B

Instances of class B are associated
with 1 or many instances of class A

Changing upper and lower bounds

Instances of class A are associated
with between j and k instances of class B

Instances of class B are associated
with 1 instance of class A

Entity diagram
Relationship cardinality

A Optional / B Optional

Occurrences of entity A are related to 0, 1 or many occurrences of entity B

Occurrences of entity B are related to 0, 1 or many occurrences of entity A

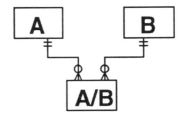

A Mandatory / B Optional

Occurrences of entity A are related to 0, 1 or many occurrences of entity B

Occurrences of entity B are related to 1 or many occurrences of entity A

Changing upper and lower bounds

Occurrences of entity A are related to between j and k occurrences of entity B

Occurrences of entity B are related to 1 occurrence of entity A

Class diagram
Recursive associations

Many to many (bill of materials)

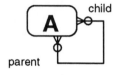

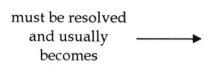

must be resolved
and usually
becomes

One to many (hierarchy)

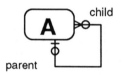

might become

One to one (chain)

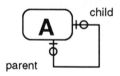

might become

Entity diagram
Recursive relationships

Many to many (bill of materials)

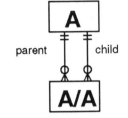

One to many (hierarchy)

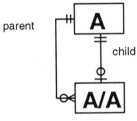

One to one (chain)

parent

A

child

A/A

Class diagram
subclasses

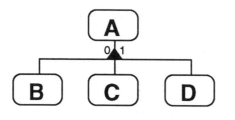

Instances are of class A, B, C or D (exhaustive and mutually exclusive subclasses). A is a concrete class and may have instances (the subclasses B, C and D are optional)

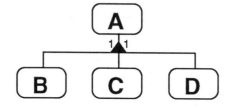

Instances are of class B, C or D (exhaustive and mutually exclusive subclasses). A is an abstract class and may not have instances

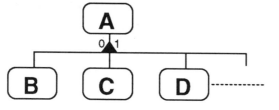

Instances are of class A, B, C or D. The dotted line indicates that the subclass partitioning (B, C and D) is not fully enumerated - more subclassses may exist but are not shown on the diagram, or a complete set of subclasses has yet to be agreed

Entity diagram
entity subtypes

Occurrences of entity type A may be related to one of the entity subtypes B, C, or D (exhaustive and mutually exclusive subtypes). Occurrences of entity A may exist without being related to a subtype entity

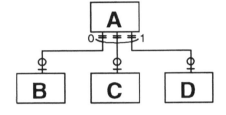

Occurrences of entity type A must be related to one of the entity subtypes B, C, or D (exhaustive and mutually exclusive subtypes). Occurrences of entity A that are not related to a subtype entity are not permitted

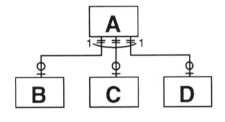

Occurrences of entity type A may be related to one of the entity subtypes B, C, or D. The dotted line indicates that the subtype partitioning (B, C, or D) is not fully enumerated - more subtypes may exist but are not shown on the diagram, or a complete set of subtypes has yet to be agreed

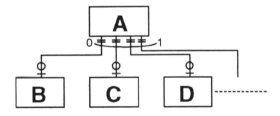

Class diagram
subclasses

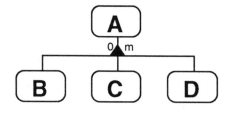

Instances can be of class A, B, C or D, or any combination of B, C and D (exhaustive and independent subclasses).
A is a concrete class and may have instances (the subclasses B, C and D are optional)

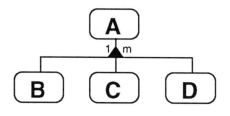

Instances can be of class B, C, or D, or any combination of B, C and D (exhaustive and independent subclasses).
A is an abstract class and may not have instances

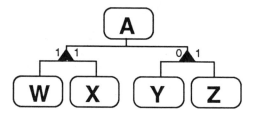

Multiple sets of subclasses. In this example, instances must be subclassified as W or X and may be optionally subclassified as Y or Z. The partitionings W/X and Y/Z are independent

Entity diagram
entity subtypes

Occurrences of entity type A may be related to one or more of the entity subtypes B, C, or D (exhaustive and independent subtypes). Occurrences of entity A may exist without being related to a subtype entity

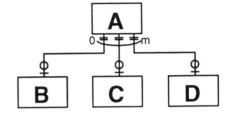

Occurrences of entity type A may be related to one or more of the entity subtypes B, C, or D (exhaustive and independent subtypes). Occurrences of entity A that are not related to a subtype entity are not permitted

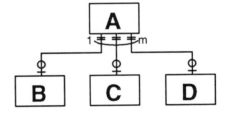

Multiple sets of entity subtypes. In this example, occurrences must be subtyped as W or X and may be optionally subtyped as Y or Z. The partitionings W/X and Y/Z are independent

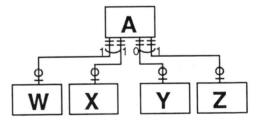

Class diagram
subclasses and
multiple inheritance

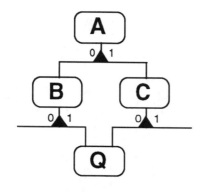

Multiple inheritance from subclasses sharing the same superclass. The subclasses B and C must be independent for this construct to be valid

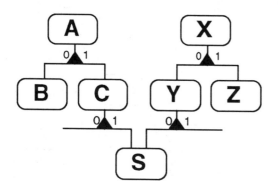

Multiple inheritance from subclasses that have different superclasses

Entity diagram
entity subtypes and multiple inheritance

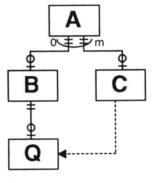

Multiple inheritance from subtypes sharing the same supertype. The sub-types B and C must be independent for this construct to be valid

Multiple inheritance from subtypes that have different supertypes

Class diagram
identity

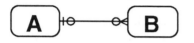   A and B are independent
classes

A and B contribute to
the identity of C
(indicated by the bar with
ends nearest to C)

Note: identity is not essential in the conceptual model, but
may be added to specify unique characteristics of instances

Entity diagram
identity

A and B are independent entity types, related by a foreign key relationship

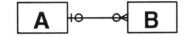

A and B contribute to the identity of C through a primary key relationship (indicated on the diagram by the relationship lines from A and B entering the top of the entity type C box)

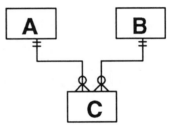

Class diagram
Exclusivity

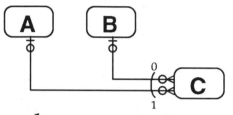

An instance of class C may be
associated with an instance of class
A or with an instance of class B,
but not with both

and

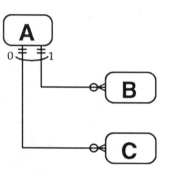

Note: exclusivity arcs are usually superseded
by the introduction of subtype entities

Transferability

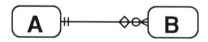

An association between an
instance of class B and an
instance of class A cannot
be transferred to another
instance of class A (an
intra-association constraint)

Entity diagram

Exclusivity

An occurrence of entity C may be related to an occurrence of entity A or to an occurrence of entity B, but not to both

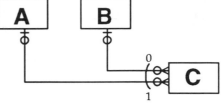

and

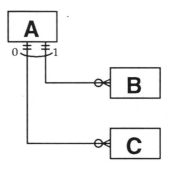

Note: exclusivity arcs are usually superseded by the introduction of subtype entities

Transferability

A relationship between an occurrence of entity B and an occurrence of entity A cannot be transferred to another occurrence of entity A (an intra-relationship constraint)

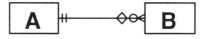

Class diagram

Association constraints

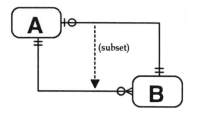

An inter-association constraint exists between the associations (e.g., one association is a subset of the other)

Time-stamping (1:n)

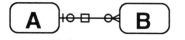

The history of the associations an instance of class B has with instances of class A is required

Time-stamping (m:n)

The history of the associations between instances of class A and instances of class B is required

Entity diagram

Relationship constraints

A constraint exists between the entities (e.g., to ensure that one relationship is a subset of the other)

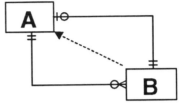

Time-stamping (1:n)

The history of the relationships an occurrence of entity B has with occurrences of entity A is required

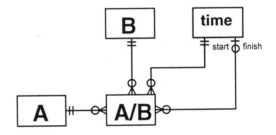

Time-stamping (m:n)

The history of the relationships between occurrences of entity A and occurences of entity B is required

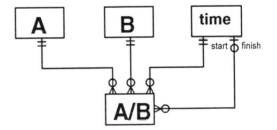

Composition

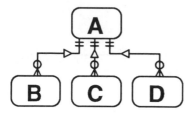

A is a composite class that has strengthened associations with classes B, C, and D. It is a useful visual clue with respect to representation, which has implications for behaviour.

Ternary association

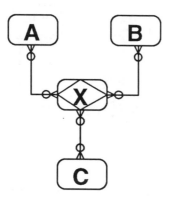

Each combination of (A, B) instances may be associated with many instances of C through the associative class X (look-across cardinality). Similarly for (A,C) with B, and (B, C) with A.

Each instance of A may particpate many times in the association (participative cardinality). Similarly for B and C.

Entity diagram

Composition

Composition structures are not permissible in a relational data model and must be modelled using 1:n relationships using foreign key and primary keys as appropriate.

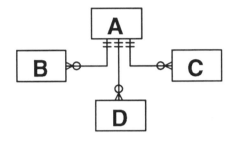

Ternary association

The ternary relationship must be resolved by the introduction of entity X which will often take as its primary key the primary keys of A, B, and C.

There is no equivalent to the look-across cardinality of the object model.

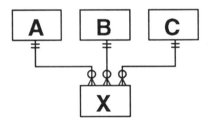

Appendix B

Case study - *The Gym*

Background

Subscriptions and fees

The Gym has two categories of member: those who are employees of organizations that have paid a corporate fee (corporate employee members), and individual members. Members in both categories pay an annual subscription, but corporate employee members get a reduced rate. The subscription rates are revised at the beginning of January each year.

The corporate fee payable by the employer organizations is also revised every January. There is a single level of corporate fee, which entitles one hundred employees of the organization to the reduced rate of membership at any one time. Larger companies with more than one hundred employees must pay separately at divisional/departmental level.

Membership can be taken out at any time of the year, but subscriptions are always backdated to the first of the month they are paid in. Thus, someone who joined on the 13th May 1993 could begin using The Gym on that date, but should renew their subscription on 1st May 1994.

Corporate fees are operative from the date the fee is paid, but are backdated to the first of the month for the purposes of fee payment in successive years. Employees will not get the benefit of reduced subscriptions until the corporate fee has actually been received from the employing organization.

Usually, The Gym receives a payment that represents a single subscription or a single corporate fee. However, sometimes large organizations send in corporate fees for all of their divisions en bloc.

Employees

Each employee is employed by a particular gym department and the gym needs to know which departments an employee has worked for in the past.

Potential new members often ask to see the gym facilities before committing themselves to joining. They are booked onto gym tours, each tour being conducted by a gym employee. A tour is limited to a maximum of six potential members and lasts approximately one hour.

New members must, by law, be trained in the use of the gym equipment. A gym employee is assigned to each new member for an hour for this purpose.

Use of gym equipment

The gym equipment falls into basic categories:

- *weights machines*, which exercise specific muscle groups by requiring users to do work against weights. This type of exercise is generally anaerobic. Users aim to repeat the exercise fifteen times at a certain weight. Once they can achieve fifteen repetitions with ease they should increase the weight. As a guide, a healthy man should be able to lift 60 kg on the leg extender fifteen times.

- *cardiovascular machines*, such as exercise bikes and power joggers. After the first few minutes, these machines give aerobic benefits. The machines are all electronically controlled and allow the user to select different programmes and standards of difficulty. Performances are measured in terms of time taken and distance travelled. For example, a good performance on the exercise bike would be five minutes for three miles on the hilly programme at standard 6.

All members are encouraged to record their performances so that their progress can be monitored by The Gym staff. It is not expected that a member would record more than one performance on one machine in the same day.

Equipment maintenance

The Gym has one or two of each of the most popular types of weights machine. It has a row of ten jogging machines and several exercise bikes and rowing machines.

There are only a few specialist companies who manufacture gym equipment and each company must be registered with its trade association. The Gym has bought machines from several of them. Within The Gym, a machine type is known by the manufacturer's name and the manufacturer's model number. Spare parts also have make and model numbers. Some of the spares can be fitted to several different machine types.

A specific machine assembly, such as an individual exercise bike, will have a serial number to distinguish it from others of the same type, as do individual spare parts and sub-assemblies. Machine assemblies must be tested once a year for safety reasons.

Data models

Firstly an object model is presented. The case study is concerned with the representation of the data and not its behaviour; consequently we have not supplied methods or event schemas. The object model is then used as the basis for a data model. As we have shown in chapter 8 on physical implementation, the attribute lists could be used to generate SQL statements to create a relational database.

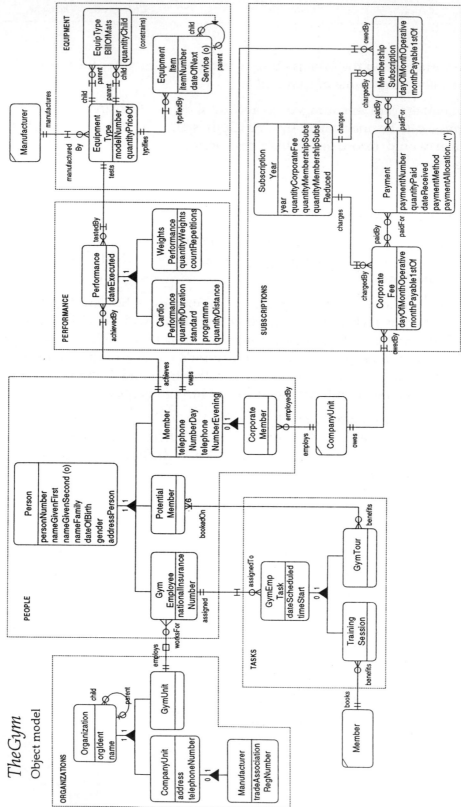

TheGym
Object model

Object model (classes and attributes)

Organization

    Organization
          orgIdent
          name
    Unique: orgIdent

    CompanyUnit isKindOf Organization
          address
          telephoneNumber

    GymUnit isKindOf Organization

    Manufacturer isKindOf CompanyUnit
          tradeAssociationRegNumber

People

    Person
          personNumber
          nameGivenFirst
    (o)   nameGivenSecond
          nameFamily
          dateOfBirth
          gender
          addressPerson
    Unique: personNumber

    GymEmployee isKindOf Person
          nationalInsuranceNumber
    Unique: nationalInsuranceNumber

    PotentialMember isKindOf Person

    Member isKindOf Person
          telephoneNumberDay
          telephoneNumberEvening

    CorporateMember isKindOf Member

Tasks

GymEmpTask
    dateScheduled
    timeStart
Unique: dateScheduled,
        timeStart,
        assignedTo GymEmployee

TrainingSession isKindOf GymEmpTask

GymTour isKindOf GymEmpTask

Equipment

EquipmentType
    modelNumber
    quantityPriceOf
Unique: modelNumber,
        manufacturedBy Manufacturer

EquipTypeBillOfMats
    quantityChild
Unique: child EquipmentType,
        parent EquipmentType

EquipmentItem
    itemNumber
(o)   dateOfNextService
Unique: itemNumber
        typifiedBy EquipmentType

Performance

Performance
    dateExecuted
Unique: dateExecuted,
        achievedBy Member,
        testedBy EquipmentType

CardioPerformance isKindOf Performance
    quantityDuration
    standard
    programme
    quantityDistance

WeightsPerformance isKindOf Performance
    quantityWeight
    countRepetitions

Subscriptions

Payment
    paymentNumber
    quantityPaid
    dateReceived
    paymentMethod
Unique: paymentNumber

CorporateFee
    dayOfMonthOperative
    monthPayable1stOf
Unique: owedBy CompanyUnit,
    chargedBy SubscriptionYear

MembershipSubscription
    dayOfMonthOperative
    monthPayable1stOf
Unique: owedBy Member,
    chargedBy SubscriptionYear

PaymentAllocation isPartOf Payment

PaymentCorpFee isKindOf PaymentAllocation
    quantityAllocated
Unique: paidFor CorporateFee,
    allocatedFor Payment

PaymentMembSubs isKindOf PaymentAllocation
    quantityAllocated
Unique: paidFor MembershipSubscription,
    allocatedFor Payment

SubscriptionYear
    year
    quantityCorporateFee
    quantityMembershipSubs
    quantityMembershipSubsReduced
Unique: Year

The Payment class has absorbed the PaymentAllocation class. This is not particularly significant with respect to representation, but it would have greater significance for the design of behaviour. The rules for allocating payments would be hidden in the Payment business object. Any change to the rules for the allocation of payments is localized to the Payment class. From our privileged position of system designer we can look inside the Payment class and see its structure:

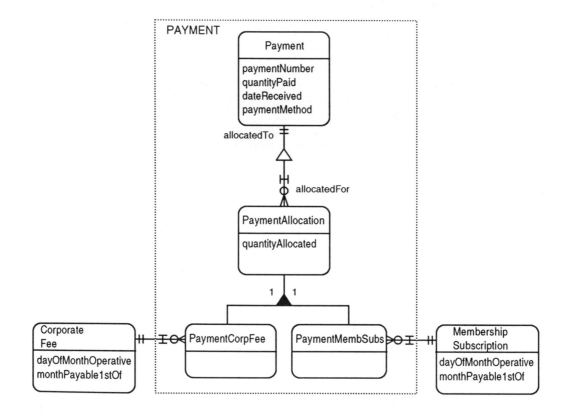

Object model (associations)

Class	function	min	max	Class	inverse function	min	max	time stamp
Organization	parent	0	m	Organization	child	0	1	
GymUnit	employs	0	m	Gym Employee	worksFor	1	1	daily
CompanyUnit	owes	0	m	CorporateFee	owedBy	1	1	
CompanyUnit	employs	0	m	Corporate Member	employedBy	1	1	
Manufacturer	manufactures	0	m	Equipment Type	manufactured By	1	1	
Gym Employee	assigned	0	m	Gym EmployeeTask	assignedTo	1	1	
Potential Member	bookedOn	0	m	GymTour	benefits	1	6	
Member	achieves	0	m	Performance	achieved By	1	1	
Member	owes	0	m	Membership Subscription	owedBy	1	1	
Member	books	0	m	Training Session	benefits	1	1	
Equipment Type	tests	0	m	Performance	testedBy	1	1	
Equipment Type	child	0	m	EquipTypeBill OfMats	parent	1	1	
Equipment Type	parent	0	m	EquipTypeBill OfMats	child	1	1	
Equipment Type	typifies	0	m	Equipment Item	typifiedBy	1	1	
Equipment Item	parent	0	m	Equipment Item	child	0	1	
Subscription Year	charges	0	m	CorporateFee	chargedBy	1	1	
Subscription Year	charges	0	m	Membership Subscription	chargedBy	1	1	

Class	function	min	max	Class	inverse function	min	max	time stamp
Payment	allocatedTo	0	m	Payment Allocation	allocatedFor	1	1	
CorporateFee	paidBy	0	m	PaymentCorp Fee	paidFor	1	1	
Payment MembSubs	paidBy	0	m	Membership Subscription	paidFor	1	1	

Data model

B.1   Organization entities

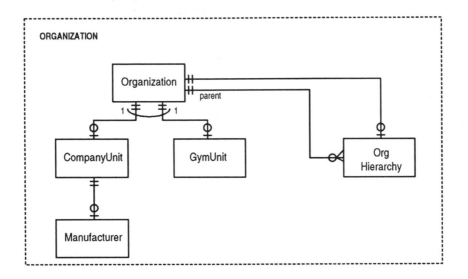

Figure B.1: *Organization*

Organization
    <u>orgIdent</u>
    name

CompanyUnit
    <u>orgIdent</u>
    address
    telephoneNumber
Foreign: orgIdent → Organization

GymUnit
    <u>orgIdent</u>
Foreign: orgIdent → Organization

Manufacturer
    <u>orgIdent</u>
    tradeAssociationRegNumber
Foreign: orgIdent → CompanyUnit

```
OrgHierarchy
        orgIdent
        orgIdentParent
Foreign:        orgIdent → Organization
Foreign:        orgIdentParent → Organization
```

Comments

- all organizations are classified as company units (external organizations and their sub-divisions) or as gym units (internal departments of The Gym);

- as manufacturer has been modelled as a subtype of CompanyUnit, employees of a manufacturer are allowed to become corporate members. Thus it will be possible to identify those corporate members that are employed by a manufacturer of gym equipment;

- by putting the OrgHierarchy at the highest level of organization supertype it will be possible to decompose all organizations hierarchically, whether they are internal or external. A hierarchical departmental structure of The Gym can be modelled, as could the hierarchical structure of an external group of companies. However, this means that the data model would allow, for example, a gym department to become part of an external company unit. Such an eventuality should probably be prevented by the imposition of a constraint (although this constraint would then need to be relaxed if The Gym were taken over by another company).

B.2   People entities

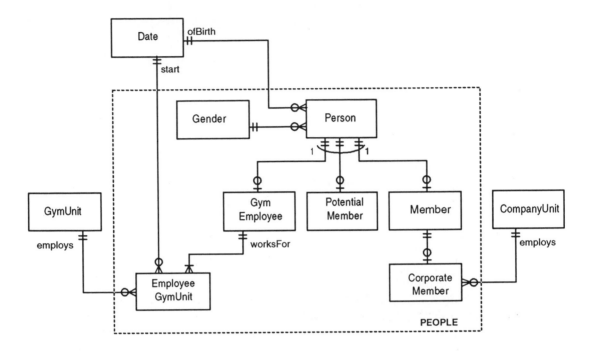

Figure B.2: *People*

Person
      <u>personNumber</u>
      nameGivenFirst
(o)   nameGivenSecond
      nameFamily
      dateOfBirth
      gender
      addressPerson
Foreign: dateOfBirth → Date
Foreign: gender → Gender

GymEmployee
      <u>personNumber</u>
      nationalInsuranceNumber
Foreign: personNumber → Person
Unique: nationalInsuranceNumber

PotentialMember
    <u>personNumber</u>
Foreign: personNumber → Person

Member
    <u>personNumber</u>
    telephoneNumberDay
    telephoneNumberEvening
Foreign: personNumber → Person

CorporateMember
    <u>personNumber</u>
    orgIdentEmploys
Foreign: personNumber → Member
Foreign: orgIdentEmploys → CompanyUnit

EmployeeGymUnit
    <u>personNumber</u>
    <u>dateStart</u>
    orgIdentEmploys
Foreign: personNumber → GymEmployee
Foreign: dateStart → Date
Foreign: orgIdentEmploys → GymUnit

Gender
    <u>gender</u>
Values: 'male', 'female'

Comments

- it might be a requirement to record multiple forenames - somebody might have been named after a football team. To allow this level of flexibility would require a new entity to be created, such as GivenName. An entity diagram for this scenario might be as follows:

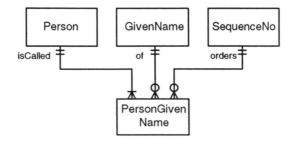

Relations are by definition unordered requiring that a sequence number be introduced. The scenario can be modelled as a class diagram using an 'ordered' constraint. In addition we have subclassified Name into GivenName and FamilyName and made theses classes independent, allowing a name such as 'Lawrence' to be classified as both a given name and a family name:

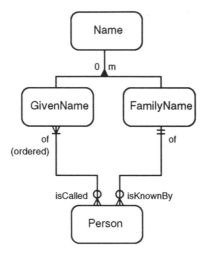

This situation can be complicated further if one considers the introduction of a cultural factor - in some countries it is standard practice to put the family name first. If we wished to record this nuance, for example for the production of personalized mailshots, the model would need to be extended still further. Thus it is only with reference to current and envisaged requirements that we can make a judgement concerning whether or not a data model has been developed in sufficient detail;

- the date that a gym employee started work for The Gym is derivable from the earliest start date of an assignment to a gym unit (gym employees must be assigned to a gym unit);

- the EmployeeGymUnit entity was introduced when resolving the time-stamped association between GymUnit and GymEmployee in the object model. The maximum frequency of time-stamping for the association was specified as daily and therefore Date was used in the data model;

- potential members have no non-key attributes, but will become owner entities later on (see Task entities).

B.3   Task entities

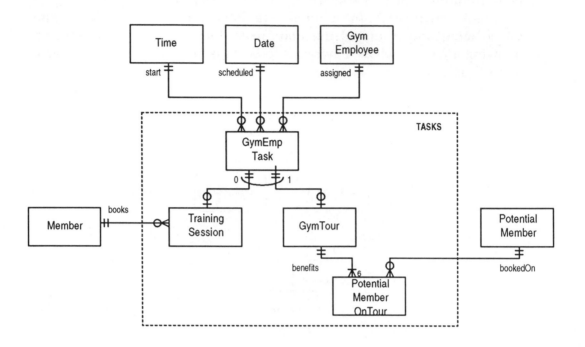

Figure B.3: *Tasks*

GymEmpTask
      <u>personNumberAssigned</u>
      <u>dateScheduled</u>
      <u>timeStart</u>
Foreign: personNumberAssigned → GymEmployee
Foreign: dateScheduled → Date
Foreign: timeStart → Time

TrainingSession
      <u>personNumberAssigned</u>
      <u>dateScheduled</u>
      <u>timeStart</u>
      personNumberBooks
Foreign: personNumberAssigned,
                dateScheduled,
                timeStart → GymEmpTask
Foreign: personNumberBooks → Member

GymTour
<u>personNumberAssigned</u>
<u>dateScheduled</u>
<u>timeStart</u>
Foreign: personNumberAssigned,
                  dateScheduled,
                  timeStart → GymEmpTask

PotentialMemberOnTour
<u>personNumberAssigned</u>
<u>dateScheduled</u>
<u>timeStart</u>
<u>personNumberBookedOn</u>
Foreign: personNumberAssigned,
                  dateScheduled,
                  timeStart → GymEmpTask
Foreign: personNumberBookedOn → PotentialMember

Comments

- it is assumed that a gym tour is not scheduled until there is at least one potential member booked on it;

- no more than six potential members may be booked on a gym tour;

- because training sessions and tours both last an hour there is no need to put a duration on this entity. However, the cardinality of the GymEmpTask subtype exclusivity group shows that tasks may exist that are neither training sessions nor gym tours - if these tasks have different durations then further attributes will be need to be introduced.

B.4   Equipment entities

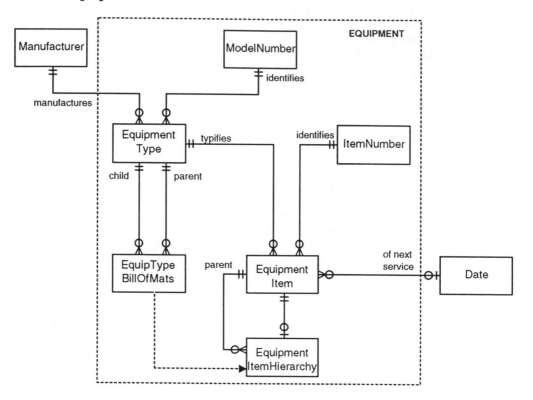

Figure B.4: *Equipment*

ModelNumber
        <u>modelNumber</u>

EquipmentType
        <u>orgIdentManufactures</u>
        <u>modelNumber</u>
        quantityPriceOf
Foreign: orgIdentManufactures → Manufacturer
Foreign: modelNumber → ModelNumber

EquipTypeBillOfMats
        <u>orgIdentManufacturesChild</u>
        <u>modelNumberChild</u>
        <u>orgIdentManufacturesParent</u>
        <u>modelNumberParent</u>
        quantityChild
Foreign: orgIdentManufacturesChild,

Foreign: modelNumberChild → EquipmentType
            orgIdentManufacturesParent,
            modelNumberParent → EquipmentType

ItemNumber
     <u>itemNumber</u>

EquipmentItem
     <u>orgIdentManufactures</u>
     <u>modelNumber</u>
     <u>itemNumber</u>
(o)   dateOfNextService
Foreign: orgIdentManufactures,
            modelNumber → EquipmentType
Foreign: itemNumber → ItemNumber
Foreign: dateOfNextService → Date

EquipmentItemHierarchy
     <u>orgIdentManufactures</u>
     <u>modelNumber</u>
     <u>itemNumber</u>
     orgIdentManufacturesParent
     modelNumberParent
     itemNumberParent
Foreign: orgIdentManufactures,
            modelNumber
            itemNumber → EquipmentItem
Foreign: orgIdentManufacturesParent,
            modelNumberParent
            itemNumberParent → EquipmentItem
Constraint: orgIdentManufactures,
            modelNumber,
            ordIdentManufacturesParent,
            modelNumberParent in
            EquipTypeBillOfMats.orgIdentManufacturesChild,
            EquipTypeBillOfMats.modelNumberChild,
            EquipTypeBillOfMats.orgIdentManufacturesParent,
            EquipTypeBillOfMats.modelNumberParent

Comment

- the EquipTypeBillOfMats shows which parts can be assembled into which higher level component structures. It is a bill of materials as a child may fit into many parent components (imagine a one kilogram weight which could be incorporated into various weights machines). The EquipmentItemHierarchy by contrast is a strict hierarchy describing which components actually make up further components. In this case a child component may only contribute to one parent (at any one time the one kilogram weight can only be used on one machine);

Given that we do not allow components to be constructed in the EquipmentItemHierarchy that violate the specification in the EquipTypeBillOfMats a constraint has been specified in the attribute list;

- model number is an identifier assigned by the manufacturer; it is outside The Gym's control. Item number is assigned within The Gym to provide an inventory of physical parts and component assemblies.

B.5   Performance entities

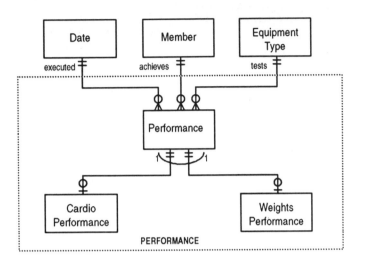

Figure B.5: *Performance*

Performance
    <u>dateExecuted</u>
    <u>personNumberAchieves</u>
    <u>orgIdentManufactures</u>
    <u>modelNumber</u>

Foreign: dateExecuted → Date
Foreign: personNumberAchieves → Member
Foreign: orgIdentManufactures,
              modelNumber → EquipmentType

CardioPerformance
    <u>dateExecuted</u>
    <u>personNumberAchieves</u>
    <u>orgIdentManufactures</u>
    <u>modelNumber</u>
    quantityDuration
    standard
    programme
    quantityDistance

Foreign: dateExecuted,
              personNumberAchieves,
              orgIdentManufactures,
              modelNumber → Performance

WeightsPerformance
    <u>dateExecuted</u>
    <u>personNumberAchieves</u>
    <u>orgIdentManufactures</u>
    <u>modelNumber</u>
    quantityWeight
    countRepetitions
Foreign: dateExecuted,
        personNumberAchieves,
        orgIdentManufactures,
        modelNumber $\rightarrow$ Performance

B.6   Subscriptions entities

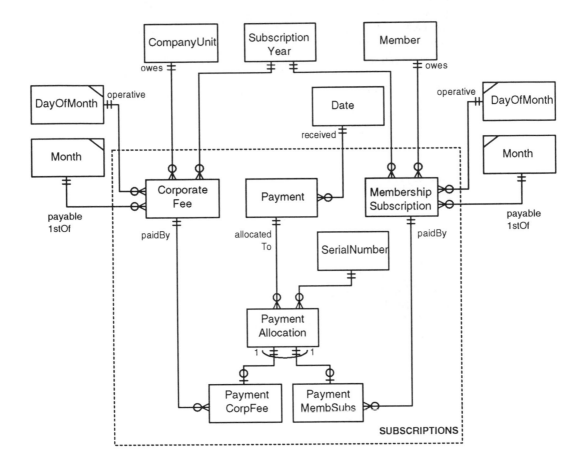

Figure B.6: *Subscriptions*

CorporateFee
     <u>orgIdentOwes</u>
     <u>year</u>
     dayOfMonthOperative
     monthPayable1stOf
Foreign: orgIdentOwes → CompanyUnit
Foreign: year → Year
Foreign: dayOfMonthOperative → DayOfMonth
Foreign: monthPayable1stOf → Month

MembershipSubscription
    <u>personNumberOwes</u>
    <u>year</u>
    dayOfMonthOperative
    monthPayable1stOf

Foreign: personNumberOwes → Member
Foreign: year → Year
Foreign: dayOfMonthOperative → DayOfMonth
Foreign: monthPayable1stOf → Month

Payment
    <u>paymentNumber</u>
    quantityPaid
    dateReceived
    paymentMethod

Foreign: dateReceived → Date

PaymentAllocation
    <u>paymentNumber</u>
    <u>serialNumberAllocation</u>
    quantityAllocated

PaymentCorpFee
    <u>paymentNumber</u>
    <u>serialNumberAllocation</u>
    orgIdentOwes
    year

Unique: paymentNumber, orgIdentOwes, year
Foreign: paymentNumber, serialNumberAllocation →
                PaymentAllocation
Foreign: orgIdentOwes, year → CorporateFee

PaymentMembSubs
    <u>paymentNumber</u>
    <u>serialNumberAllocation</u>
    personNumberOwes
    year

Unique: paymentNumber, personNumberOwes, year
Foreign: paymentNumber, serialNumberAllocation →
                PaymentAllocation
Foreign: personNumberOwes, year → MembershipSubscription

SerialNumber
    <u>serialNumber</u>

Comments:

- Each Payment Allocation must satisfy either a Corporate Fee or a MembershipSubscription, but not both. The combination of PaymentNumber, OrgIdent and year is held to be unique, preventing more than one allocation from the same payment to a given corporate fee. Likewise the combination of paymentNumber, personNumberOwes and year is held to be unique, preventing more than one allocation from the same payment to a given membership subscription.

B.7   Time entities

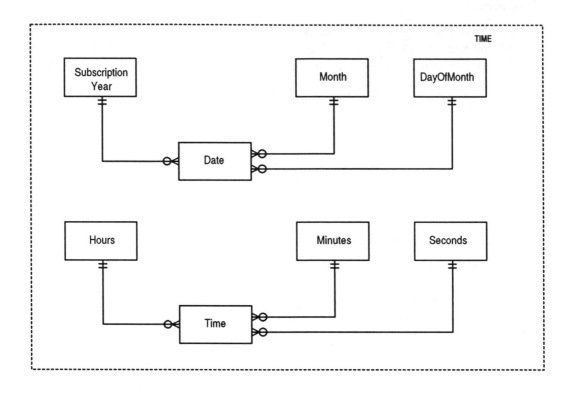

Figure B.7: *Time*

SubscriptionYear
        <u>year</u>
        quantityCorporateFee
        quantityMembershipSubs
        quantityMembershipSubsReduced

Month
        <u>month</u>
        monthName

DayOfMonth
        <u>dayOfMonth</u>

Date
    <u>date</u>
    year
    month
    dayOfMonth
Foreign: year → SubscriptionYear
Foreign: month → Month
Foreign: dayOfMonth → DayOfMonth

Hour
    <u>hour</u>

Minute
    <u>minute</u>

Second
    <u>second</u>

Time
    <u>time</u>
    hour
    minute
    second
Foreign: hour → Hour
Foreign: minute → Minute
Foreign: second → Second

Comments:

- subscriptions are assumed to be changed on January 1st and have therefore been held in the SubscriptionYear entity;

- the Date entity has an artificial structured key as well as its natural foreign keys - this has been done to make the use of the Date entity more convenient elsewhere in the model (otherwise it would be necessary to specify year, month, and day each time a date is required);

- the same comment applies to Time as to Date.

B.8   Entity Descriptions

CardioPerformance
Subtype of Performance; a performance on a cardio-vascular machine.

CompanyUnit
All or part of an organization which may pay a fee to The Gym to allow up to one hundred of its employees to join The Gym at a reduced rate of subscription for the calendar year following the payment.

CorporateFee
A many-to-many resolver between year and organization, this entity shows which organizations have contracted to pay or to continue paying corporate fees in the year. If the organization starts paying midway through a year then the fee is a pro rata amount of the full year's fee. Each whole or part or part month remaining in the year must be paid for.

CorporateMember
A person who has contracted to join the gym at a reduced rate as an employee of an organization that has corporate membership.

Date
A day of the Gregorian calendar.

DayOfMonth
Key-only entity holding values of the attribute dayOfTheMonth.

EmployeeGymUnit
Many-to-many resolver between Employee and GymUnit, showing which employee is assigned to which gym unit and when the assignment began.

EquipmentItem
A particular physical occurrence of an EquipmentType; an assembly, sub-assembly or component of a piece of gym equipment owned by The Gym.

EquipmentItemHierarchy
Subtype of EquipmentItem, which resolves the one-to-many relationship between items: that one may currently be made up of many others but itself forms a part of at most one other.

EquipmentType
The model for a number of EquipmentItems.

EquipTypeBillOfMats
This entity resolves the many-to-many relationship between EquipmentTypes: that one is made up of many others and may itself be a part of several others. The entity shows how many of the child type go into the assembly of the parent.

Gender
Key-only entity holding values of the attribute gender.

GymEmployee
Subtype of Person; someone who works or has worked for The Gym.

GymEmpTask
Allocation of approximately one hour of a GymEmployee's time to perform a given duty.

GymTour
Gym tours are arranged for groups of potential members to show them the facilities.

GymUnit
Subtype of Organization; an organization unit representing all or part of The Gym.

Hour
Key-only entity storing values of the attribute hour.

ItemNumber
Key-only entity storing values of the attribute itemNumber.

Manufacturer
Subtype of CompanyUnit; a CompanyUnit which manufactures gym equipment.

Member
Subtype of Person; a person who has completed a membership application form and been approved as a member of The Gym.

MembershipSubscription
The fee owed by a member for a year's membership of The Gym at either the full or reduced rate.

Minute
Key-only entity holding values of the attribute minute.

ModelNumber
Key-only entity holding values of the attribute modelNumber.

Month
A twelfth part of the year.

Organization
A group of individuals joined in a common purpose.

OrgHierarchy
A subtype of Organization, this entity resolves the one-to-many recursive relationship between Organizations: that one may own many others but is itself owned by at most one other.

Payment

A sum of money, in pounds sterling, received by The Gym.

PaymentAllocation

The assignment of all or part of a payment to a debt.

PaymentCorpFee

Subtype of PaymentAllocation, showing which corporate fee a payment allocation has helped to satisfy.

PaymentMembSubs

Subtype of PaymentAllocation, showing which membership subscription a payment allocation has helped to satisfy.

Performance

A recorded level of achievement by a gym member on a given equipment type on a given date. It is assumed that the member will only want to record his/her best performance on a given day.

Person

An individual human being.

PotentialMember

A person who is not yet a member of the gym but who has expressed an interest in joining.

PotentialMemberOnTour

Many-to-many resolver between PotentialMember and GymTask, showing who is booked on which tour.

Second

Key-only entity holding values of the attribute second.

SerialNumber

Key-only entity holding values of the attribute serialNumber.

SubscriptionYear

A year of the Gregorian calendar.

Time

A key-only entity holding values of the attribute time.

TrainingSession

A subtype of GymTask, a TrainingSession involves one Member and one GymEmployee and lasts approximately an hour. It is a legal requirement for The Gym to give training to all new members before they use the equipment unsupervised, unless the new member can produce a certificate of competence.

WeightsPerformance

Subtype of Performance; a performance on a weights machine.

B.9   Attribute Descriptions

address
> The physical location, as identified for postal purposes, of a CompanyUnit.

addressPerson
> The physical location, as identified for postal purposes, of a person's home.

countRepetitions
> The number of times a weight has been moved out of and back into equilibrium during a performance.

date
> The year, month and day of a date of the Gregorian calendar.

dayOfMonth
> Unique identifier of a DayOfMonth.

gender
> The physical sexual classification of an animal.

hour
> Unique identifier of an Hour; one twenty-fourth of a day; how much of a day has passed.

itemNumber
> Unique identifier, within orgIdentManufactures and modelNumber, of an item of equipment. A number assigned to an equipment item by gym staff.

minute
> Unique identifier of a Minute; one sixtieth of an hour; how many minutes have elapsed in a particular hour.

modelNumber
> Unique identifier, within orgIdentManufactures, of a type of gym equipment. The number by which the manufacturer identifies that type of equipment.

month
> Unique identifier of a month; one twelfth of a year; how much of a year has passed.

monthName
> The name of the month of the year, such as February.

name
> The trading name of an organization.

nameFamily
> One or more words used to identify (though not necessarily uniquely) the family into which a person was born.

nameGivenFirst
> One or more words used with nameFamily to identify (though not necessarily uniquely) a person.

nameGivenSecond
> One or more words used with nameFamily and nameGivenFirst to identify (though not necessarily uniquely) a person.

nationalInsuranceNumber
> Code assigned to a citizen of the UK over sixteen years of age or who has already gained employment by the national welfare administration system. Unique identifier of a GymEmployee.

orgIdent
> Unique identifier of an organization.

paymentMethod
> Nature and perhaps identity of the ultimate guarantor of a Payment, such as cash, credit card or American Express.

paymentNumber
> Unique identifier of a Payment.

personNumber
> Unique identifier of a Person.

programme
> The pattern of the performance, which can be pre-programmed on many cardiovascular machines. For example, hilly, flat or plateau.

quantityAllocated
> How much of a Payment is attributed to a PaymentAllocation.

quantityChild
> How many of an EquipmentType go to make up a parent EquipmentType.

quantityCorporateFee
> The amount in pounds sterling owed by a CompanyUnit in a given SubscriptionYear.

quantityDistance
> How far a Member is deemed to have travelled during a CardioPerformance.

quantityDuration
> How long a CardioPerformance has lasted.

quantityMembershipSubs
The amount in pounds sterling payable by a member who is not employed by an organization that has paid a corporate fee for membership of The Gym for the whole of the year in question.

quantityMembershipSubsReduced
The amount in pounds sterling payable by a member who is employed by an organization that has paid a corporate fee for membership of the gym for the whole of the year in question.

quantityPaid
The amount in pounds sterling of a payment.

quantityPriceOf
The amount of an EquipmentType's price.

quantityWeight
The weight against which work was done during a WeightsPerformance.

second
Unique identifier of a Second.

serialNumber
Unique identifier of a SerialNumber.

standard
The level of difficulty of a CardioPerformance.

telephoneNumber
The telephone system address of the CompanyUnit.

telephoneNumberDay
The telephone system address which can be used to contact a member during weekday working hours.

telephoneNumberEvening
The telephone system address which can be used to contact a member out of weekday working hours.

time
A number of hours, minutes and seconds of the day.

tradeAssociationRegNumber
An identifier assigned to a Manufacturer of gym equipment by its trade association.

year
Unique identifier of a Year.

B.10   Relationship Descriptions

CompanyUnit *employs* CorporateMember

> Corporate members are considered to be employed by a company unit if they have full-time or part-time contracts of employment. Temporary staff qualify as employees if they have a contract for a period of six months or more.

CompanyUnit *owes* CorporateFee

> A company unit owes a corporate fee for the SubscriptionYear specified in the standard agreement signed with The Gym and for every subsequent year until the agreement is cancelled in writing by either party.

CorporateFee *paidBy* PaymentCorpFee

> A corporate fee is satisfied, in whole or in part, by a PaymentCorpFee.

Date *executed* Performance

> A date is the date on which a Performance was executed.

Date *ofBirth* Person

> A date is the date when a person was born.

Date *ofNextService* EquipmentItem

> A date is the next date that an equipment item is due to be serviced.

Date *received* Payment

> A date is the date when a Payment was received by The Gym.

Date *scheduled* GymEmployeeTask

> A date is the date on which a GymEmployeeTask is due to be carried out by a GymEmployee.

Date *start* EmployeeGymUnit

> A date is the date from which an employee is assigned to work in a particular part of The Gym.

DayOfMonth *is part of* Date

> A day of the month is part of a date.

DayOfMonth *operative* CorporateFee

> A day of the month is the earliest day in the month that a CorporateFee is paid that a CompanyUnit's employees become eligible to pay membership subscriptions at a reduced rate. It is usually the date on which the CorporateFee was paid in full.

DayOfMonth *operative* MembershipSubscription

> A day of the month is the earliest day in the month that a MembershipSubscription is paid that the user can begin using The Gym's facilities. It is usually the date on which the MembershipSubscription was paid in full.

EquipmentType *child* EquipTypeBillOfMats
> An EquipmentType can go to make up another EquipmentType.

EquipmentItem *parent* EquipmentItemHierarchy
> An EquipmentItem currently contains another EquipmentItem.

EquipmentType *parent* EquipTypeBillOfMats
> An equipmentType can contain another EquipmentType.

EquipmentType *tests* Performance
> An EquipmentType typifies the equipment item actually used during a member's recorded performance.

EquipmentType *typifies* EquipmentItem
> An EquipmentType is the model, or specification, for a given physical EquipmentItem.

Gender *of* Person
> Gender describes the physical sexual characteristics of a Person.

GymEmployee *assigned* GymEmployeeTask
> A Gym Employee is scheduled to carry out, or has already carried out, a Gym Employee Task.

GymEmployee *worksFor* EmployeeGymUnit
> A GymEmployee, throughout his or her period of employment, works for the whole or a part of The Gym. Employment with an employee's first unit is deemed to begin on the day specified in the contract of employment, provided that the contract has already been signed, and continue until the employee is assigned to another unit of The Gym. When the employee's last assignment finishes, the person ceases to be a GymEmployee.

GymTour *benefits* PotentialMemberOnTour
> A Gym Tour will, or has, been organized in order to demonstrate to one or more potential members the facilities of The Gym.

GymUnit *employs* EmployeeGymUnit
> A unit of The Gym may have, or have had, one or more employees assigned to it.

Hour *is part of* Time
> A hour is part of a time.

ItemNumber *identifies* EquipmentItem
> An item number is assigned within The Gym to each of the physical EquipmentItems that it owns. The item number is stamped or engraved onto each piece of equipment, or a label bearing the number is attached to the item.

Manufacturer *manufactures* EquipmentType
> A manufacturing company makes many EquipmentTypes. Each EquipmentType is manufactured by only one manufacturer.

Member *achieves* **Performance**
A Member may record many cardio and weights Performances, though only one per EquipmentType per day.

Member *books* **TrainingSession**
A Member has been or will be trained during one or more training sessions. Each training session is for the benefit of one member.

Member *owes* **MembershipSubscription**
A Member becomes liable for a MembershipSubscription once he or she has signed an agreement to join The Gym. Existing members' subscriptions fall due on the first day of the month that is the anniversary of the agreement having been signed.

MembershipSubscription *paidBy* **PaymentMembSubs**
A MembershipSubscription is satisfied, in whole or in part, by a PaymentMembSubs.

Minute *is part of* **Time**
A minute is part of a time.

ModelNumber *identifies* **EquipmentType**
A ModelNumber is assigned to each EquipmentType by the manufacturer of that equipment type.

Month *is part of* **Date**
A Month is part of a Date.

Month *payable1stOf* **MembershipSubscription**
A month of the year is the anniversary of a member joining The Gym. In subsequent years, subscriptions fall due on the first of this month.

Month *payable1stOf* **CorporateFee**
A month of the year is the anniversary of a CompanyUnit signing an agreement with The Gym. In subsequent years, corporate fees fall due on the first of this month.

Organization *parent* **OrgHierarchy**
An Organization is made up of other Organizations.

Payment *allocated to* **PaymentAllocation**
A Payment may be subdivided into separate PaymentAllocations.

PotentialMember *bookedOn* **PotentialMemberOnTour**
A PotentialMember may have been, or may be scheduled to go, on a tour of The Gym.

Second *is part of* **Time**
A number of seconds is part of a Time.

SerialNumber *identifies* PaymentAllocation.

An arbitrary serial number is used to identify each of the allocations of a Payment.

SubscriptionYear *charges* CorporateFee

A SubscriptionYear is the year whose subscription rates were used to calculate a CorporateFee.

SubscriptionYear *charges* MembershipSubscription

A SubscriptionYear is the year whose subscription rates were used to calculate a MembershipSubscription.

SubscriptionYear *is part of* Date

A year is part of a Date.

Time *start* GymEmployeeTask

A time is the time on the scheduled date at which a GymEmployeeTask is due to be carried out by a GymEmployee.

Appendix C

Meta-model

C.1   Meta-model of a logical data model

This appendix summarizes the meta-model of a logical data model which was described in chapter 14. A populated meta-model is included for illustrative purposes.

The attribute list for the meta-model shown in figure C.1 is as follows:

```
        Attribute
                attributeName
                entityName
                ifOptional
                ifDerived
        (o)     description
        (o)     dataType
        (o)     sizeOutput
        (o)     precisionOutput
        (o)     valueMaximum
        (o)     valueMinimum
        (o)     example
        Foreign:        entityName → Entity
        Foreign:        dataType → DataType
        Foreign:        valueMinimum → Value
        Foreign:        valueMaximum → Value


        AttributeInKey
                entityName
                serialNumberKey
                serialNumberKeyItem
                attributeName
        Foreign:        entityName,
                        serialNumberKey,
                        serialNumberKeyItem → KeyItem
        Foreign:        attributeName → Attribute
        Constraint:     entityName,
                        attributeName in
                        Attribute.entityName,
                        Attribute.attributeName


        AttributeValue
                value
                attributeName
        Foreign:        value → Value
        Foreign:        attributeName → Attribute
```

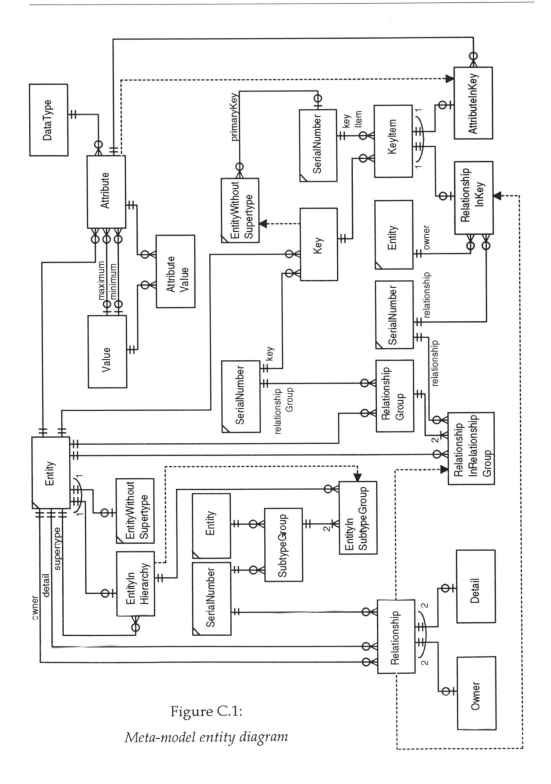

Figure C.1:

Meta-model entity diagram

DataType
> dataType

Detail
> entityNameOwner
> entityNameDetail
> serialNumberRelationship

(o)   relationshipLabelDetail
(o)   minimumCardinality
(o)   maximumCardinality
(o)   policyOnInsertion
(o)   policyOnDeletion

Foreign: entityNameOwner,
            entityNameDetail,
            serialNumberRelationship → Relationship

Entity
> entityName

(o)   description
(o)   example
(o)   diagramNameHome
       ifPhysicalImplementation

EntityInHierarchy
> entityName
    entityNameSupertype

Foreign: entityName → Entity
Foreign: entityNameSupertype → Entity

EntityInSubtypeGroup
> entityNameSubtypeGroupOwner
> serialNumberSubtypeGroup
> entityName

Foreign: entityNameSubtypeGroupOwner,
            serialNumberSubtypeGroup → SubtypeGroup
Foreign: entityName → EntityInHierarchy
Constraint: entityName,
            entityNameSubtypeGroupOwner in
            EntityInHierarchy.entityName,
            EntityInHierarchy.entityNameSupertype

EntityWithoutSupertype
    <u>entityName</u>
(o)   serialNumberPrimaryKey
Foreign: entityName → Entity
Foreign: serialNumberPrimaryKey → SerialNumber
Constraint: entityName,
    serialNumberPrimaryKey in
    Key.entityName,
    Key.serialNumberKey

Key
    <u>entityName</u>
    <u>serialNumberKey</u>
Foreign: entityName → Entity
Foreign: serialNumberKey → SerialNumber

KeyItem
    <u>entityName</u>
    <u>serialNumberKey</u>
    <u>serialNumberKeyItem</u>
Foreign: entityName,
    serialNumberKey → Key
Foreign: serialNumberKeyItem → SerialNumber

Owner
    <u>entityNameOwner</u>
    <u>entityNameDetail</u>
    <u>serialNumberRelationship</u>
    relationshipLabelOwner
    ifLabelPropagated
(o)   minimumCardinality
(o)   maximumCardinality
(o)   policyOnInsertion
(o)   policyOnDeletion
Foreign: entityNameOwner,
    entityNameDetail,
    serialNumberRelationship → Relationship
Unique: entityNameOwner,
    entityNameDetail,
    relationshipLabelOwner

Relationship
    <u>entityNameOwner</u>
    <u>entityNameDetail</u>
    <u>serialNumberRelationship</u>
    relationshipDescription
    ifTransferable

Foreign:	entityNameOwner → Entity
Foreign:	entityNameDetail → Entity
Foreign:	serialNumberRelationship → SerialNumber

RelationshipGroup
    <u>entityNameRelationshipGroupOwner</u>
    <u>serialNumberRelationshipGroup</u>

(o)	minimumCardinality
(o)	maximumCardinality
Foreign:	serialNumberRelationshipGroup → SerialNumber
Foreign:	entityNameRelationshipGroupOwner → Entity

RelationshipInKey
    <u>entityName</u>
    <u>serialNumberKey</u>
    <u>serialNumberKeyItem</u>
    entityNameOwner
    serialNumberRelationship

Foreign:	entityName,
	serialNumberKey,
	serialNumberKeyItem → KeyItem
Foreign:	entityNameOwner → Entity
Foreign:	serialNumberRelationship → SerialNumber
Constraint:	entityNameOwner,
	entityName,
	serialNumberRelationship in
	Relationship.entityNameOwner,
	Relationship.entityNameDetail,
	Relationship.serialNumberRelationship

RelationshipInRelationshipGroup
    <u>entityNameRelationshipGroupOwner</u>
    <u>serialNumberRelationshipGroup</u>
    <u>entityName</u>
    <u>serialNumberRelationship</u>

Foreign:	entityNameRelationshipGroupOwner,
	serialNumberRelationshipGroup → RelationshipGroup
Foreign:	entityName → Entity
Foreign:	serialNumberRelationship → SerialNumber

Constraint: entityNameRelationshipGroupOwner,
 entityName,
 serialNumberRelationship in
 Relationship.entityNameOwner
 Relationship.entityNameDetail
 Relationship.serialNumberRelationship
 or in
 Relationship.entityNameDetail
 Relationship.entityNameOwner
 Relationship.serialNumberRelationship

SerialNumber
 serialNumber

SubtypeGroup
 entityNameSubtypeGroupOwner
 serialNumberSubtypeGroup
(o) minimumCardinality
(o) maximumCardinality
 ifCompleteEnumeration
Foreign: entityNameSubtypeGroupOwner → Entity
Foreign: serialNumberSubtypeGroup → SerialNumber

Value
 value

C.2 The meta-model illustrated

Now consider the entity diagram in figure C.2, which is a representation of the well-used customer order scenario. Assume that the attribute list for this entity diagram is:

Customer
 customerNumber
 name
 address
(o) telephoneNumber

AccountCustomer
 customerNumber
 quantityCreditLimit
Foreign: customerNumber → Customer

VATRegisteredCustomer
    <u>customerNumber</u>
    registeredVATNumber
Foreign: customerNumber → Customer
Unique: registeredVATNumber

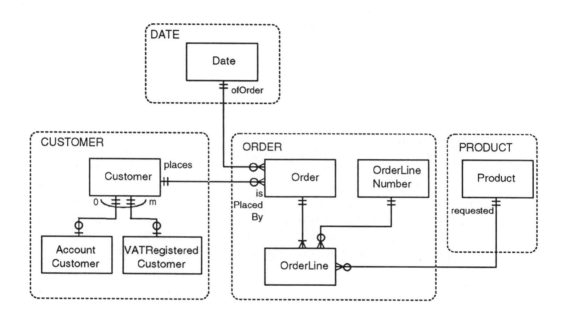

Figure C.2: *Customer order scenario*

Order
    <u>orderNumber</u>
    dateOfOrder
    customerNumberPlaces
Foreign: customerNumberPlaces → Customer
Foreign: dateOfOrder → Date

OrderLine
    <u>orderNumber</u>
    <u>orderLineNumber</u>
    productNumber
    quantityRequested
Foreign: orderNumber → Order
Foreign: orderLineNumber → OrderLineNumber
Foreign: productNumber → Product

Unique: orderNumber,
               productNumber

Product
    <u>productNumber</u>
    productDesc
    quantityCostPrice

OrderLineNumber
    <u>orderLineNumber</u>

Date
    <u>date</u>

Populating the tables of the meta-model would result in the following data being held about the customer order scenario. Note that derivable data has not been included in the tables - all foreign keys are derivable from relationships. So, for example, you will not see the attribute customerNumberPlaces in the Order entity as this attribute can be derived from the relationship "Customer places Order". Nor will you see the attribute orderNumber in the orderLine entity, despite it being part of the key of OrderLine, as this attribute is derivable from the identifying relationship "Order isMadeUpOf OrderLine". The attribute list representation of the data model introduces redundancy - this does not matter as the attribute list is a report that is produced from a repository based on a non-redundant meta-model (at least in its logical form).

Entity

entityName	diagramName Home (o)	ifPhysical Implementation	
Date	dateSubject	N	•••
Customer	customerSubject	Y	
AccountCustomer	customerSubject	Y	
VATRegisteredCustomer	customerSubject	Y	
Order	orderSubject	Y	
OrderLineNumber	orderSubject	N	
OrderLine	orderSubject	Y	
Product	productSubject	Y	

EntityInHierarchy

entityName	entityNameSupertype
AccountCustomer	Customer
VATRegisteredCustomer	Customer

EntityWithoutSupertype

entityName	serialNumber PrimaryKey (o)
Date	1
Customer	1
Order	1
OrderLineNumber	1
OrderLine	1
Product	1

DataType

dataType
character
integer
realNumber
yesNoFlag
soundSample
videoClip
image
date

Attribute

attributeName	entityName	dataType (o)	size Output (o)	precision Output (o)	···
customerNumber	Customer	character	8		
name	Customer	character	30		
address	Customer	character	40		
telephoneNumber	Customer	character	15		
quantityCreditLimit	AccountCustomer	integer			
registeredVATNumber	VATRegistered Customer	character	16		
orderNumber	Order	integer			
date	Date	date			
orderLineNumber	OrderLineNumber	integer			
quantityRequested	OrderLine	realNumber	9	3	
productNumber	Product	character	6		
productDesc	Product	character	35		
quantityCostPrice	Product	realNumber	8	2	

Relationship

entityNameOwner	entityNameDetail	serial Number Relationship	if Transferable	relationship Description
Date	Order	1	N	.....
Customer	Order	1	N	.....
OrderLineNumber	OrderLine	1	N	.....
Order	OrderLine	1	N	.....
Product	OrderLine	1	Y	.....

Owner

entityName Owner	entityName Detail	serial Number Rel^{n}ship	relationship LabelOwner	ifLabel Prop- agated	minimum Card- inality (o)	maximum Card- inality (o)	
Date	Order	1	ofOrder	Y	1	1	...
Customer	Order	1	places	Y	1	1	
OrderLine Number	OrderLine	1	identifies	N	1	1	
Order	OrderLine	1	isMadeUpOf	N	1	1	
Product	OrderLine	1	requested	N	1	1	

Detail

entityName Owner	entityName Detail	serial Number Rel^{n}ship	relationship LabelDetail (o)	minimum Cardinality (o)	maximum Cardinality (o)	
Date	Order	1		0	m	...
Customer	Order	1	isPlacedBy	0	m	
OrderLine Number	OrderLine	1		0	m	
Order	OrderLine	1		1	m	
Product	OrderLine	1		0	m	

Key

entityName	serialNumberKey
Customer	1
VATRegisteredCustomer	1
Date	1
Order	1
OrderLineNumber	1
OrderLine	1
OrderLine	2
Product	1

KeyItem

entityName	serialNumber Key	serialNumber KeyItem
Customer	1	1
VATRegisteredCustomer	1	1
Date	1	1
Order	1	1
OrderLineNumber	1	1
OrderLine	1	1
OrderLine	1	2
OrderLine	2	1
OrderLine	2	2
Product	1	1

AttributeInKey

entityName	serial NumberKey	serialNumber KeyItem	attributeName
Customer	1	1	customerNumber
VATRegisteredCustomer	1	1	registeredVATNumber
Order	1	1	orderNumber
OrderLineNumber	1	1	orderLineNumber
Date	1	1	date
Product	1	1	productNumber

RelationshipInKey

entityName	serialNumber Key	serialNumber KeyItem	entityName Owner	serialNumber Relationship
OrderLine	1	1	Order	1
OrderLine	1	2	OrderLine Number	1
OrderLine	2	1	Order	1
OrderLine	2	2	Product	1

SubtypeGroup

entityNameSubtype GroupOwner	serialNumber SubtypeGroup	minimum Card- inality (o)	maximum Card- inality (o)	ifComplete Enumeration
Customer	1	0	m	Y

EntityInSubtypeGroup

entityNameSubtype GroupOwner	serialNumber SubtypeGroup	entityName
Customer	1	AccountCustomer
Customer	1	VATRegisteredCustomer

Appendix D

Alternative diagramming notations

In this appendix the notation used in this book is contrasted with SSADM Version 4 and Oracle CASE*Method to give those modellers familiar with these methods a quick way of comparing the notations. The customer order scenario introduced in appendix C (figure C.2) is used (reproduced here as figure D.1).

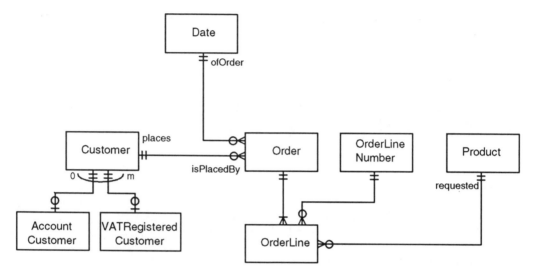

Figure D.1: *Entity diagram*

By suppressing the root entity Date and the key-only entity OrderLineNumber the entity diagram can be represented as in figure D.2.

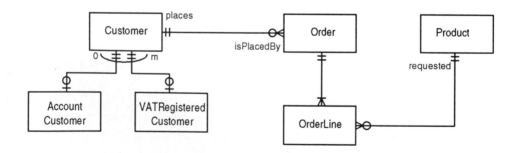

Figure D.2: *Entity diagram - root entities and key only masters suppressed*

The relationships in the entity diagram in figure D.2 are interpreted as:

Each customer may place many orders
Each order must be placed by one customer

Each order must contain one or more order lines
Each order line must be contained on one order

Each product may be requested by many order lines
Each order line must be for one product

The subtypes are independent (over-lapping) and the subtype group is optional (occurrences of Customer that do not have an associated subtype are permitted):

An account customer is a kind of customer
A VAT registered customer is a kind of customer

a customer may be an account customer, a VAT registered customer, or both

Subtypes are indicated by a special type of 1:1 relationship which has a fixed cardinality - optional for the owner; mandatory for the detail. The cardinality of the subtype group is given by an arc (note: 1:1 relationships that do not reflect subtype structures are shown as 1:n relationships in which n is constrained to a maximum cardinality of 1 - see appendix A for a full specification of the notation used in this book) for which minimum and maximum cardinalities should be specified.

Primary key relationships are shown entering the top of the entity box and foreign key relationships are shown entering the side of the entity box. Thus it is possible to tell from inspection of the entity diagram that:

the key of Customer does not contribute to the key of Order
the key of Product does not contribute to the key of OrderLine
the key of Order does contribute to the key of OrderLine

D.1   SSADM Version 4

Using the SSADM Version 4 notation the diagram can be represented as in figure D.3. In the SSADM notation optionality (minimum cardinality of zero) is indicated by a dotted line. Subtype entities are implemented using 1:1 relationships. Because 1:1 relationships are used for subtypes and for 1:n relationships that have been reduced to 1:1, it can be difficult to recognize where subtypes occur from inspection of an SSADM data model diagram.

Mutually exclusive subtypes can be modelled by the addition of an exclusivity arc; making the 1:1 relationships into solid lines would indicate a mandatory subtype grouping.

"Dead crows" tend to be fairly common in SSADM data models and the example in figure D.3 has been drawn to show the Product/Order Line relationship entering the bottom of the Order Line entity (something that we discourage). This SSADM notation makes it difficult to see where one entity contributes to the identity of another entity.

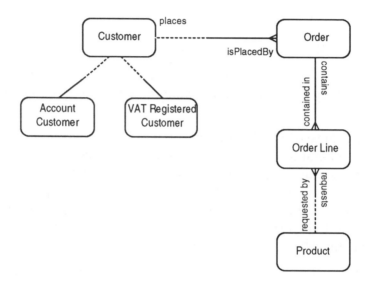

Figure D.3: *SSADM Version 4 logical data structure (LDS)*

D.2   Oracle CASE*Method

The Oracle CASE*Method notation is similar to the SSADM notation with the exception of subtypes, which are represented explicitly using boxes within boxes (a similar notation is supported by IEM and the IEF CASE tool). However, it is not possible to represent the semantics of figure D.2 using the Oracle notation. In the Oracle notation subtype groups are assumed to be mandatory and mutually exclusive which means that figure D.4 should be interpreted as:

> customers must be either account customers or VAT registered customers, but not both

Extensions to the boxes within boxes notation can be made to show optional subtype groups and overlapping (independent) subtypes. However, the authors tend not to use the boxes within boxes style for representing subtypes as it can get rather messy with complex structures and it is not easy to show all the nuances of cardinality for subtype groups (this is largely a matter of personal taste).

Where one entity contributes to the identity of another entity then a bar can be added to the relationship line, as is the case with Order and Order Line.

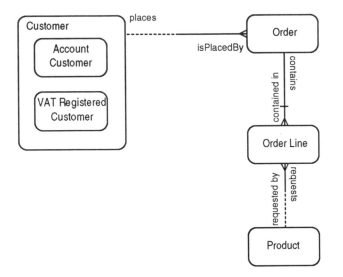

Figure D.4: *Oracle CASE*Method*

D.3   Diagramming notations and CASE tools

A diagramming notation should be thought of as a graphical representation derived from an underlying repository. From the repository different reports, such as entity diagrams can be created to suit different purposes. Indeed, once the meta-model has been developed there is no reason why a repository-based CASE tool should not be able to support many diagramming notations alternative forms of presentation. The flexibility of the CASE tool will depend in part upon the flexibility of the meta-model that underlies the repository. Some CASE tools can be tailored to suit the analyst's preferred style of diagramming or to meet the data modelling standards imposed by the organization. Where the CASE tool allows the analyst to tailor the notation it begins to move into the province of meta-CASE.

Index